Pamela L. Higgins
Editor

Libraries and Electronic Resources:
New Partnerships, New Practices, New Perspectives

Libraries and Electronic Resources: New Partnerships, New Practices, New Perspectives has been co-published simultaneously as *Journal of Library Administration*, Volume 35, Numbers 1/2 2001.

Pre-publication
REVIEWS,
COMMENTARIES,
EVALUATIONS . . .

" **A** useful introduction to new models for scholarly communication, standards development in electronic publishing and digital libraries, and the role of consortial and other kinds of partnerships in advancing digital library standards. Most of the authors describe specific projects or initiatives in which they have played a leading role, such as BioOne, the California Digital Library's eScholarship Program, or national site licensing efforts in The Netherlands, Australia, and the United Kingdom."

Edward Shreeves, MLS, PhD
Director
Collections & Information Resources
University of Iowa Libraries

Libraries
and Electronic Resources:
New Partnerships, New Practices,
New Perspectives

Libraries and Electronic Resources: New Partnerships, New Practices, New Perspectives has been co-published simultaneously as *Journal of Library Administration,* Volume 35, Numbers 1/2 2001.

The *Journal of Library Administration* Monographic "Separates"

Below is a list of " separates," which in serials librarianship means a special issue simultaneously published as a special journal issue or double-issue *and* as a "separate" hardbound monograph. (This is a format which we also call a "DocuSerial.")

"Separates" are published because specialized libraries or professionals may wish to purchase a specific thematic issue by itself in a format which can be separately cataloged and shelved, as opposed to purchasing the journal on an on-going basis. Faculty members may also more easily consider a "separate" for classroom adoption.

"Separates" are carefully classified separately with the major book jobbers so that the journal tie-in can be noted on new book order slips to avoid duplicate purchasing.

You may wish to visit Haworth's Website at . . .

http://www.HaworthPress.com

. . . to search our online catalog for complete tables of contents of these separates and related publications.

You may also call 1-800-HAWORTH (outside US/Canada: 607-722-5857), or Fax 1-800-895-0582 (outside US/Canada: 607-771-0012), or e-mail at:

getinfo@haworthpressinc.com

Libraries and Electronic Resources: New Partnerships, New Practices, New Perspectives, edited by Pamela L. Higgins (Vol. 35, No. 1/2, 2001). *An essential guide to the Internet's impact on electronic resoruces management–past, present, and future.*

Diversity Now: People, Collections, and Services in Academic Libraries, edited by Teresa Y. Neely, MLS, PhD, and Kuang-Hwei (Janet) Lee-Smeltzer, MS, MSLIS, (Vol. 33, No. 1/2/3/4, 2001). *Examines multicultural trends in academic libraries' staff and users, types of collections, and services offered.*

Leadership in the Library and Information Science Professions: Theory and Practice, edited by Mark D. Winston, MLS, PhD (Vol. 32, No. 3/4, 2001). *Offers fresh ideas for developing and using leadership skills, including recruiting potential leaders, staff training and development, issues of gender and ethnic diversity, and budget strategies for success.*

Off-Campus Library Services, edited by Ann Marie Casey (Vol. 31, No. 3/4, 2001 and Vol. 32, No. 1/2, 2001). *This informative volume examines various aspects of off-campus, or distance learning. It explores training issues for library staff, Web site development, changing roles for librarians, the uses of conferencing software, library support for Web-based courses, library agreements and how to successfully negotiate them, and much more!*

Research Collections and Digital Information, edited by Sul H. Lee (Vol. 31, No. 2, 2000). *Offers new strategies for collecting, organizing, and accessing library materials in the digital age.*

Academic Research on the Internet: Options for Scholars & Libraries, edited by Helen Laurence, MLS, EdD, and William Miller, MLS, PhD (Vol. 30, No. 1/2/3/4, 2000). *"Emphasizes quality over quantity. . . . Presents the reader with the best research-oriented Web sites in the field. A state-of-the-art review of academic use of the Internet as well as a guide to the best Internet sites and services. . . . A useful addition for any academic library." (David A. Tyckoson, MLS, Head of Reference, California State University, Fresno)*

Management for Research Libraries Cooperation, edited by Sul H. Lee (Vol. 29, No. 3/4, 2000). *Delivers sound advice, models, and strategies for increasing sharing between institutions to maximize the amount of printed and electronic research material you can make available in your library while keeping costs under control.*

Integration in the Library Organization, edited by Christine E. Thompson, PhD (Vol. 29, No. 2, 1999). *Provides librarians with the necessary tools to help libraries balance and integrate public and technical services and to improve the capability of libraries to offer patrons quality services and large amounts of information.*

Library Training for Staff and Customers, edited by Sara Ramser Beck, MLS, MBA (Vol. 29, No. 1, 1999). *This comprehensive book is designed to assist library professionals involved in presenting or planning training for library staff members and customers. You will explore ideas for effective general reference training, training on automated systems, training in specialized subjects such as African American history and biography, and training for areas such as patents and trademarks, and business subjects.* Library Training for Staff and Customers *answers numerous training questions and is an excellent guide for planning staff development.*

Collection Development in the Electronic Environment: Shifting Priorities, edited by Sul H. Lee (Vol. 28, No. 4, 1999). *Through case studies and firsthand experiences, this volume discusses meeting the needs of scholars at universities, budgeting issues, user education, staffing in the electronic age, collaborating libraries and resources, and how vendors meet the needs of different customers.*

The Age Demographics of Academic Librarians: A Profession Apart, by Stanley J. Wilder (Vol. 28, No. 3, 1999). *The average age of librarians has been increasing dramatically since 1990. This unique book will provide insights on how this demographic issue can impact a library and what can be done to make the effects positive.*

Collection Development in a Digital Environment, edited by Sul H. Lee (Vol. 28, No. 1, 1999). *Explores ethical and technological dilemmas of collection development and gives several suggestions on how a library can successfully deal with these challenges and provide patrons with the information they need.*

Scholarship, Research Libraries, and Global Publishing, by Jutta Reed-Scott (Vol. 27, No. 3/4, 1999). *This book documents a research project in conjunction with the Association of Research Libraries (ARL) that explores the issue of foreign acquisition and how it affects collection in international studies, area studies, collection development, and practices of international research libraries.*

Managing Multicultural Diversity in the Library: Principles and Issues for Administrators, edited by Mark Winston (Vol. 27, No. 1/2, 1999). *Defines diversity, clarifies why it is important to address issues of diversity, and identifies goals related to diversity and how to go about achieving those goals.*

Information Technology Planning, edited by Lori A. Goetsch (Vol. 26, No. 3/4, 1999). *Offers innovative approaches and strategies useful in your library and provides some food for thought about information technology as we approach the millennium.*

The Economics of Information in the Networked Environment, edited by Meredith A. Butler, MLS, and Bruce R. Kingma, PhD (Vol. 26, No. 1/2, 1998). *"A book that should be read both by information professionals and by administrators, faculty and others who share a collective concern to provide the most information to the greatest number at the lowest cost in the networked environment." (Thomas J. Galvin, PhD, Professor of Information Science and Policy, University at Albany, State University of New York)*

OCLC 1967-1997: Thirty Years of Furthering Access to the World's Information, edited by K. Wayne Smith (Vol. 25, No. 2/3/4, 1998). *"A rich–and poignantly personal, at times–historical account of what is surely one of this century's most important developments in librarianship." (Deanna B. Marcum, PhD, President, Council on Library and Information Resources, Washington, DC)*

Management of Library and Archival Security: From the Outside Looking In, edited by Robert K. O'Neill, PhD (Vol. 25, No. 1, 1998). *"Provides useful advice and on-target insights for professionals caring for valuable documents and artifacts." (Menzi L. Behrnd-Klodt, JD, Attorney/Archivist, Klodt and Associates, Madison, WI)*

Economics of Digital Information: Collection, Storage, and Delivery, edited by Sul H. Lee (Vol. 24, No. 4, 1997). *Highlights key concepts and issues vital to a library's successful venture into the digital environment and helps you understand why the transition from the printed page to the digital packet has been problematic for both creators of proprietary materials and users of those materials.*

The Academic Library Director: Reflections on a Position in Transition, edited by Frank D'Andraia, MLS (Vol. 24, No. 3, 1997). *"A useful collection to have whether you are seeking a position as director or conducting a search for one." (College & Research Libraries News)*

Emerging Patterns of Collection Development in Expanding Resource Sharing, Electronic Information, and Network Environment, edited by Sul H. Lee (Vol. 24, No. 1/2, 1997). *"The issues it deals with are common to us all. We all need to make our funds go further and our resources work harder, and there are ideas here which we can all develop." (The Library Association Record)*

Interlibrary Loan/Document Delivery and Customer Satisfaction: Strategies for Redesigning Services, edited by Pat L. Weaver-Meyers, Wilbur A. Stolt, and Yem S. Fong (Vol. 23, No. 1/2, 1997). *"No interlibrary loan department supervisor at any mid-sized to large college or university library can afford not to read this book." (Gregg Sapp, MLS, MEd, Head of Access Services, University of Miami, Richter Library, Coral Gables, Florida)*

Access, Resource Sharing and Collection Development, edited by Sul H. Lee (Vol. 22, No. 4, 1996). *Features continuing investigation and discussion of important library issues, specifically the role of libraries in acquiring, storing, and disseminating information in different formats.*

Managing Change in Academic Libraries, edited by Joseph J. Branin (Vol. 22, No. 2/3, 1996). *"Touches on several aspects of academic library management, emphasizing the changes that are occurring at the present time. . . . Recommended this title for individuals or libraries interested in management aspects of academic libraries." (RQ American Library Association)*

Libraries and Student Assistants: Critical Links, edited by William K. Black, MLS (Vol. 21, No. 3/4, 1995). *"A handy reference work on many important aspects of managing student assistants. . . . Solid, useful information on basic management issues in this work and several chapters are useful for experienced managers." (The Journal of Academic Librarianship)*

The Future of Resource Sharing, edited by Shirley K. Baker and Mary E. Jackson, MLS (Vol. 21, No. 1/2, 1995). *"Recommended for library and information science schools because of its balanced presentation of the ILL/document delivery issues." (Library Acquisitions: Practice and Theory)*

The Future of Information Services, edited by Virginia Steel, MA, and C. Brigid Welch, MLS (Vol. 20, No. 3/4, 1995). *"The leadership discussions will be useful for library managers as will the discussions of how library structures and services might work in the next century." (Australian Special Libraries)*

The Dynamic Library Organizations in a Changing Environment, edited by Joan Giesecke, MLS, DPA (Vol. 20, No. 2, 1995). *"Provides a significant look at potential changes in the library world and presents its readers with possible ways to address the negative results of such changes. . . . Covers the key issues facing today's libraries . . . Two thumbs up!" (Marketing Library Resources)*

Access, Ownership, and Resource Sharing, edited by Sul H. Lee (Vol. 20, No. 1, 1995). *The contributing authors present a useful and informative look at the current status of information provision and some of the challenges the subject presents.*

Libraries as User-Centered Organizations: Imperatives for Organizational Change, edited by Meredith A. Butler (Vol. 19, No. 3/4, 1994). *"Presents a very timely and well-organized discussion of major trends and influences causing organizational changes." (Science Books & Films)*

Declining Acquisitions Budgets: Allocation, Collection Development and Impact Communication, edited by Sul H. Lee (Vol. 19, No. 2, 1994). *"Expert and provocative. . . . Presents many ways of looking at library budget deterioration and responses to it . . . There is much food for thought here." (Library Resources & Technical Services)*

The Role and Future of Special Collections in Research Libraries: British and American Perspectives, edited by Sul H. Lee (Vol. 19, No. 1, 1993). *"A provocative but informative read for library users, academic administrators, and private sponsors." (International Journal of Information and Library Research)*

Catalysts for Change: Managing Libraries in the 1990s, edited by Gisela M. von Dran, DPA, MLS, and Jennifer Cargill, MSLS, MSed (Vol. 18, No. 3/4, 1994). *"A useful collection of articles which focuses on the need for librarians to employ enlightened management practices in order to adapt to and thrive in the rapidly changing information environment." (Australian Library Review)*

Monographic "Separates" list continued at the back

Libraries and Electronic Resources: New Partnerships, New Practices, New Perspectives

Pamela L. Higgins
Editor

Libraries and Electronic Resources: New Partnerships, New Practices, New Perspectives has been co-published simultaneously as *Journal of Library Administration,* Volume 35, Numbers 1/2 2001.

The Haworth Information Press
An Imprint of
The Haworth Press, Inc.
New York • London • Oxford

Published by

The Haworth Information Press®, 10 Alice Street, Binghamton, NY 13904-1580 USA

The Haworth Information Press® is an imprint of The Haworth Press, Inc., 10 Alice Street, Binghamton, NY 13904-1580 USA.

Libraries and Electronic Resources: New Partnerships, New Practices, New Perspectives has been co-published simultaneously as *Journal of Library Administration,* Volume 35, Numbers 1/2 2001.

The development, preparation, and publication of this work has been undertaken with great care. However, the publisher, employees, editors, and agents of The Haworth Press and all imprints of The Haworth Press, Inc., including The Haworth Medical Press® and Pharmaceutical Products Press®, are not responsible for any errors contained herein or for consequences that may ensue from use of materials or information contained in this work. Opinions expressed by the author(s) are not necessarily those of The Haworth Press, Inc. With regard to case studies, identities and circumstances of individuals discussed herein have been changed to protect confidentiality. Any resemblance to actual persons, living or dead, is entirely coincidental.

Cover design by Thomas J. Mayshock Jr.

Library of Congress Cataloging-in-Publication Data

Libraries and electronic resources : new partnerships, new practices, new perspectives / Pamela L. Higgins, editor.
    p. cm.
    Co-published simultaneously as Journal of library administration, v. 35, nos. 1/2 2001.
    Includes bibliographical references and index.
    ISBN 0-7890-1728-8 (alk. paper) – ISBN 0-7890-1729-6 (pbk : alk. paper)
    1. Libraries and electronic publishing. 2. Scholarly electronic publishing. 3. Electronic publishing–Licenses. 4. Digital libraries. 5. Libraries–Special collections–Electronic information resources. I. Higgins, Pamela L., 1954- II. Journal of library administration.
Z716.6 .L495 2002
025.17′44–dc21
                                                 2002006312

Indexing, Abstracting & Website/Internet Coverage

This section provides you with a list of major indexing & abstracting services. That is to say, each service began covering this periodical during the year noted in the right column. Most Websites which are listed below have indicated that they will either post, disseminate, compile, archive, cite or alert their own Website users with research-based content from this work. (This list is as current as the copyright date of this publication.)

(continued)

Special Bibliographic Notes related to special journal issues (separates) and indexing/abstracting:

- indexing/abstracting services in this list will also cover material in any "separate" that is co-published simultaneously with Haworth's special thematic journal issue or DocuSerial. Indexing/abstracting usually covers material at the article/chapter level.
- monographic co-editions are intended for either non-subscribers or libraries which intend to purchase a second copy for their circulating collections.
- monographic co-editions are reported to all jobbers/wholesalers/approval plans. The source journal is listed as the "series" to assist the prevention of duplicate purchasing in the same manner utilized for books-in-series.
- to facilitate user/access services all indexing/abstracting services are encouraged to utilize the co-indexing entry note indicated at the bottom of the first page of each article/chapter/contribution.
- this is intended to assist a library user of any reference tool (whether print, electronic, online, or CD-ROM) to locate the monographic version if the library has purchased this version but not a subscription to the source journal.
- individual articles/chapters in any Haworth publication are also available through the Haworth Document Delivery Service (HDDS).

Libraries
and Electronic Resources:
New Partnerships, New Practices,
New Perspectives

CONTENTS

ABOUT THE EDITOR

Pamela L. Higgins, MLS, MAS is Assistant Director for External Relations at the Johns Hopkins University's Sheridan Libraries. She is the former Head of Library Systems at the Sheridan Libraries and was previously Head of Access Services at Johns Hopkins Welch Medical Library. Currently, Ms. Higgins assists the Dean of University Libraries with advocacy and outreach activities relating to national information policy and scholarly communication issues, and directs the Sheridan Libraries' participation in local, regional and national consortia. Since 2000, she has also been responsible for developing a new framework for licensing electronic resources across all the Johns Hopkins libraries.

Introduction

Pamela L. Higgins

In *The Social Life of Information,* John Seely Brown and Paul
Duguid (2000) examine the social context of information and provide a
provocative view of the impact of information technology on our lives
and our institutions. Among the myths of the information age they identify is the origin myth, or the myth of separation. They write:

> Historians frequently trace the beginnings of the information age
> not to the Internet, the computer, or even the telephone, but to the
> telegraph. With the telegraph, the speed of information essentially
> separated itself from the speed of human travel. People traveled at
> the speed of the train. Information began to travel at the speed of
> light. In some versions of this origin story (which tends to forget
> that fire and smoke had long been used to convey messages over a
> distance at the speed of light), information takes on not only a
> speed of its own, but a life of its own. (It is even capable, in some
> formulations, of "wanting to be free.") And some scholars contend
> that with the computer, this decisive separation entered a second
> phase. Information technologies became capable not simply of
> transmitting and storing information, but of producing informa-
> tion independent of human intervention. No one doubts the impor-
> tance of Samuel Morse's invention. But with the all-but-death of
> the telegraph and the final laying to rest in 1999 of Morse code, it
> might be time to celebrate less speed and separation and more the
> ways information and society intertwine. Similarly, it's important
> not to overlook the significance of information's power to breed
> upon itself. But it might be time to retreat from exuberance (or de-

[Haworth co-indexing entry note]: "Introduction." Higgins, Pamela L. Co-published simultaneously in
Journal of Library Administration (The Haworth Information Press, an imprint of The Haworth Press, Inc.)
Vol. 35, No. 1/2, 2001, pp. 1-4; and: *Libraries and Electronic Resources: New Partnerships, New Prac-
tices, New Perspectives* (ed: Pamela L. Higgins) The Haworth Information Press, an imprint of The
Haworth Press, Inc., 2001, pp. 1-4. Single or multiple copies of this article are available for a fee from The
Haworth Document Delivery Service [1-800-Haworth, 9:00 a.m. - 5:00 p.m. (EST). E-mail address:
getinfo@haworthpressinc.com].

pression) at the volume of information and to consider its value more carefully. The ends of information, after all, are human ends. The logic of information must ultimately be the logic of humanity. For all information's independence and extent, it is people, in their communities, organizations and institutions, who ultimately decide what it all means and why it matters. (p. 17)

Librarians have always been keenly aware of the intertwining of information and society and indeed, the Internet adds new dimensions to those relationships. The nascent digital libraries at the dawn of the 21st century are challenged to devise new financial strategies to address the crisis in scholarly communication, to create new organization structures to manage the digital library, and indeed to drive the creation of new institutional frameworks as electronic resources become an integral and permanent part of library collections. This volume captures the current context of electronic resources in libraries from the perspective of new models in scholarly communication, emerging standards in e-publishing, access to digital library collections, the global phenomenon of consortial site licensing initiatives, and new roles for libraries and librarians associated with digital libraries of instructional resources. The issue of preserving digital resources–of guaranteeing that electronic documents will become a permanent part of the human record–while critical to the ultimate success of digital libraries, is not addressed in depth in this volume. The complex questions surrounding digital preservation of works born digital as well as those converted from print warrant another work devoted exclusively to that topic.

TRANSFORMING SCHOLARLY COMMUNICATION

These articles illustrate the breadth of engagement by libraries in scholarly publishing through their participation in the creation, production, dissemination and use of scholarly and scientific information. Jim Neal examines the evolution of relationships between university presses and research libraries, recognizing that electronic scholarly communication presents conflicts between presses and libraries in matters of economic, information policy, and publishing issues. Marilu Goodyear and Adrian Alexander assert that the commercialization of scholarly publishing is at the heart of the economic problems faced by academic libraries and discuss alternatives for scholarly publishing by scholarly societies in terms of BioOne, a partnership which presents a new model for the university, academic libraries and the commercial sector.

Catherine Candee describes the California Digital Libraries' eScholarship program, which fosters faculty-led innovation in scholarly publishing. She highlights experimental work with discipline-based repositories to support self-publishing, and the management and archiving of digital content. Important questions regarding the creation of a comprehensive system for the management of electronic scholarly information are discussed.

Mary Summerfield, Carol Mandel and Paul Kantor offer a perspective on the potential of scholarly online books resulting from the Columbia University Online Books Evaluation Project. Lifecycle costs of traditional print books and online books for publishers and libraries, scholars' behavior and reaction to online books and marketplace reactions to the concept of online books are presented.

Zsuzsa Koltay and Tom Hickerson describe Project Euclid, a joint electronic publishing initiative of Cornell University Library and Duke University Press for mathematics journals. They discuss a new role for libraries in the life cycle of scholarly communication and identify the new expertise necessary in order for libraries to be successful in that role.

STANDARDS EMERGE

Allen Renear and Gene Golovchinsky present a comprehensive look at content standards for electronic publishing and provide critical insights into how conflicts and competition among the players can slow the adoption of standards. They discuss the development of the Open e-Book Forum's *Publication Structure,* an XML-based specification for e-books, and urge the active participation of the library community, as consumers of e-books and, increasingly as producers of e-books, in influencing standards development.

INCREASED ACCESS TO SCHOLARLY INFORMATION–THE CREATION OF INTEROPERABLE DIGITAL LIBRARIES

The creation of digital libraries and their proliferation in a distributed fashion introduces major challenges for accessing the resources held therein. Ed Fox and Hussein Suleman discuss the importance of search and retrieval mechanisms for digital libraries and the multifaceted issues of digital library interoperability in the context of the Open Archives Initiative.

GLOBAL CONSORTIAL INITIATIVES

This series of articles illustrates global consortial activities in the arena of site licenses for electronic resources. Arnold Hirshon traces the development of the international "consortium of consortia" phenomenon that is ICOLC. Noting the resurgent interest in consortial activities created by the advent of widespread licensing of electronic resources, he offers insights into the key factors that affect why and how consortia are managed. Specific site licensing experiences in the Netherlands, Australia, the United Kingdom, and Canada illustrate striking similarities as well as distinct differences in such initiatives, as discussed by Hans Geleijnse, Diane Costello, Hazel Woodward, and Deb deBruijn, respectively.

TRANSFORMING TEACHING AND LEARNING

With e-publishing and e-resources come e-learning and the creation of digital libraries of instructional resources. Based on their experience in creating a digital library of teaching resources, David McArthur, Bill Graves, and Sarah Giersch argue that librarians need not be disintermediated by new developments in information technology. They assert that successful new models for digital libraries will result from the intertwining of the skills of library professionals with educators, creating new collaborative roles for librarians in the educational process.

REFERENCE

Brown, John Seely and Paul Duguid. *The Social Life of Information*. Boston: Harvard Business School Press, 2000.

THE COMMUNITY ENGAGES: SCHOLARLY PUBLISHING IN THE EARLY 21ST CENTURY

Symbiosis or Alienation: Advancing the University Press/ Research Library Relationship Through Electronic Scholarly Communication

James G. Neal

SUMMARY. University presses and research libraries have a long tradition of collaboration. The rapidly expanding electronic scholarly communication environment offers important new opportunities for co-operation and for innovative new models of publishing. The economics of libraries and scholarly publishers have strained the working relationship and promoted debates on important information policy issues. This article explores the context for advancing the partnership, cites examples

James G. Neal is Vice President for Information Services and University Librarian, Columbia University, 535 West 114th Street, New York, NY 10027 (E-mail: jneal@columbia.edu).

[Haworth co-indexing entry note]: "Symbiosis or Alienation: Advancing the University Press/Research Library Relationship Through Electronic Scholarly Communication." Neal, James G. Co-published simultaneously in *Journal of Library Administration* (The Haworth Information Press, an imprint of The Haworth Press, Inc.) Vol. 35, No. 1/2, 2001, pp. 5-18; and: *Libraries and Electronic Resources: New Partnerships, New Practices, New Perspectives* (ed: Pamela L. Higgins) The Haworth Information Press, an imprint of The Haworth Press, Inc., 2001, pp. 5-18. Single or multiple copies of this article are available for a fee from The Haworth Document Delivery Service [1-800-HAWORTH, 9:00 a.m. - 5:00 p.m. (EST). E-mail address: getinfo@haworthpressinc.com].

5

of joint efforts in electronic publishing, and presents an action plan for working together. *[Article copies available for a fee from The Haworth Document Delivery Service: 1-800-HAWORTH. E-mail address: <getinfo@ haworthpressinc.com> Website: <http://www.HaworthPress.com> © 2001 by The Haworth Press, Inc. All rights reserved.]*

KEYWORDS. Research libraries, university presses, electronic scholarly communication

During the period 1989-1995, while the author served as the library director at Indiana University, a series of periodic discussions was organized between the press and library administrators from the Big 10/CIC universities. At the outset, the debates focused on the very practical aspects of publisher-customer relationships and the shared angst of dealing with the financial pressures of the science, technology and medical (STM) journals. By the end of this period, the potential of electronic publishing was being recognized and the notion of aggressive press/library partnerships was being embraced. Clearly, a new symbiosis, a fresh and more intimate mutualism was being conceived.

This article will focus on the evolution of this interdependence between university press and research library under the impact of revolutions in information technology, global learning and electronic scholarship. Examples of publishing partnerships that have been forged will be described, and new strategies for collaboration will be recommended. It is important to recognize that electronic scholarly communication also carries the seeds of alienation, of important conflicts and competition between presses and libraries on economic, information policy and publishing issues.

North American universities have since their founding embraced the importance of well-supported and professionally staffed libraries as central to institutional academic and research excellence. These libraries over decades have selected and acquired information resources on a global scale that respond to the current and anticipate the future needs of faculty, students and researchers. These materials are organized, stored and preserved for dependable access, and library staff provide dissemination, interpretation and instructional services to enable effective use. Under the impact of electronic technologies and digital resources, these libraries are also now serving as gateways to information which is increasingly created, stored and delivered online. The processes of information acquisition, synthesis, navigation and archiving are increasingly focused on networked and interactive access to digital multimedia information at point of need. This has provoked a more market-based, customized and entrepreneurial approach to the packaging and delivery of information.

The Association of Research Libraries (ARL) is a not-for-profit membership organization comprising the libraries of North American research institutions which operates as a forum for the exchange of ideas and as an agent for collective action. The mission of ARL is "to shape and influence forces affecting the future of research libraries in the process of scholarly communication." ARL programs and services promote equitable access to, and effective use of recorded knowledge in support of teaching, research, scholarship, and community services. The Association articulates the concerns of research libraries and their institutions, forges coalitions, influences information policy development, and supports innovation and improvement in research library operations. ARL programs include the Office of Scholarly Communication, the Scholarly Publishing and Academic Resources Coalition (SPARC) and the Federal Relations and Information Policy Development Program. Other activities focus on access and technology, including the Coalition for Networked Information, collections and preservation, including the Global Resources Program, staffing and management, and performance measures.

University presses in North America have developed over the last century as the publishing arms of their parent institutions, acquiring, developing, designing, producing, marketing and distributing works in a wide range of disciplines and for a variety of markets. This has included monographs and journals of scholarly and intellectual merit, often for small audiences of specialists interested in concentrated fields of research. University presses also publish trade books for general readers, undergraduate and advanced textbooks, reference works, fiction and poetry, important authors from around the world in translation, and regional and local works. Often in partnership with learned societies, scholarly associations, and research libraries, these presses are focused on serving the public good by generating and disseminating knowledge. As academic publishing has focused more aggressively on electronic capture, distribution, and use of works, university presses have rapidly expanded their capacity in this area.

The Association of American University Presses (AAUP) is a nonprofit membership organization comprising university presses, scholarly societies, research institutions and museums, all committed to publication in service to the academic and scholarly communities. The AAUP seeks to promote the work and influence of university presses and to help members respond effectively to the changing economy and environment for scholarly publishing. It maintains a program of cooperative advertising, promotion and marketing of publications. It offers a combination of educational sessions, networking opportunities, and social and intellectual exchange at its annual meetings and professional development regional workshops. It collects and analyzes data on the operations and output of university presses and on the state of scholarly publishing. It monitors important information policy and legislative developments, with a particular focus in the area of copyright.

Both the ARL and the AAUP have provided important leadership and direction over the past five years as the academic and publisher communities have sought to rethink the future scholarly communication systems. A series of forums has been organized which have brought together stakeholders and encouraged aggressive debate and the forging of key principles for moving forward. These meetings have pursued two fundamental tracks: the specialized scholarly monograph in crisis and emerging systems of scholarly communication. The former was focused on research and publication in humanities and social science fields, and the latter on the future of journals and the distribution of research in science, technical and medical disciplines.

Discussions on the future of the scholarly monograph have highlighted the challenging economics of the specialized book, the cost of production in combination with the declining market, and the impact of technology and experimental approaches to publishing books online. Debates on STM journal publishing resulted in two important publications, both proposing important new principles and directions for scholarly communication. The Pew Higher Education Policy Perspectives on "To Publish and Perish," published in March 1998 (http://www.arl. org/scomm/pew/pew.html) advocated the following: moving the debate beyond "the library problem" so as to embrace the entire academic community, disentangling the notions of quality and quantity in the work of faculty, leveraging university resources by creating a more coherent and collaborative market for scholarly publications, retaining more control over intellectual property within the academy, investing in electronic forms of peer-reviewed scholarly communication, and decoupling publication and quality assessment of scholarly work. *The (Tempe) Principles for Emerging Systems of Scholarly Publishing* (March 2000) (http://arl.cni.org/scomm/tempe.html) proposed: cost containment; electronic strategies to expand access, interoperability and searchability; archiving and permanent availability; appropriate levels of manuscript evaluation; balance between the interests of copyright owners and users in the digital environment and the sustenance of fair use; reduced time from submission to publication; greater emphasis on quality of faculty publications and a reduced emphasis on quantity; and privacy in the use of materials. In all cases, representatives from research libraries and university presses were active participants in the debates and endorsed the results. The outcomes suggest important areas for library and press collaboration, particularly in the areas of electronic publishing, preservation, and information policies.

Since 1995, there have been numerous collaborative electronic publishing programs involving university presses and research libraries. The following examples highlight the breadth of activities that have been launched. They also illustrate some common characteristics, including the importance of foundation and other external funding in launching the projects, the dependence on shared investment in infrastructure and expertise, an emphasis on policies that are supportive of the access and use needs of the higher education community, the effort to reach new and non-traditional markets, and the commitment to integrate new functionality and experimental approaches. There are other electronic publishing programs that have been implemented or are in development, and searches of press or library Web sites will provide information about these growing number of initiatives.

Project Muse is a collaborative program launched in 1995 between the Johns Hopkins University Press and the Milton S. Eisenhower Library to provide network-based access to the scholarly journals published by the JHU Press and other university presses, many of which are publications of scholarly societies. With initial funding from the National Endowment for the Humanities and the Mellon Foundation, it is designed to take advantage of new technological developments in the creation, storage, distribution and use of electronic information. It seeks to provide a rich searching environment and a user-supportive interface. A broad range of subscription options are provided for individual libraries and library consortia. Muse enables a liberal use and re-use approach within the bounds of the subscribing organization. Launched with 40 titles in the humanities and the social sciences, it has now expanded to nearly 200 titles with over 800 subscribing libraries worldwide. Organized as an experiment built on venture capital, it is now a publishing effort operating at a modest profit while also returning new income to the society sponsors of the journals.

MIT Cognet at the Massachusetts Institute of Technology provides an electronic community for researchers in cognitive and brain sciences, with in-depth current and classic text resources, and an interactive forum for scholars and students in the field. A comparable initiative at Columbia is Earthscape, an online resource on the global environment with materials selected and gathered from a variety of sources, including research reports, educational content, datafiles and images, as well as links, an earth affairs magazine, and tools for communication. These dynamic databases of resources are offered to libraries, organizations and individuals on a subscription basis.

Columbia International Affairs Online (CIAO) is a comprehensive online source for theory and research in international affairs. It publishes working papers from university research institutes, occasional paper series from non-governmental organizations (NGOs), foundation-based research projects, conference proceedings, abstracts, and other grey literature items. Each section of CIAO is updated with new material on a regular schedule. The goals are timeliness, access to difficult to locate materials, quality control, and integrated access to a diverse body of literature. Both CIAO and Earthscape are now part of a larger initiative called EPIC, the Electronic Publishing Initiative at Columbia. EPIC is a collaboration that involves the Columbia University Press, the Libraries and Academic Information Systems. Its mission is to create new kinds of scholarly and educational publications through the use of new media technologies in an integrated research and production environment, and to make these digital publications self-sustaining through subscription sales to institutions and individual users.

Another noteworthy project is eScholarship at the University of California. Hosted by UC's California Digital Library, it is dedicated to facilitating scholar-led innovations in scholarly communication, including disciplinary-based knowledge archives of e-prints surrounded by functional tools and value-added products and features. In addition, eScholarship has expanded to embrace digital journals, digital books and data sets. The coverage includes archaeology, dermatology, international and area studies, tobacco control research and an electronic cultural atlas. It includes support tools for submission, expanded peer review, discovery and access, and use of scholarship. It is developing new alerting citation and annotation services for scholars, and integration and summarization services for students.

Two important initiatives in history that have included significant research library input must also be cited. First is the History Cooperative, a partnership among the American Historical Association, the Organization of American Historians, the University of Illinois Press, and the National Academy Press launched in March 2000. It seeks to integrate historical scholarship and innovative technology to create an important scholarly source for historians on the Web. The initial focus is to make the full text of current issues of the *American Historical Review* and the *Journal of American History* available electronically to association members and to institutions that subscribe to the print versions of the journals. The History E-Book Project is a collaborative effort of the American Council of Learned Societies, five scholarly societies, and initially seven university presses, with significant funding from the Mellon Foundation, to make quality monographs in history available in electronic format. In its initial phase, it seeks to convert to electronic format 500 backlist titles of major importance to historical studies, and to publish 85 completely new electronic works by senior scholars that use technologies to communicate the results of scholarship in new ways.

There are many additional examples of electronic publishing activities at university presses that involve research libraries as collaborators, advisors or important consumers. The presses are increasingly outsourcing the electronic distribution of the backfiles of their monographs to new electronic book aggregators, such as netLibrary and ebrary. Similarly, electronic versions of journals published by university presses are being made available to journal vendors/distributors as part of comprehensive journal packages, and backfiles of core journal titles in selected disciplines have been integrated into the JSTOR database. The publications are also being distributed through services like Questia, which provide direct student licenses for these resources with productivity tools to enhance effective use. An increasing number of university presses are making important texts and reference works available on a subscription basis. The digital library activities of research libraries that seek to make important special collections and unique holdings available for global access are spawning a number of important publishing initiatives. The digital center at the University of Michigan Libraries and the various electronic text centers at the University of Virginia Libraries are outstanding examples. The digitization capabilities of libraries are forging new hybrid structures like the new press at the University of Cincinnati Libraries that will seek to market electronic publications and the developing Eisenhower Library Press at Johns Hopkins that is working with faculty to publish such works as collections of symposium papers and specialized scholarly monographs which face increasing difficulty in finding publishers.

The HighWire Press at Stanford University is an extraordinary example of library leadership in defining new strategies for quality electronic scholarly publishing. In partnership with scientific societies and publishers, HighWire has over a five year period defined excellence in electronic STM publication. With over 250 journal sites online, HighWire integrates high resolution images and multimedia so important to science researchers, advanced searching capabilities, powerful interactivity, and links among authors and articles and citations. The availability of backfiles free on the Web for these important scientific titles is a brave and pace-setting venture.

The Scholarly Publishing and Academic Resources Coalition (SPARC) is a global alliance of research institutions, libraries and other organizations that encourages competition in the scholarly communication market. SPARC develops new solutions to scientific journal publishing, facilitates the use of technology to expand access, and partners with publishers to bring top quality, low-cost research to a greater audience of scholars. This is accomplished through competitive STM publishing initiatives and demonstration projects that support the access and use needs of the scholarly community and that introduce innovative publishing models. This is accomplished through publishing partnerships with editorial boards, societies and universities, the provision of advisory and marketing services, and the availability of committed sales through SPARC member purchases. SPARC also advances a "Create Change" campaign to educate faculty about the scholarly publishing situation and to provide tools and options for action. SPARC has encouraged "Leading Edge" initiatives that demonstrate innovative business models that benefit scholarly communication, and seed-funded "Scientific Communities" projects that support aggregation and linking of scientific content and that encourage collaboration among scientists, scholarly societies, and academic institutions. The most recent initiative of "Declaring Independence" seeks to encourage researchers/authors and editorial boards to move away from commercial publishers and to relocate their publications to society and university presses.

University press and research library collaboration on electronic scholarly publication must be understood in the context of a variety of scholarly, economic, technological and political developments. The urge to publish among faculty must be understood. Scholars need to communicate with colleagues, and publication is part of the academic culture in which researchers have been nurtured. Scholars seek the preservation of their ideas; prestige and recognition; documentation of their eligibility for tenure, promotion, compensation increases, advancement, and competitiveness for grants; and, in some cases, profit from their work. Similarly, the expectations of scholars for technology must be appreciated. These include more and better content, access, convenience, new capabilities, cost reduction, and individual and organizational productivity.

There are important changes in the environment of higher education and scholarship that must be factored into these publishing activities. Not only do more faculty and students have access to more sophisticated technology and robust networks, but more and more information is being captured digitally and integrated with sophisticated searching and productivity tools. Push, hypertext, multimedia, artificial intelligence and customization technologies, for example, are revolutionizing the ways students and scholars work. Of particular note is the important trend to open access: open content, open archives, open source, open research, open course content, open standards, open URLS, and open reference linking. Combined with the concept of a shared knowledge conservancy, this push to barrier-free availability of information is a powerful force.

Scholars recognize the importance of the enhanced accessibility and availability of electronic information, but they increasingly advocate more rigorous application of the advantages of digital media in scholarly publishing. They want more sophisticated searchabiltiy, integration of multimedia and interactivity, spatial and navigational capabilities, and expanded interdisciplinary content and linkability. They also seek the portability, durability, readability, archivability, ownability, and affordability that print publication provides. Scholarly activity, regardless of the medium, is the creation of knowledge and the evaluation of its validity, the preservation of information, and the transmission of information to others.

Universities continue to push educational offerings to larger and off-campus markets, to part-time professionals studying at home or at work, to high school students, and to the lifelong learning community. Distributed learning requires content creation, storage and management of course materials, sophisticated search and query techniques, distribution and access strategies, and more effective rights management. These are new opportunities for university presses and academic libraries.

Research libraries continue to confront severe budgetary challenges as they seek to build collections of relevance and quality for their faculty and students. The volume of publishing combined with the cost of journals and books, the budgetary challenges at universities, and the need to invest in new electronic products, has contributed to noteworthy trends in collection development activities. There continue to be significant cuts in journal subscriptions and reductions in the purchase of monographs. As libraries consider expanded licensing of digital publications, they are concerned about: the need for both current and historical coverage, the ability to continue to pay for both the print and electronic versions, the usability of these products, the shifting technology, the prospective erosion of fair use exceptions, the consolidation in the industry, the ability and willingness of publishers to enable broad linking of content, the integrity of publications, and the inability to preserve works for long-term access. The research library community has consistently sustained its core interests in the future of publishing: a competitive market, easy distribution and reuse, innovative applications of technology, quality assurance and permanent archiving.

The research community has rallied behind a variety of strategies including market conforming activities that seek to introduce more competition into scholarly publishing, market distorting activities such as expanded consortial purchasing, system transforming programs like the discipline pre-print servers, and system busting efforts like the peer-to-peer sharing of information. New models are displacing commercial domination of the market. These include academic servers where universities take responsibility for capturing the work of their own researchers or global publications in a discipline, and expanded and renewed involvement by scholarly societies and university presses. Pre-print servers for author posting of work, peer-review lite models like PubMed Central through their expansion and relevance to the behaviors of scholars, or scholar capture and archiving of their own work on personal Web sites could all revolutionize the future communication systems.

Under the impact of these developments, university presses face their own extraordinary challenges. Institutional support has declined or disappeared and subsidies from other sources are not dependable. Library purchasing of monographs has declined, and the super-bookstores and online book services have become critical markets. The rights and coursepack income is threatened with decline as more faculty members and libraries create electronic reserve and course Web pages that link to licensed content. There is a need to invest in new technologies and expertise and to create an on-demand publishing capacity. Publishers need to increasingly manage both the content and distribution systems in new ways. Presses, as a result, have turned to increased book prices, lower discounts, more efficient book production methods, reductions in staff, acquisition of works with greater sales potential, and more frequent inventory sales. There is an increasing dichotomy in scholarly value as measured by awards and market value as measured by sales. Presses are struggling with such issues as how to price online products, how to archive electronic works, how to deal with rights management and permissions, how to market and negotiate with consortia, how to manage complex licensing and legal issues, how to build the necessary technology and expertise infrastructure, how to develop new business models, how to market to individuals effectively, how to sustain multiple formats, and how to respond to threats from consolidating commercial scholarly publishers. University presses provide invaluable selection, refinement, marketing and promotion services for the scholarly community, and these roles must be sustained and strengthened.

The core business of university presses is book publishing and as electronic capture and distribution dominates, they need to understand some of the critical issues in the research library community. Will libraries want to purchase or lease? Will books be self-published or commercially marketed? Will the focus be on the conversion of backfiles or the creation of new electronic works? Will these books remain primarily text, or will multimedia content be expanded? Will works be created for use in proprietary or open formats and readers? Will access and use be primarily online or offline? Will book publishing be focused on access to individual works or the creation of searchable databases of works? Will the use model be consultation or circulation? Will the content be archived or fluid?

These questions highlight the increasing importance of information policy issues and the common ground that university presses and research libraries should seek in these critical areas. Issues include intellectual property and the importance of preserving the balance in copyright law among the interests of authors, publishers, and users; the development of the Internet and the telecommunications policies that govern access and availability; privacy and freedom of speech; federal funding for information technology and scholarly research; and the recruitment and retention of information technology expertise. The success of joint electronic publishing programs will be influenced by each of these policy arenas.

The debates over the adaptation of copyright law to the digital environment are particularly challenging, and are a potential source of conflict between university presses and research libraries. International agreements seeking to harmonize national copyright policies have spawned a series of significant legislative initiatives in the U.S. which threaten to undermine the application of fair use for education and research. Licensing and contract law are increasingly dominating the access and use of electronic information by students and scholars. And technological controls in the form of new digital rights management systems threaten to further undermine legitimate uses of information.

It is essential that both presses and libraries recognize some of the new principles and measures that define the e-commerce environment. The quality of a work is increasingly defined by both the content and its functionality, that is, what a reader can do with it. The value of a work is increasingly evaluated on the basis of quality and traffic, that is, the number of hits on the Web site. The price of a work can no longer just be determined by the costs of the inputs, but also must factor in the perception in the marketplace of quality, value and reputation. This means that presses and libraries need to be increasingly focused on the ability to attract resources, on the ability to build successful business plans, to identify and manage competition and to secure needed venture capital.

Libraries and presses face important challenges in expanding their working relationships behind innovative and successful electronic publishing programs. They have very different relationships with their institutions, particularly in the financial area. The organizational culture of the academic and scholarly library can conflict with the business and "bottom line" mandate at the press. The differences in size of staff and even physical location on campus are important factors. Both are seeking to integrate technology into historically paper-based enterprises, but libraries have access to significant institutional, private and federal funds to ease this transition.

University presses and research libraries, in cooperation with their national associations, must develop an action plan for future collaboration with a focus on electronic scholarly publishing. In this spirit, the following twenty recommendations are presented for discussion to the Association of Research Libraries and the Association of American University Presses. Each recommendation includes an indication whether it is an institutional and/or national action.

1. The ARL and AAUP should convene an annual policy meeting among the leaders from both communities to develop priorities and strategies for collaboration (National), presses and libraries at a university should meet on an annual basis as a follow-up to the national meeting to develop a local plan. (Institutional)
2. A key outcome of this meeting both at the national and local level should be the identification of joint innovative electronic publishing projects. (National and Institutional)

3. The ARL and AAUP on the national level, and campus libraries and presses should encourage counterpart participation and reporting on governance and policy boards. (National and Institutional)

4. The ARL and AAUP should work together to define a shared information policy agenda for the two communities and to draft a coordinated advocacy strategy at the federal level. (National)

5. The ARL and AAUP on the national level, and campus libraries and presses should create forums for consultation with researchers and authors to explore their roles and interests as creators and consumers of scholarly works. (National and Institutional)

6. The ARL and AAUP on the national level, and campus libraries and presses should cooperate in the creation of high-quality continuing professional development and training programs for staff. (National and Institutional)

7. The ARL and AAUP on the national level, and campus libraries and presses should cooperate in the creation of high-quality education and training opportunities for library and publishing professionals from around the world and for faculty, researchers and students, with a focus on electronic publishing issues. (National and Institutional)

8. The ARL and AAUP should work together on the revision and updating of principles which govern the licensing of electronic works and on the identification or refinement of a model contract. (National)

9. The ARL and AAUP should work together on the identification and adoption of standards in those areas which impinge on electronic scholarly publishing, including technology and metadata. (National)

10. Campus libraries and presses should develop a technology and expertise infrastructure for systematic usability testing of electronic publications. (Institutional)

11. The ARL and AAUP on the national level, and campus libraries and presses should work together to outline a research and development program with a focus in areas of technology and software development, the impact of electronic publishing on education and research, and measuring use, for example. (National and Institutional)

12. The ARL and AAUP on the national level, and campus libraries and presses should work together to identify and solicit funding

from individual, foundation, corporate and federal/state sources to support joint activities. (National and Institutional)

13. Campus libraries and presses should seek out opportunities to integrate or share expertise in critical areas like metadata, technology and discipline specialists. (Institutional)

14. The ARL and AAUP on the national level, and campus libraries and presses should develop joint programs for the preservation and archiving of electronic content, particularly for works produced from cooperative publishing efforts. The projects now being funded by Mellon are excellent prototypes. (National and Institutional)

15. The ARL and AAUP on the national level, and campus libraries and presses should collaborate with SPARC to encourage and enable journal and book authors and editors to move from commercial to university presses. (National and Institutional)

16. The ARL and AAUP on the national level, and campus libraries and presses should collaborate on a systematic electronic book publishing program including both retrospective and current works, and emphasizing both specialized monographs and grey literature. (National and Institutional)

17. The ARL and AAUP on the national level, and campus libraries and presses should develop a suite of content and information services for the expanding distance learning community. (National and Institutional)

18. Campus libraries and presses should work together to capture, organize, distribute and archive new scholarly works such as courseware, software, datafiles and simulations. (Institutional)

19. The ARL and AAUP on the national level, and campus libraries and presses should develop a national document delivery service for scholars which features ease of use, rapid response and customizable elements. (National and Institutional)

20. The ARL and AAUP should collaborate along with other national organizations on the development and implementation of the Scholars Portal concept now in discussion (see Jerry Campbell's article in January 2001 issue of *Portal: Libraries and the Academy*) (http://muse.jhu.edu/journals/portal_libraries_and_the_ academy/v001/1.1campbell.html) that will create a scholarly responsive and productive tool for locating information on the Web. (National)

BioOne:
A New Model for Scholarly Publishing

Marilu Goodyear
Adrian W. Alexander

SUMMARY. This article describes a unique electronic journal publishing project involving the University of Kansas, the Big 12 Plus Libraries Consortium, the American Institute of Biological Sciences, Allen Press, and SPARC, the Scholarly Publishing and Academic Resources Coalition. This partnership has created BioOne, a database of 40 full-text society journals in the biological and environmental sciences, which was launched in April, 2001. The genesis and development of the project is described and financial, technical, and intellectual property models for the project are discussed. Collaborative strategies for the project are described. *[Article copies available for a fee from The Haworth Document Delivery Service: 1-800-HAWORTH. E-mail address: <getinfo@haworthpressinc.com> Website: <http://www.HaworthPress.com> © 2001 by The Haworth Press, Inc. All rights reserved.]*

KEYWORDS. Electronic publishing, scholarly publishing, biological literature, environmental science literature

Marilu Goodyear is Vice Chancellor for Information Services and Chief Information Officer, University of Kansas, 223 Strong Hall, Lawrence, KS 66045 (E-mail: goodyear@ku.edu).

Adrian W. Alexander is Executive Director, The Big 12 Plus Libraries Consortium, Linda Hall Library, 5109 Cherry Street, Kansas City, MO 64110 (E-mail: alexandera@lindahall.org).

[Haworth co-indexing entry note]: "BioOne: A New Model for Scholarly Publishing." Goodyear, Marilu, and Adrian W. Alexander. Co-published simultaneously in *Journal of Library Administration* (The Haworth Information Press, an imprint of The Haworth Press, Inc.) Vol. 35, No. 1/2, 2001, pp. 19-35; and: *Libraries and Electronic Resources: New Partnerships, New Practices, New Perspectives* (ed: Pamela L. Higgins) The Haworth Information Press, an imprint of The Haworth Press, Inc., 2001, pp. 19-35. Single or multiple copies of this article are available for a fee from The Haworth Document Delivery Service [1-800-HAWORTH, 9:00 a.m. - 5:00 p.m. (EST). E-mail address: getinfo@haworthpressinc.com].

BACKGROUND

In the last twenty years the basic issues related to the economics of scholarly publishing have become familiar to most academic librarians, particularly those involved in collection development. A constantly expanding universe of scholarly information (particularly in the sciences), the continually rising cost of scholarly information, and the inability of academic library budgets to keep pace with inflation are elements of the problem that have all been well documented and discussed continuously over the past fifteen years or so, at least. One of the more recent and concise overviews of the scholarly publishing conundrum was written by Joseph Branin of SUNY-Stony Brook (currently Director, Ohio State University Library) and Mary Case of the Association of Research Libraries (ARL) in 1998 and published in Notices of the American Mathematical Society in April 1998.[1]

One theme of the Branin/Case article is that the commercialization of scholarly publishing in the sciences is "at the core of the economic problem" faced by academic libraries.[2] A key paragraph in the statement relates directly to the issue of the commercialization of scholarly publishing raised by Branin and Case:

> We must urge faculty to submit articles to professional society publications, support ventures into electronic publishing, and pay close attention to and question pricing policies of the publications in their specialties. Faculty, especially those who serve as leaders in their professional societies, must urge those societies to take responsibility for maintaining or creating low cost venues for print or electronic publication of refereed journals of research finding and scholarly thought.[3]

This section of the document calls attention to the fact that many journals previously published by scholarly societies are now produced by major commercial publishers on behalf of those societies. When this happens, it usually results in a higher price tag for the libraries subscribing to the journal. This issue is exacerbated when smaller scholarly societies are faced with the need or desire to move their journals to electronic formats. Most smaller societies cannot afford the investment of funds it takes to move to electronic publishing unassisted. They also lack technical expertise and the ability to develop software appropriate for electronic distribution. Commercial publishers are able to offer not only the financial support for the transitions, but the technical systems to support electronic journals. Partnering with commercial publishers, with the price increase to the journal which almost always follows, often offers a tempting solution to this dilemma for scholarly societies.

Encouraging scholarly societies to seek alternatives (both for print and electronic formats) to more expensive commercial publishing partners is in the best interest of academic libraries from the standpoint of cost containment, but what should those alternatives be? Is there a larger role for the academy itself in this process, and what is that role? How might it impact university presses and academic computing centers, as well as libraries themselves? Are there other stakeholders that can play a part as well?

Academic libraries have become more involved directly in the scholarly publishing process only in the past few years. *Project Muse* is a collaboration begun in 1995 between the Johns Hopkins University Press and the Milton S. Eisenhower Library of that university to provide electronic versions of the 40+ journals published by the press in the humanities, social sciences, and sciences. *Project Muse* provides a central search interface for its journals, all of which are mounted on a central server at JHU.[4] Also in 1995, Stanford University's library launched *Highwire Press* with the electronic production of the highly cited *Journal of Biological Chemistry*. Highwire now provides access to almost 150 scholarly journals, many of which are society-published. Indeed, Highwire describes its partners as "scientific societies and responsible publishers."[5] Unlike *Project Muse,* however, Highwire does not utilize a central database for its journals. Instead, many of the journals are mounted by its partner societies on their own Web sites, with central searching of the various titles provided via Highwire's site. These notable projects provide two distinct models for changing scholarly publishing. This article outlines a third model that takes advantage of the collaborative energy of research libraries, academic computing resources, scholarly societies *and* commercial publishing.

GENESIS AND HISTORY OF THE BioOne PROJECT

BioOne is the result of an alliance of five organizations related to scholarly communication, representing scholarly societies, the university (both its faculty and its libraries), and the commercial sector.

- American Institute of Biological Sciences (http://www.aibs.org), publisher of the journal *BioScience,* is a federation of scientific societies that facilitates the exchange and dissemination of research among its members and with the public at large.
- SPARC, the Scholarly Publishing and Academic Resources Coalition (http://www.arl.org/sparc/) is a coalition of libraries that promotes and facilitates expanded competition in the scientific journals market. Libraries created SPARC to promote competition in the scholarly publishing marketplace by creating lower priced alternatives to high-cost journals. Using libraries' buying power, SPARC's goal is to nurture the creation of high-quality, low-priced publication outlets for peer-reviewed scientific, technical, and medical research. SPARC's approximately 200 member libraries pledge support for SPARC publisher-partners, helping their print and electronic journals achieve viability from the start.
- The Big 12 Plus Libraries Consortium (http://www.big12plus.org) represents 29 major research libraries with common objectives related to scholarly communications in the western United States. A major strategic initiative of the Consortium is to address scholarly communication issues in cooperation with the provosts of its member institutions.
- The University of Kansas (http://www.ku.edu) is a major comprehensive research and teaching university committed to research as a means of mutually reinforcing the scholarly inquiry underlying and informing the educational experience based in Lawrence, Kansas. The University has strong information technology capabilities and leadership that strongly supports new models of scholarly publishing.
- Allen Press (http://www.allenpress.com) is one of the nation's leading providers of publishing production services to societies that self-publish their journals, based in Lawrence, Kansas. It specializes in the production of superior charts, tables, photographs, and other non-textual material for print and electronic distribution.

The original concept for the project evolved from an initial conversation between AIBS and Allen Press. The American Institute of Biological Sciences serves approximately 125,000 biologists worldwide. AIBS societies represent the major biology groups outside the molecular biology and biochemistry research communities. Collectively these societies publish about 85 journals, many of which are the leading journals in their respective fields.

Allen Press, Inc. produces scholarly journals for over 300 societies and other scientific organizations. Allen Press has been involved in electronic publishing since 1997. Currently, it works with over twenty-five scholarly societies on electronic journal production; altogether Allen Press currently produces in print and/or electronic form, over 75 AIBS journals. Allen Press is known and respected for its ability to produce high quality journals while supporting its client societies' goal of providing information at a reasonable price to subscribers. Some commercial publishers view Allen Press as a competitor because it supports the activities of not-for-profit societies, sometimes against the interests of these large journal publishers.

Early discussions between AIBS and Allen Press confirmed several common interests and ideas related to the dissemination of scholarly information:

- The vast majority of AIBS societies do not yet provide electronic versions of their journals. There is growing interest among the societies to begin developing this option.
- Commercial publishers have approached some AIBS societies about providing electronic publishing services. A few societies, in fact, have already signed deals with commercial publishers, with much higher subscription prices for their journals being the result.
- AIBS societies and Allen Press share a common goal of retaining control of the intellectual property of AIBS journals in the hands of the societies and their members.
- Establishing separate Web sites for AIBS-related journals would be cost-prohibitive for the societies.
- There is a need for aggregated access to AIBS-related journals, due to the amount of "cross-usage" by users of those journals.

In April 1999, AIBS and Allen Press drafted jointly a "concept paper" that proposed the creation of a single, aggregated database of the approximately 80 highly-cited AIBS journals, to be produced in full-text electronic format, searchable via a common interface and available via the Internet, using commonly available Web browsers. The database would provide integrated content via links among fully searchable SGML-encoded articles, with a fully navigable electronic archive. Allen Press would develop and maintain the production database, utilizing the electronic publishing resources and expertise they had developed already. The launch was targeted for January 2001, with the full content for the 1999 and 2000 subscription years included in the first release of the database.

Due to the long-term potential size of the database, however, a second technology partner was needed to provide high-speed network access. Additionally, development funding to build the database was estimated initially to total almost $1 million, a sum that AIBS and Allen Press could not handle alone. Because of previous conversations about scholarly publishing issues between Allen Press and its "neighbor" in Lawrence, the University of Kansas, the concept paper was sent to William J. Crowe, then Vice-Chancellor for Information Services and Dean of Libraries at Kansas. Crowe immediately recognized the potential for a unique "public/private sector" collaborative opportunity involving scholarly societies, academic libraries, the university community and a for-profit publisher. The involvement of the University of Kansas (KU) achieved two immediate purposes. First, it provided BioOne with eventual access to Internet2 via KU's connection to that high-speed network. (Internet2® is a not-for-profit consortium, led by over 180 U.S. universities, with participation by over 60 leading companies. Internet2 is not a separate physical network and will not replace the Internet. Internet2 brings together institutions and resources from academia, industry and government that helped foster today's Internet in its infancy, and recreates the partnership to develop new technologies and capabilities that can then be deployed in the global Internet.[6]) More immediately, however, it brought AIBS and Allen Press together quickly with two important partners representing the key research library market, SPARC and the Big 12 Plus Libraries Consortium (BTP).

SPARC's overall aim to create a more competitive scholarly communication marketplace, ensure fair use of electronic resources, and apply technology to improve the process of scholarly communication in a cost-effective way could be operationalized through support of BioOne. BioOne needed the investment and support of the SPARC 180-member library membership base.

The University of Kansas has a long history of strong support for library cooperative activities, particularly with its research library partners in the middle west. It is one of the original members of the Big 12 Plus Libraries Consortium, based in Kansas City, and consisting now of 29 large research libraries (most of which are ARL members) located in 15 states in the Midwest, Southwest, and Western regions. In 1998, the consortium identified scholarly communication as a key program area in which to cooperate. At their spring meeting in Kansas City in April 1999, the Big 12 Plus library deans/directors received a briefing on the BioOne concept paper and endorsed the concept enthusiastically. There was strong consensus that the consortium should involve itself in various aspects of the project, including a commitment of consortium financial resources to development of the database. As one Big 12 Plus library dean noted, "This is the most important thing that we can be doing together right now."

Soon after this, the concept was discussed at a meeting of the SPARC Working Group at the spring meeting of the Association of Research Libraries in Kansas City, Missouri. Members of the working group expressed considerable interest in a role for SPARC in the further development of the project, and charged SPARC Enterprise Director Richard K. Johnson to continue working with the BioOne partners.

Since that time, the five BioOne partners have met on a monthly basis, and communicate regularly by means of regular conference calls and what now number thousands of e-mail messages, as development of the enterprise continues in earnest toward the launch date of April 2, 2001. The remainder of this article, however will discuss the conceptual, organizational, and technical elements of an enterprise that took shape in two short years.

ORGANIZATION OF BioOne

The Legal Entity

A non-binding memorandum of understanding (MOU) was signed by the partners in June 1999, which formalized the mutual intent of the partners to continue work on development of the enterprise. BioOne is a District of Columbia nonprofit corporation certified in August 1999. Tax exempt status (IRS 501(c)(3) and DC) was obtained in Summer 2000. BioOne's business office is located within the offices of ARL in Washington, DC, where it will remain at least through 2001. BioOne received conditional registration of its trade name and trademark by the US PTO in October 2000, subject to permanent registration by demonstration and statement of "use in commerce" as database subscriptions begin in April of 2001. BioOne's registered domain name and site is http://www. bioone.org.

Governance

BioOne has ten non-compensated Directors on its Board, with two representatives appointed by each of the Founding Organizations. The

Directors serve a two-year term and are appointed by the Founding Organizations. Three officers have been elected by the Board of Directors. Currently, the Chair of the Board is Kent E. Holsinger, Professor, Department of Ecology and Evolutionary Biology, University of Connecticut at Storrs. Adrian W. Alexander, Executive Director of the Big 12 Plus Libraries Consortium, serves as Treasurer and Marilu Goodyear, Vice Chancellor for Information Services and Chief Information Officer at the University of Kansas, serves as Secretary.

Management and Staff

BioOne has one employee. Chief Operating Officer and President, Heather Joseph began in August 2000 after a nation-wide recruitment. Previously, Ms. Joseph was Director of Publishing at the American Society for Cell Biology and held senior publishing positions with the Society for Neuroscience, Elsevier Science and the American Astronomical Society. She is active in the Society for Scholarly Publishing and the Council of Science Editors. BioOne was fortunate to find a leader with such extensive experience in electronic publishing and in working with the scholarly community in dissemination of scholarship. BioOne plans to add additional employees as the growth of the project warrants.

Over a dozen representatives of the Founding Organizations have comprised a non-compensated Working Group that was invaluable during BioOne's start-up and early development stage. The work of organizing the project was accomplished through the following division of responsibilities with overall coordination and advice from the Working Group.

The American Institute of Biological Sciences provided the major link to the professional societies in the area of biology, ecology and environmental science. It has played the lead role, along with BioOne's President, in acquiring content for the project. The Big 12 Plus Library Consortium has provided financial support, expertise in development of the marketing model, and advice from member libraries on a wide variety of issues. SPARC recognized BioOne as a "SPARC Scientific Communities Partner" and has provided financial, strategic and tactical support, as well as sharing a lead role in development financing and market communications. SPARC also has provided a business development consultant to assist the Working Group. The University of Kansas has provided strategic, technological and operational advice as well as development of the intellectual property concept and the licenses. KU also serves as primary Internet host, system operator and initial database repository under an arms-length Service Agreement. Allen Press is providing technological and business advice, and serves as contractor for Web site design/development and database fabrication/text conversion/production under an arms-length Vendor Agreement.

As the project becomes operational, Working Group members will have a new role of "advice providers" on financial, marketing, and technical matters. Additionally, BioOne maintains its commitment to seeking and responding to the advice and opinions of the constituent groups. Three Advisory Groups have been appointed in this regard.

A Publisher Advisory Group will advise BioOne on such matters as product features, financial models, avoidance of risks and costs in electronic publishing, governance, finding common ground in meeting the needs of small and large organizations, and tools that might be offered to enhance editorial and publishing process efficiency.

A Technology Advisory Group will advise BioOne on such issues as:

- architecture and new system developments
- linking mechanisms between citations of digital works and the works themselves, and Abstracting and Indexing (A & I) services
- standards
- technical aspects of digital archiving
- access management
- meta-data standards
- technical issues associated with helping users gain authorized access to networked information (identification/authentication/authorization issues).

A Library Advisory Group will assist BioOne in giving advice on the following matters:

- *Pricing:* how to balance issues of adequate revenue for the publishers and sufficient funds for continued system development with reasonable pricing for libraries
- *Licenses*: advice on subscriber license terms best suited to meet end-users needs
- *Interface development*: ways to improve the BioOne interface to better present content to end users
- *System usability*: ways to improve existing functionality and suggest additional functionality to best meet end-user needs

- *Content*: Where should BioOne place it's priorities in attracting new journals; what other kinds of content and links would be most helpful to today's scholar?

FINANCES AND PRICING

The unique nature of the BioOne partnership, involving both for-profit and not-for-profit organizers, has dictated the need for an innovative financial model that meets the requirements of scholarly societies and libraries alike. Since BioOne itself has been established as a non-profit company, the basis for its financial model will be cost recovery, with pricing of the database set accordingly. Pricing and costs will be reviewed regularly by the BioOne Board of Directors. But this goal can only be achieved while also meeting the particular needs of BioOne's partners in the scholarly community, including both societies and libraries. Several key issues had to be considered in developing a financial model for BioOne and meeting the needs of the stakeholders.

Development Funding

A key strategy in the development of the financial model has been that these development costs should not, if possible, be amortized into the price of the database, and BioOne should launch the product with no outstanding debt. Instead, the BioOne partners would cover those costs in other ways. Start-up costs have been substantially reduced by the in-kind contributions of the Founding Organizations as noted above. All of the founding organizations (AIBS, Allen Press, BTP, KU, and SPARC) have made important *in-kind* contributions to the effort in terms of time, travel, etc. Additionally, particular partners have made even larger "investments" that have contributed significantly to the development of BioOne to date. Allen Press, for example, will be converting the electronic content files from participating societies to SGML/XML, and they have pledged to underwrite a significant part of this work for the societies that are already publishing their journals (both print and electronic) through Allen Press. Likewise, KU will provide important in-kind contributions in its role as the "host" for the BioOne database, which will be maintained 24×7 by the university's Academic Computing Services staff. Finally, SPARC has, from the outset, provided valuable business start-up advice through the use of a publishing consultant paid by SPARC.

One of the most unique features of the BioOne financial model has been the participation of the marketplace itself in providing development funding. In the Fall of 1999, SPARC launched a solicitation effort to its 180 member libraries. SPARC members were asked to contribute from $1,000 to $5,000 in charter support, based upon library materials budget, and an optional $5,000 in sponsor support to BioOne from that part of their funding already ear-marked for SPARC projects. In return, these libraries will receive a discount on their BioOne subscriptions during the first five years. This financial support was supplied by 127 libraries.

Additional start-up financial support has been acquired from the Big 12 Plus Libraries Consortium and by the provosts of the Big 12 universities. BioOne's marketing partners, Amigos Library Services and OCLC, have also provided significant financial contributions.

Revenue for Societies

A critical success factor for the development of BioOne is the engagement and retention of a significant number of scholarly societies and their journals. The industry trend toward electronic journals has not always been embraced by the scholarly community, and the societies that form the core of BioOne's efforts are no exception. For many of these societies, their journal is their primary revenue stream and there is a need to ensure revenue from electronic publication as print revenues decrease. Given these needs of the societies, the BioOne working group developed a unique "revenue sharing" program that will give fully 50% of all net sales receipts back to the societies, with the remainder going to cover the ongoing costs of operating and maintaining BioOne. The amount that each individual society receives annually will be based on a formula that takes into account both the number of hits on a journal title and the number of pages that title "contributes" to the BioOne database. This percentage is much higher than that which societies typically receive when their journal is published commercially. Additionally, BioOne will provide "insurance" to societies against large-scale cancellations of print subscriptions to their journals. Societies participating in the BioOne project that experience cancellation rates for their print journals that are above average (based on their historical cancellation experience for the past three years) during the first two years that they are part of BioOne will be eligible for reimbursement for those cancellations from the revenue pool.

Pricing Model

BioOne will be sold as a complete database that will grow as more journals are added. In order to maintain enough "critical mass" of content to insure that smaller societies as well as larger societies benefit from BioOne, individual journal titles or titles from individual societies will not be priced separately. Also, BioOne electronic journal titles will not be linked to print subscriptions of the same journal for pricing purposes. Instead, the product will be marketed as a totally "unbundled from print" database.

Initially, the primary selling and distribution focus will be on the research library and institutional market, predominantly in higher education. Because of the power of the library consortium phenomenon all over the world, consortia will be central to BioOne's marketing and sales efforts. This core marketing strategy was one of the reasons that BioOne selected an organization such as Amigos Library Services to serve as the exclusive distributor for BioOne in the U.S. institutional market and OCLC as its international sales and marketing partner.

CONTENT OF THE DATABASE

The BioOne Journals Database is a unique electronic aggregation of richly linked, interrelated journals consolidated and uniformly available for the first time. This collection represents many important primary sources organized by discipline–in this case, organismal and integrative biology, including ecology and the environment. BioOne will initially present each journal's current volume, updated as issued, plus, generally, one back volume. As the years progress, back volumes will remain accessible indefinitely. Additional titles will be added during 2001 and beyond and some backfile conversion is anticipated. The BioOne Journals Database will continue to expand to potentially hundreds of titles as the product develops. Backfile conversion is also anticipated.

Electronic licensing efforts have been directed primarily to members of AIBS and to other nonprofits that want to participate in BioOne. AIBS has some 80 scientific organizations as members, with a combined membership well exceeding 150,000, and more than 85 publications with peer-reviewed research. No publisher or title will be excluded if appropriate for inclusion in the aggregation and compatible with BioOne's values, objectives and business model. However, content-providers are concentrated initially among nonprofit self-publishers, for which there is a strong mutuality of inter-dependence with scientists, libraries and BioOne itself. These nonprofit self-published journals will likely always form the database's core.

TECHNICAL DESCRIPTION OF THE PRODUCT

BioOne has a commitment to utilize open standards such as SGML, HTML, ODBC, SQL, and citation/reference identifiers such as PMID, SICI, DOI, OpenURL, etc., in its content and systems development. All journal articles and other document types (book reviews, letters, notes, errata, etc.) are encoded using a modified version of ISO 12083 SGML, designed to identify the journal header and article elements of the items in the database, as well as citation/reference identifiers to articles both internal and external to the database.

All articles in the database are accessible from computable URLs according to the National Center for Biotechnology Information (http://www.ncbi.nlm.nih.gov/PubMed/linking.html) URL specifications so that automatic links can be generated from library systems or A&I services. While items will be encoded using SGML for indexing and archival purposes, HTML and PDF versions are provided for ease of display and printing using standard Web browsers. All characters not supported by standard Web browsers will be rendered as graphics. Allen Press had already developed a large graphic library of almost 5,000 special characters used in science publishing for this purpose. Complex equations and tables will be stored and displayed as graphics, converted from Postscript for exact reproduction of the printed version.

Numerous standard links will be available in the BioOne database, including:

- TOC to HTML abstracts, HTML full-text, and PDF text
- HTML abstract to HTML full-text and PDF text
- HTML full-text to PDF text
- Tables, figures, equations, citations to references to them
- Citations to full-text of any article in any journal on the system
- Citations to Medline data (titles, abstracts, works by the same author)
- Bi-directional links between errata and original article
- Author index to abstracts, full-text and PDF text
- Keyword index to abstracts, full-text and PDF text.

The article citation/reference links, such as DOIs, will be made available to external (A & I) services to provide easy linking to the on-line full text of articles discovered as a result of searches in traditional A&I databases. This is a critical feature for researchers in need of broad, deep, detailed information in a timely fashion. Adherence to standards also means that BioOne will be a highly portable resource capable of migrating as technology and encoding standards advance.

While fabrication of the SGML files will take place at Allen Press, the production database will actually "live" at the University of Kansas, maintained by the University's Academic Computing Services (ACS) department. This arrangement will enable high-speed access to the BioOne database through KU's participation in both Internet 1 and 2. Both Allen Press and the University of Kansas serve as providers of the technological base of the product through contracts with BioOne which were generated in an "arms-length" process with appropriate due diligence analysis.

BioOne's sales and distribution contractors are responsible for customer support–Amigos in the U.S. and Canada and OCLC for all international subscribers. This includes responding to inquiries, problems, complaints and questions on all matters regarding the site license, pricing, invoicing, IP address management, service features, etc. BioOne's database contractor, Allen Press, is responsible for user support (in consultation with BioOne and the University of Kansas, host contractor, when necessary). Extensive online help screens are available with the product. All parties are committed to provide the highest practical levels of quality and responsiveness in customer and user support.

THE POLICY BASE FOR BioOne

Intellectual Property

The BioOne intellectual property model seeks to provide wide distribution of the scholarly material in the database while at the same time provides continuing control over the content for the author and the society. BioOne encourages the societies to ask only for distribution rights from authors. Societies (or authors) will retain ownership of the printed text and electronic encoded versions of each journal. The society will transfer exclusive rights for the first twelve months for electronic distribution to BioOne. After that period, the society may utilize the encoded text as they wish. During the initial twelve months, they may also utilize the electronic text on their own Web site.

On the subscriber side, BioOne will grant rights to the subscribers for personal, non-commercial research use. The license will allow all regular use as well as:

- Printing and downloading
- Interlibrary Loan
- Electronic Reserves
- Distance Education uses
- Specific provisions for all fair use.

BioOne has sought input on license language from the library community through a review by the SPARC license committee and librarians from the Big 12 Plus.

Linking Policy

In order to create enhanced value, BioOne is considering a number of arrangements to create links from the journal article content in our database to a variety of secondary sources. The creation of a robust set of links to and from the data in the BioOne database greatly enhances its value to the scientific research community, and provides opportunities for increased awareness and exposure to the database's content. Therefore the BioOne Board of Directors has approved a policy of linking to any and all collections, as long as the subject matter is deemed appropriate and as long as the cost of linking does not represent a significant financial impediment to BioOne.

Privacy Policy

BioOne seeks to protect entirely the privacy of individual users. A statement on the Web site explains our information gathering and dissemination practices, and delineates clearly what information will or will not be used, and how. BioOne will share and publish aggregated usage and demographic information, but none pertaining to individual users will be released in any form to any outside party or used for any marketing purpose.

User Reports and Statistics

BioOne will maintain usage records and provide usage statements to both publishers and subscribers. Publisher statements of usage by title will be issued periodically, including a formal annual report. Subscriber usage statements will be issued regularly and according to the current guidelines of the International Coalition of Library Consortia (ICOLC), and possibly, the ARL E-metrics project when issued. BioOne also will report its status, accomplishments and usage periodically in public communications, including postings on the Web site.

CONCLUSION

BioOne has attracted considerable attention since the announcement of the project. Its unique nature has attracted attention and articles have appeared about the project in *Science, Library Journal Academic Newswire, Nature, The London Times, The Chronicle of Higher Education,* and the *Journal of Electronic Publishing.*

The partners in the BioOne enterprise have taken the challenge to protect and promote scholarly communication through the effective management of the academy's intellectual property to heart in the conceptualization and development of this project. While opinions differ on what strategies are best, most librarians, educators and scientists agree that transformation of the scholarly communications process and marketplace is critically needed. BioOne has been formed around a concept of strength through collaboration and shared values.

The underlying strategies upon which the model has been constructed include:

- Build a business model upon on the belief that high-impact, low-cost scientific journals must and can remain viable and independent;
- Balance the priorities and requirements of all vested groups;
- Provide an electronic aggregation of journals maximizing the potential of the networked environment and addressing a high need in the electronic environment;
- Achieve financial momentum and security;
- Remain dedicated to nonprofit values and motivation;
- Deploy the highest levels of technological and marketing resources, expertise and capabilities;
- Operate with a low fixed-cost structure;
- Repay library supporters with excellent service and cost recovery-based pricing;

• Repay participating publishers with e-publishing opportunities and society-enhancing revenue-sharing.

BioOne represents a unique collaboration between scientific societies, higher education, and commercial publishing. It will bring to scientists and students a valuable aggregation of high-impact bioscience research journals in the form of a cost-effective, hyper-linked Internet resource. Most importantly, it will help to keep ownership of information in the hands of the scholarly societies whose members produce that information, while making it more accessible for those who use it, and keeping it affordable for the libraries that buy it.

NOTES

1. Joseph J. Branin and Mary Case, "Reforming Scholarly Publishing in the Sciences: A Librarian Perspective," *Notices of the American Mathematical Society,* 45 (April 1998): 475-486.

2. Ibid., 478-479.

3. Ibid.

4. http://www.press.jhu.edu/muse.html.

5. http://highwire.stanford.edu/intro.dtl.

6. http://www.internet2.edu/.

The California Digital Library and the eScholarship Program

Catherine H. Candee

SUMMARY. The eScholarship program was launched in 2000 to foster faculty-led innovation in scholarly publishing. An initiative of the University of California (UC) and a program of the California Digital Library, the eScholarship program has stimulated significant interest in its short life. Its modest but visible accomplishments garner praise from many quarters, within and beyond the University of California. In perhaps the best indication of its timeliness and momentum, there are more proposals submitted to eScholarship today than the CDL can manage. This early success is due in part to the sheer power of an idea whose time has come, but also to the unique approach on which CDL was founded and the eScholarship initiative was first launched. *[Article copies available for a fee from The Haworth Document Delivery Service: 1-800-HAWORTH. E-mail address: <getinfo@haworthpressinc.com> Website: <http://www.HaworthPress.com> © 2001 by The Haworth Press, Inc. All rights reserved.]*

KEYWORDS. Scholarly publishing, scholarly communication, digital library, electronic scholarship, electronic publishing, digital publishing, Web publishing

---

Catherine H. Candee is Director of Scholarly Communication Initiatives, California Digital Library, University of California, Office of the President, 300 Lakeside Drive, 6th Floor, Oakland, CA 94612-3550 (E-mail: catherine.candee@ucop.edu).

[Haworth co-indexing entry note]: "The California Digital Library and the eScholarship Program." Candee, Catherine H. Co-published simultaneously in *Journal of Library Administration* (The Haworth Information Press, an imprint of The Haworth Press, Inc.) Vol. 35, No. 1/2, 2001, pp. 37-59; and: *Libraries and Electronic Resources: New Partnerships, New Practices, New Perspectives* (ed: Pamela L. Higgins) The Haworth Information Press, an imprint of The Haworth Press, Inc., 2001, pp. 37-59. Single or multiple copies of this article are available for a fee from The Haworth Document Delivery Service [1-800-HAWORTH, 9:00 a.m. - 5:00 p.m. (EST). E-mail address: getinfo@haworthpressinc.com].

INTRODUCTION

We are at an amazing moment in history. In the modern industrial world, digital technologies have been absorbed into the mainstream in a way that leaves few lives untouched. Virtually every sector of our society–academic, commercial, governmental, and public–has been transformed by the way its institutions manage information. Leaders are challenged not just to direct their institutions and enterprises, but to transform them–to exploit new technologies, to produce more for less, to feed the rising expectations of the savvy information consumer for better, faster, cheaper information. This is particularly true for those in the business of information, and perhaps nowhere more than in libraries.

Digital libraries of the new millennium bear little resemblance to their 20th century former selves. Most libraries in the early digital era of the 1990s functioned as they had historically–as collectors and managers of published intellectual content. Stirred by unending budget crises, mindful of their mission to support research and teaching, and steeled by a determination to preserve collections and the access to them, libraries became early adopters of digital technologies which could facilitate those ends and, they hoped, could finesse the budget crises.

The budget crisis is still with us in the 21st century. But, during the past decade, many libraries became adept implementers of those technologies, clever developers of systems and tools for providing service based on the expanding collections of digital resources, and ardent agents for change in the commercially controlled system of scholarly communication. Today, these 21st century digital libraries find themselves in new and expanding roles, including a role once reserved for publishers: selector of content for digital publication and publisher of new material.

At the University of California, both the depth of the crisis and the opportunity for change were understood in the mid 1990s. United in determination to take action, and grounded in an acute sense of the historical moment, founders of the California Digital Library (CDL) created a virtual, or co-library, for the UC system. The creation of the CDL provided a framework to focus the system's tremendous resources in a way which could allow its libraries to maintain their high quality of library service while they worked to change the system of scholarly communication that threatened them and the entire institution. The hope and the aim was to capture some of the hundreds of millions of dollars passing through the university, to the university library, and on into the hands of commercial publishers, and to redirect it to its stated purpose–support of research and teaching through effective high-quality library service.

HISTORY

In 1997, the California Digital Library (CDL) was charged by University of California President Richard C. Atkinson to develop a comprehensive system for the management of digital scholarly information. The formal launching of the CDL followed an extensive consultative and collaborative process of analysis and review by individuals and departments throughout the UC system, and specific recommendations of the LPAI,[1] an advisory body of distinguished faculty and librarians.

The crisis driving the CDL formation was not new; UC libraries had been suffering the effects of unchecked serial price increases for decades. Nor were the efforts to supersede the crisis; scattered efforts appeared aimed at exploiting technical possibilities and some even suggested possibilities for circumventing the endless budget crises. But the establishment of CDL reflected a deepening grasp of the challenges facing the university, a recognition of the opportunity represented by new technologies and the World Wide Web, and a profound commitment to respond to both. The CDL opened its digital doors to the public in January 1999.

At first, CDL aimed to provide the kind of content and services universities had come to expect of libraries. As a co-library for the 9-campus UC system,[2] CDL was able to achieve economies of scale by centralizing the acquisition and licensing of a growing quantity of digital content. By the end of its first two years CDL had mounted an impressive array of digital content and digital library services to aid the user in discovery and retrieval of its vast distributed resources. The University of California's Melvyl system includes a union catalog for the UC system, associated indices such as the California Periodicals database which lists almost 900,000 unique titles held in the more than 550 participating California libraries, and associated resources including more than 50 abstracting and indexing databases and more than 5,000 full text journals. There is also a growing collection of digitized finding aids and, in some cases, associated digital content in the Online Archive of California, a database of digital descriptions of archival collections from campuses and institutions across the state. In addition to centralizing licensing, storage and access functions, the CDL provides infrastructure and policies to guide the developing possibilities for shared collections, for ongoing development of the expanding digital library services, and a mechanism for a new level of cooperation among the soon to be 10 campus-based libraries of the UC system.

However, the charge to CDL was always understood to mean more than simply reformatting existing collections, or licensing more journals for more users. From the start, the charge to CDL included reaching beyond the bounds of traditional library services into the pockets and corners of the changing university community to find more effective ways to support teaching and research. This mandate required applying technologies in ways not yet anticipated, and in ways that only the would-be users of the newly enhanced services could ultimately determine. The technologies would have to be made available at the point that they would be used most effectively–in the laboratory, in the classroom, in the hands of the authors themselves–and it was the library's mission to determine the moment and the method for positioning the organizational and technical support to be most effective. This experiment took programmatic form as the eScholarship initiative in the spring of 2001.

THE eSCHOLARSHIP EXPERIMENT

The University of California is an ideal spot for the eScholarship experiment. In addition to its 170,000+ students, the University of California claims among its current faculty 300 members of the Academy of Sciences, 20 Nobel Prize winners, and senior editors of approximately 12% of the world's top scholarly journals.[3] Any effort to effect significant change in scholarly publishing would need to make good use of these assets.

Indeed, the approach taken in the launching of CDL and its eScholarship program has been key to its embrace by faculty and researchers, within UC and beyond. For the eScholarship experiment in particular, Richard E. Lucier, the founding University Librarian and Executive Director of the CDL, drew on his experience in the 1980s at Johns Hopkins University with the Genome Project.[4] Lucier grasped then the unique and protracted nature of the process unfolding as the genome researchers groped their way to the creation of a gene map. He surmised, apparently correctly, that the process now unfolding in the UC system and elsewhere could not be directed or prescribed but would unfold more productively if it were framed and supported by an organizational and technical infrastructure.

The other prong of the evolving eScholarship approach was to monitor and experiment with the rapidly developing digital technologies themselves. CDL technologists kept a trained eye on emerging software and tools that might enable the kind of experiment envisioned by eScholarship, and which in turn might be best tested and developed in the real life challenges of electronic dissemination. The eScholarship experiment became the embodiment of this two-pronged approach.

There were other advanced experiences and models to draw on and they, too, had to be understood in their particularity. One such model was the automated e-print archive at Los Alamos, now known as arXiv, for physics, mathematics, computer science and nonlinear science. arXiv had been online and automated for nearly ten years and was widely perceived to have transformed scholarly communication in high-energy physics. Paul Ginsparg, considered the inventor of arXiv and himself a physicist, suggested as early as 1996 that "the role of journals as communicators of information has long been supplanted in certain fields of physics" and goes on to state that in certain fields of physics they have ceased to hold the franchise for validation of information for purposes of job and grant application.[5]

These claims have been largely validated in the high-energy physics community. But they were the exception, not nearly the rule, in science, in physical science, or even within all the fields of physics. To draw lessons from this important experience and to make effective use of the available technologies, CDL had to comprehend what about the arXiv experience was unique, and what about it was universal. Indeed, this approach was incorporated into the spine of the developing eScholarship initiative. Concern for the uniqueness of each discipline, for the unique structure of the literature for every field, for the unique way in which scholars in those fields use and adapt technical tools, was converted into real knowledge of those particularities through a phenomenon of the early eScholarship program called "Faculty Forums."

WHAT DO SCHOLARS WANT?

Throughout 1999 and in early 2000, Lucier and CDL staff, working with campus based library staff, conducted faculty forums in fields ranging across all disciplines. There was a great deal of interest among UC faculty in what the university might do to relieve the deleterious effects of the budget crisis. There was frustration with the sheer volume of scholarly information, and therefore interest in CDL efforts to develop systems and tools to help manage the explosion of resources. Faculty who had already embarked on innovative digital publishing projects of their own, or who were preparing to, were eager to gain library support or collaboration in those efforts.

The CDL scouts made an unsurprising but very important finding which has remained central to the vision and program of eScholarship. Coupled with the desire to spread ideas farther and faster for less–the most obvious benefits suggested by new digital technologies–there was widespread, almost unanimous, concern with two essential components of the current system of scholarly communication: peer review and permanence. This was not a surprise, and wouldn't be to anyone following the discussion of the future of the electronic journal. It has been said over and over again, but Hal Varian said it most succinctly in a paper presented at Emory University in 1997. Of the academic publishing system's filtering function, Varian said, "work cannot be cumulative unless authors have some faith that prior literature is accurate."[6] The finding was no less significant because it was so familiar. It simply confirmed that, no matter what shape or platform digital resources might occupy, or what unique models of publication evolved in the eScholarship program, concern for the quality–however it would be determined–and the persistence of digital content deposited with CDL were paramount for UC scholars.

Other concerns raised in the forums were as different as night and day, and often contradictory. For instance, while one concern voiced was that the credibility problem facing digital publishing would have to be met with aggressive quality indicators, the belief that electronic journals can provide the same vetting process as traditional journals, perhaps more efficiently, was also expressed. Some UC-based editors found electronic publishing to be less expensive; others expressed concern with the startup costs of electronic publishing. The range of concerns reinforced the perception that in order to build on the experiences gone before, eScholarship would have to customize its engagement with each scholarly community with the appropriate technical and organizational supports.

AN APPROACH THAT WORKS

CDL's approach to this constellation of needs and concerns was to: disassemble the components of the current system of scholarly communication–the creation, dissemination, certification and archiving; the authors, reviewers, certifiers, and the users who read and cite the authors; the publishers and disseminators; the libraries and information services who index and archive the literature; and the university and organizations which employ and fund the research upon which this is all based–and reassemble the components in new and untested ways to determine the most effective and advantageous way possible.[7] If the appropriate technologies could be brought into play with any community of scholars in a way which preserved the best parts of the current system, but allowed for a redesign and reconfiguration to best meet their research and communication needs, the academy would realize the greatest gains. The challenge lay in determining the right mix of players, services and technologies.

This was not an easy task. The structure of the literature varies tremendously from field to field, as does the individual and community-wide preparedness to experiment with new methods of communication. Both factors influence the kind of technologies sought by those communities and the speed with which the new technical tools are adopted; sometimes the factors are inextricably linked, and at other times the two seem to act independently of one another. For the eScholarship interventions to be fruitful, all of these factors had to be understood and incorporated to some degree into the program.

Indeed, early eScholarship efforts have been finely tuned to discovering the needs, objective and subjective, of emerging eScholarship communities. Monitoring of the technical advances that might enable those efforts, a broader CDL effort now led by a specialized strategic development team, has informed and influenced which proposals are accepted and how they are implemented. But a one-size-fits-all solution has never dictated the program. This two-pronged approach has allowed us to opportunistically test emerging software and to contribute to its development, while advancing the specific needs of eScholarship communities. This custom mapping of emerging technologies to the faculty inspired initiatives began to accelerate the eScholarship experiment in early 2001. A more surprising development–the growing demand by partners to publish a range of new scholarly products within the eScholarship program–presented more evidence of the changes astir in scholarly communication and spurred the rapid differentiation of several digital publishing models within the program. Promising developments in our partnerships and collaborations, with scholarly communities, with researchers in computer science, and with UC Press, paralleled the maturation of the eScholarship publishing models

Perhaps the best way to illustrate the development and direction of the eScholarship effort is to describe the technical model and infrastructure undergirding the program. Then we can explore the various ways in which the technical components and publishing models are being developed by the unique requirements of the scholars governing its use. The process, which often takes place on the level of calls for specific functionality, drives the software and tool development within the eScholarship program as well as identification of the policies and practices which will govern their use. Since the eScholarship program uses almost exclusively open source software, which is in turn being constantly modified by the broader universe of its adopters and users, there is a complex mix of forces shaping the reassembling of the scholarly communication system.

TECHNICAL MODEL AND INFRASTRUCTURE

The eScholarship initiative was founded on the hypothesis that discipline-based archives which encourage self-publishing hold great promise for stimulating open dissemination of scholarship, for focusing and simplifying the problem of long term preservation and persistent access to that scholarship, and for expanding the possibilities for integration within and across disciplines, institutions and platforms.

The program was built on a three-tiered technical infrastructure comprised of the following:

1. Disciplinary-based e-print repositories which allow open dissemination of scholarship through direct author or institutional submission and archiving.
2. Tools for submission, peer-review, discovery and use of scholarship.
3. New scholarly products drawn from the content deposited in the e-print archives. In addition to spawning familiar forms such as journals and monographs, the archives would encourage creative bundling of the scholarship into original forms and compilations, new uses for annotation and citation services, and alerting, integration and summarization services for students.

DIGITAL REPOSITORIES

As mentioned earlier, the eScholarship experiment draws a good deal of inspiration from the enormously positive effect that the Los Alamos arXiv has had on scholarly communication in physics. Building on the model, if not the actual technical architecture, eScholarship proposes to experiment with repositories to support self-publishing, managing and archiving of digital content in any discipline. As such, the discipline-based Digital Repository is perhaps the most essential component of the technology infrastructure for the kind of experimentation and innovation eScholarship exists to support.

Among the services available in eScholarship's repositories as of January 2001 are: submission of content via standard Web browser, author/submitter registration; submission of descriptive information for content; submission verification; and editing of user record by owner and staff. Users can browse by subject, conduct a search on a range of variables: title, authors, abstract, keywords, subject categories, document type, conference, department, editors, institution, status (unpublished, in press, published), refereed (yes/no), publication, year; results can be sorted by author's name, title, year (most recent first), year (oldest first). Services still in development include a commenting function and a system and mechanism for version control. In general we expect and will support the evolution of services as suggested by experience, consultation with the community of contributors and users, and changes in technology.

In January 2001, discipline-based repositories were opened using the self-archiving software called "ePrints" recently released by the Electronics and Computer Science Department of the University of Southampton. The software is already running under Cogprints, the Cognitive Science ePrints Archive, and is inter-operable with other Open Archive Initiative (OAI) compliant archives. There is more information about the software at eScholarship's Web site http://escholarship.cdlib.org/and at http://www.eprints.org/.

The ePrints software from Southampton offered a lot of the necessary functionality, and appeared to be modular enough to allow additional functionality to be added without too much difficulty. The configuration variables are completely separate from the core code, so upgrades to the software could be implemented rather simply. Indeed, the beta release of ePrints in Fall 2000 came just in time for the CDL team to customize three instances for eScholarship communities. The eScholarship team continues to monitor developments in software and tools for managing archives such as these, and is prepared to migrate to new systems and platforms as necessary. However, despite the experimental nature of the eScholarship repositories, the content deposited within them is being–and will continue to be–archived and persistently available from the first deposit.

The first three repositories are being made available to scholars in Dermatology, International and Area Studies (IAS), and Tobacco Control Research. These communities have widely divergent needs and thus require different functionality and tools in their support. An editorial or advisory board has been named to oversee the development of each of the repositories and to help formulate policies and guidelines to govern its use. These scholars and others in each of the communities grapple with critical issues of use and intervention, (e.g., filtering and editorial control, version control, powers of an author to delete or replace old versions) for deposits made to their repository in order to ensure its integrity and to match the culture of the field. In fact, the development path of each of the three tiers of our technical infrastructure varies according to the discipline it serves, as does the interaction between the layers of technical infrastructure and thus the entire infrastructure itself. This is reflected most clearly in the various organizational and technical models for the scholarly products to be drawn from the content in the repositories, but it is evident as well in the levels of filtering applied to the different repositories.

In the case of the *Dermatology Online Journal,* which migrated to CDL servers from its birthplace at University of California at Davis (UCD) last July, the journal will be an overlay to the broader contents of the dermatology open repository. In California International and Area Studies (CIAS) publications, digital monographs will be the primary packaging of content drawn from the international and area studies repository; and within the Tobacco Research and Control community, the repository will be available for new research stimulated by the vast amount of new primary source material available digitally in the new Legacy National Tobacco Documents Library at the University of California, San Francisco (UCSF).

As more repositories are added, and the current repositories are further developed, we will feed back into the community the lessons we've learned along the way. In the end, we hope the eScholarship effort will contribute broadly to the academy's growing need and effort to transform scholarly communication. For now, the lessons which can be drawn are primarily in the realm of process and approach.

Here is a closer look at the communities for which prototype repositories are being developed, the publishing models emerging around those repositories (and a few developing independently of the open archive infrastructure) and the issues emerging regarding the use and development of the entire technical apparatus for eScholarship.

Dermatology

One of the first communities to use an eScholarship repository is a UC-centered but internationally-based group in dermatology. This community is currently represented by the editorial board of the *Dermatology Online Journal* (DOJ, http://dermatology.cdlib.org/), the electronic journal published since 1995 by UC Davis. DOJ is a first tier scholarly journal indexed in Medline that provides opportunities for experimenting with access to rich supplementary materials such as the images and data sets associated with clinical medicine. Led by journal founder Art Huntley, the journal migrated to CDL servers in January 2001.

With the January 2001 release of the eScholarship Web site, support of *Dermatology Online Journal* (DOJ) and the associated community was extended to include a prototype *Dermatology Digital Repository*. The editorial board for DOJ has agreed to guide this effort to experiment with open archives in dermatology, which shares with other fields in clinical medicine a grave concern for quackery and general liability for pubic safety. The articles and papers deposited herein, which will be digitally archived and persistently available on CDL servers independently of the journal, may also have been submitted to DOJ but will remain open to the public during the entire review process. Papers accepted for publication in DOJ will be physically maintained in the archive though they will have the signature formatting of the journal and will be identified as a published article.

Articles or commentaries in the repository, whether or not they are submissions to DOJ or other science or medical journals, will be given a brief review by members of the editorial board to establish a confidence rating which can be associated with the otherwise unvetted content in the open archive. During its first year, the archive will be closely monitored by the editorial board to determine if this is the appropriate level of filtering.

International and Area Studies (IAS)

Led by scholars from over 20 centers and organized research units (ORUs) on eight UC campuses, eScholarship's international and area studies collaborators focus on the importance of increasingly sophisticated understandings of the dynamics of other societies–and the regional and global political, economic, and cultural systems in which we live. In July of 2000, in collaboration with the University of California Press, eScholarship made available digital versions of titles in the IAS Research Monograph Series. Free access to these works through the eScholarship program reflects IAS goals of encouraging the rapid dissemination of international research in the social sciences and the humanities, with a special concern for making these works available to researchers in the societies under discussion. To date, the full text of twelve IAS monographs have been made available at the eScholarship site.

With its January 2001 release, eScholarship also announced the formal opening of a Digital Repository for the IAS community and the inauguration of a California International and Area Studies (CIAS) Electronic Publications Program. The CIAS publications program is a UC system-wide initiative designed to accelerate and expand the dissemination of information, ideas, and analyses generated by the dozens of international and area studies conferences, workshops, seminars, and lecture series sponsored each year by the University of California.

IAS scholars hope to digitally publish books in the CIAS monographic series directly from the papers and manuscripts maintained in repository. The introduction of the 12 existing monographs helped "seed" the IAS-eScholarship site, in that the digital monographs illustrate the types of products which can be created from working papers and articles deposited in the IAS repository. The "born-digital" monographs will be subjected to the same rigorous peer-review as their print cousins, but will be more rapidly and widely available then ever before. Through use of the two-tiered repository and digital publishing program, CIAS "expects to enrich the presentation of research materials and encourage greater international intellectual exchange and research collaboration."

Tobacco Control Research

For more than a decade, tobacco researchers and tobacco control advocates have been changing the look of public health efforts in California and beyond through a combination of scientific research and extensive public education. A cornerstone of the public information effort has been the release and archiving of tobacco industry documents made public during the 1990s and housed at the Tobacco Control Archive

(TCA) sponsored by University of California at San Francisco's Library & Center for Knowledge Management.

The Tobacco Control Archive, now a part of a broader Legacy National Tobacco Documents Library, collects, preserves, and provides access to papers, unpublished documents and electronic resources relevant to tobacco control issues primarily in California. In addition to the industry documents, the archive also includes organizational records and personal papers, discoverable through the Electronic Finding Aids of the *Online Archive of California*.

California, a world leader in reducing smoking rates, was catapulted to center stage by the passage in 1988 of Proposition 99. The proposition established state funding for tobacco research and control activities and funds the renowned Tobacco Related Disease Research Program (TRDRP). Administered through the University of California Office of the President, TRDRP has funded basic and applied research in biological and biomedical sciences, social and behavioral sciences, public health, epidemiology, and public policy at 60 California non-profit institutions. It was an original grantor for the once fledgling effort at UCSF to build the tobacco archive. Now, support of the national tobacco archive at UCSF has taken a huge leap.

In January 2001, the UCSF partners were awarded $15 million by the American Legacy Foundation, a national public health foundation, to formally establish and extend the national tobacco documents library at UCSF. In association with the vastly expanding collection of primary source material at UCSF, millions of dollars have been awarded by the National Cancer Institute to fund original research based on those newly available materials in the UCSF archive. To facilitate the new research and scholarship made possible by the digitized resources at the archive and the NCI funding of it, eScholarship will be providing to the tobacco research and tobacco control community a repository for the deposit, management and archiving of the new digital content. A special advisory body has been identified to guide the development and use of the digital repository at CDL for original tobacco control research and will have its first meeting in summer 2001.

DETERMINING THE GREATER GOOD

One of the challenges for the eScholarship program is to reconcile the hesitation within these communities for making unvetted findings publicly available with the program's interest in testing the hypothesis regarding the usefulness of a technical and organizational infrastructure for enabling direct and open access to original research. The issue is not merely one of policy; it quickly becomes a practical matter of allocation of resources. Decisions range from rationing the time and money spent discovering the felt needs of the community, which may or may not be universal, to determining the amount of effort that should be applied in the programming and customization of repository tools for filtering and editing. Not all communities are prepared to launch or make use of a completely open archive of unfiltered content from their field, nor do they have the resources to support an external mechanism for providing the desired filter. While robotic solutions for filtering are not yet adequate, communities needing some level of filtering are making use of what was supposed to be an administrative-level management tool of the ePrints software, i.e., a buffer which allows an authorized party to manually manage submission into the archive. When an author submits a paper to the repository's buffer, it will remain there while e-mail notification is automatically sent to the authorizing person who will perform the briefest technical and editorial screening to determine its acceptability for submission to the open repository.

There are benefits, for both eScholarship and for the community, to monitoring the buffer: for the community of authors and users of the archive there is an opportunity to filter dangerous (medically) or offensive submissions; for eScholarship there is an opportunity to monitor the ease of use for the intended author as they attempt registration and submission of new papers. The potential risks to rapid dissemination and to the integrity of the open archive concept of applying to fine a filter is being weighed by the community and by the eScholarship program. For eScholarship, in addition to the important policy issues coming into focus, there are issues at stake regarding resource expenditure in development of technical tools and enhancements to the core software. In the short run, the eScholarship team is working on an appropriate division of responsibilities between CDL and the communities/authors themselves for management of the buffer.

DIGITAL MONOGRAPHS

Despite the almost endless possibilities for presentation and packaging of digital scholarly content, there are no indications that interest in the scholarly monograph is waning. In fact, this is an arena in which eScholarship is actively enabling reconfiguration of the scholarly publication process. One aspect of this involves enabling of rapid, cost-effective and re-purposable publication of scholarly monographs by effective use of digital technologies. *Tobacco War: Inside the California Battles* was eScholarship's first experiment in this regard and through it we are exploring the use of cutting-edge Extensible Markup Language (XML) tools for creating highly structured and flexible publications. The book is entirely XML encoded and is greatly enhanced by links in the book to the original materials upon which it is based.

Using the Cocoon Publishing Framework, open source software for publishing on line XML encoded text, all monographs coming onto eScholarship servers are now being published in XML and will thus allow maximum efficiency in delivery to the desktop, while maintaining flexibility for re-purposing of the files for future platforms. This is a central concern for eScholarship as we strive to efficiently meet our commitments to provide persistent access to the content we host and to take full advantage of technical improvements for its delivery. (To see an example of an XML-encoded text delivered through the Cocoon Publishing Framework, see *Tobacco War: Inside the California Battles* at http://escholarship.cdlib.org/ucpress/tobacco-war.xml.)

But another and perhaps more significant restructuring is taking place in the institutional and organization realm: the partnership between CDL and the University of California Press (UC Press), which has developed around the publication of these digital monographs but extends now across all digital publishing models. In the partnership with UC Press, we are helping to re-engineer editorial and production roles while we endeavor to exploit the latest technologies for rapid publication of the monographs and the possibilities for new types of bundling. This collaboration is beneficial for the entire university system as it minimizes the chance of duplication of research and development in the volatile arena of 21st century scholarly publishing, which is focused almost entirely on the digital production of new content and the restructuring of the relationships between the authors and the institutions of the academy. Beginning in May 2001, the entire collection of digitized UC Press titles are being XML encoded and will join *Tobacco War* and the twelve IAS digital monographs on CDL servers.

Another example of the interesting and increasingly complex nature of the eScholarship projects, and of the developing publishing partnership with UC Press, is the Japanese American Relocation Digital Archive (JARDA) publishing project. The JARDA's digital objects, which ultimately will include more than 20,000 images and electronics, are being drawn from the collections of the California State Historical Society, California Historical Society, the California State Archive, California

State University, Fullerton, California State University, Sonoma, the Japanese American National Museum (JANM), The Bancroft Library at UC Berkeley, UCLA, The Young Research Library Department of Special Collections, University of the Pacific, and University of Southern California–all members of the California Digital Library (CDL) Online Archive of California (OAC). The eScholarship, UC Press and the Online Archive of California (OAC) collaboration aims to foster publication of original content from OAC. The publishing is clearly facilitated by the growing quantity and accessibility of unique virtual collections, such as JARDA, but it is set in motion by the concentrated collaborative effort to bring scholars together with the newly available digitized primary resources and to provide them the technical tools necessary to make use of those resources. A meeting of the key California-based scholars and curators in this field is taking place in April 2001 to advise the further development of the JARDA, to influence and shape publishing efforts from this important collection of primary source material, and to advise on the development of the appropriate interfaces for the archive.

An additional dimension to this already rich collaboration will be added by an associated collaborative effort to develop a K-12 interface and a Teacher Toolkit for use with the JARDA. The Interactive University, located at UC Berkeley is funding the effort to provide a customized interface and tools which will allow teachers anywhere to easily customize a curriculum for making effective use of the JARDA in their primary and secondary school teaching.

DIGITAL JOURNALS: WHERE DO THEY FIT IN?

Scholarly journals will continue to be a central piece of equipment in the scholarly communication apparatus for some time to come. With Internet-based journals it is possible to fully exploit the capabilities of digital technologies while maintaining their most enduring enhancement–peer-review. Indeed, the *Dermatology Online Journal* mentioned earlier is a key part of the eScholarship program. With scholars in the dermatology community, who are beginning to make use of an open repository, we are focusing on creative uses of the interplay between the self-published content of the repository and the peer-reviewed content of the overlay journal.

We are also exploring the extent to which digital technologies can stretch and change this established publishing archetype. Technically, there is no reason that digital journals cannot include the same author/reader services of the repositories and ultimately be able to associate text-based communications with a full range of media forms. eScholarship is engaged in an exciting project in this regard. With scholars in UCLA's Institute of the Environment we are approaching the fall 2001 launch of a new journal for Environmental Studies. The digital journal is a model for experimentation in inter-disciplinary studies and for exploitation of new technologies for journal publishing. The main restriction in this project is the development pace and path for the technical tools themselves; both journal publishing projects are supported by a Scholarly Publishing and Academic Resources coalition (SPARC) grant to eScholarship that was designed to spur digital science publishing ventures based in academe. But, just as there are issues surrounding the development of the open repositories, there is also a range of interests and concerns expressed about the direction of and prioritization of technical enhancements for journals and monographs.

One of the forces driving the Institute of the Environment's endeavor to launch a born-digital journal is the capacity of digital technologies and Web publication to greatly enhance the communication of findings in this multi-disciplinary arena. In fact, the pattern of print journal dissemination and use, and its interplay with the structure of disciplines and therefore academic departments, make it nearly impossible for the mix of scholars in this field–atmospheric chemists, biologists, civil engineers, statisticians, information scientists, public health and public policy experts–to communicate effectively in print beyond their hyper-specialized fields. A born-digital multidisciplinary journal for Environmental Studies can make good use of Web technologies to reach across disciplines and it may help cohere this hybridized arena of study.

Articles in the new environmental studies journal will include images, audio and video streaming, and archival data. Ultimately the journal will make use of more sophisticated tools to allow use of 3-D modeling and interaction and manipulation of the associated data. All will be available for free on the Web and will be discoverable through the greatest possible mix of subject-based abstracting and indexing tools, as well as Internet-based search engines, to maximize discovery across the associated disciplines.

DATA SETS

As scholars and researchers themselves begin to utilize the full capacity of digital technologies, publishing takes on even more diverse forms. Virtually every proposal now before eScholarship includes some notion of primary data publication–as a scholarly creation itself or in association with journal articles, with monographs, or as supplementary files deposited with a repository paper. eScholarship is attempting to identify and grapple with the myriad technical, legal, policy and logistical issues that arise with the publishing of data sets.

One eScholarship community which is unique in the way it pushes the boundaries of traditional scholarly publishing is the Electronic Cultural Atlas Initiative (ECAI) an international effort led by UC Berkeley Professor Lewis Lancaster. By its own description, ECAI is "committed to the development of a new model for scholarly communication which facilitates collaboration among researchers across disciplines, which is international in scope, and which can function in a networked digital library environment. At the core of ECAI's innovations are the ECAI Information Technology Architecture and its central unifying element, the ECAI Metadata Clearinghouse System, which together support ECAI's mission to foster collaboration and to create a new paradigm for data access through visual time/place interfaces."[8]

Beginning in 2001, the CDL will provide housing for and persistent access to standards-based humanities and social science data sets created by scholars working with the ECAI. Rich databases, representing decades of research never seen before, which can finally be published and digitally shared across the globe, hold the potential to spawn a proliferation of new findings and new scholarship around the world. The first such project, now in production, is the publication of the Korean Buddhist Canon. Rubbings made from the original wood block carvings, which themselves are the original depiction of the canon, will be viewable as scanned images. Associated with the images will be the entire transcription of the 52 million characters of the canon which was independently keyed in and is maintained in a separate database. A hyper-linked polyglot dictionary will allow easy look-up of the meaning of the characters, as well as the chronological appearance and the original geographical location of the first appearance of each of the characters. A 200-page manuscript on the history of the canon will accompany the images and the transcription, and all of it will be visually rendered in a map-like display created by Geographic Information Systems (GIS) type tools. In addition to the joint publication of unique data sets such as these and the housing of other data sets and unique collections, the tools and software which allow use and manipulation of the data are also being made available through the ECAI-eScholarship partnership.

In the course of this productive partnership, eScholarship hopes to contribute to the effort to establish metadata standards and protocols which will facilitate the widest possible access to ECAI data sets and which are in alignment with best digital library practices for access and persistence. To the degree that they are a part of the publishing effort, eScholarship will support development of the tools, such as the TimeMap application–a GIS-type application with a temporal dimension–created by one of the ECAI scholars. These tools, many of which were already in development but are now being fostered under the ECAI umbrella, have been incorporated as they are understood to advance the ECAI agenda. Similarly, as with other eScholarship partnerships, this alliance is being fostered in recognition of its potential to contribute to the broader effort to improve scholarship.

Perhaps the greatest challenge in the publication of data sets of this type is yet to come. As the technical obstacles to serving data, which can be displayed, manipulated, and analyzed by any reader, are overcome–and this is no trivial matter–a whole new set of issues will arise. If a platform is to be provided for such data manipulation, and if new findings are to be discovered in the course of this manipulation, how will these new findings be associated with the original findings? Will the new findings also need to be preserved? What responsibility does CDL bear for preserving these new findings which will have come into being on CDL-hosted servers? How should it be determined when there is a new finding that warrants archiving? What sort of intellectual property concerns will arise when it is unclear what proportion of the new findings are the result of human creative activity such as interpretation, or the result of another human's creative activity in the form of their software engineering or programming which manipulates and displays the available data, or the result of the meticulous gathering of the data and its self-conscious storage in a useful database structure? Even if there is no dispute over ownership, how will attribution be handled?

The answers to these questions are not at all obvious, and often even the questions are not obvious. Many more certainly lurk beneath the surface. Furthermore, behind the obvious policy issues to be addressed are scores of practical and technical issues to be solved. But the lure and promise of Web technologies to enable such rich cross fertilization and to inspire new scholarship are stronger than the trepidation that comes with setting such a process in motion. The sharing of new content on the Web–whether it is a short paper submitted to an open repository, or data collected over a professional lifetime–always brings with it some risks.

To await an answer to these hypothetical questions, though, is to risk losing an opportunity to stimulate exciting new scholarship. Perhaps the risks bring with them an opportunity. Perhaps the inevitable muddling of the genesis and ownership of ideas will lead us back to the gift culture upon which our academic institutions were originally formed. If this is one result of the eScholarship experiment it will certainly have been worthwhile.

TOWARD A SUSTAINABLE MODEL

This article began with the assertion that eScholarship's promising early successes were owing, at least in part, to the approach undergirding it. eScholarship has, from the start, been grounded by a sober understanding of this moment in history. Indeed, the entire development of the CDL has been anchored by an appreciation for, and an ability to draw upon, the technical tools available and the considerable expertise aggregated in the decades long history of UC's technical accomplishments. And there has been a healthy appreciation for experience external to UC–both in its particularity and its universality–and a willingness to learn from it. But also included in this list of features is a grave concern for the business of paying for the new modes of scholarly publishing.

One of the commitments asked of all eScholarship partners is that they collaborate with CDL to develop funding sources for the projects. One such effort is underway in the UC Press-CIAS-eScholarship collaboration to secure grant funding for a focused experiment to develop a business model for the CIAS Electronic Publications Program. With partners in ECAI, grant funding is being sought for many different aspects of the program, e.g., publication of data sets, tool development, meetings and conferences, K-12 interface development.

But it is widely understood that these experimental configurations are not sustainable in isolation from the rest of the scholarly communication system. eScholarship is an experimental program and each of its successes and failures will likely be only prods and probes for the kind of systemic re-engineering that must take place. If the CDL is to fulfill its mission and develop a comprehensive system for the management of digital scholarly information, it must address itself to the entire constellation of financial, business, legal and technical structures on which such a system resides. We do not know exactly how the changes will come and it is not clear that there will be a pivotal event or moment which will set millions of scholars in motion against the tide of the current commercially driven system.

Once there were dreams of wholesale realignments, where scholarly societies and university libraries would emerge as collaborative publishers and archivists of the scholarly record, to the exclusion of the commercial interests which have adulterated the current system. The natural alliance of universities and scholarly societies is still central to the eScholarship vision, and we remain optimistic that change is certain. But we are anchored in the realization that this is a very early stage of system-wide change, that change is taking place in pockets here and there, and that many new forms of communication will emerge alongside the old forms and in as many varieties as there are fields of study before the academic community settles on the preferred menu of options. If the eScholarship experiment is successful, it will have shown enough authors and readers that there are indeed alternatives to the current system and that they are within reach. When masses of researchers and scholars begin demanding a new level of support from the institutions that support their teaching, research, and publishing, those institutional alliances will inexorably come into play.

MANY SURPRISES, MORE QUESTIONS

One pleasant surprise in the eScholarship endeavor has been the extent to which many scholars in the humanities and social sciences were already experimenting with digital publishing. Indeed, much of the eScholarship effort is aimed at concentrating technical and organizational support at critical junctures in those faculty-led experiments. This has provided fertile ground for the eScholarship experiment, the most obvious result of which is the formulation of almost endless, provocative questions about how to go about improving scholarly communication.

The questions are sometimes difficult to formulate and more difficult to answer. How much experimenting is enough to show what is possible? Who must be convinced? If editors and authors moved en masse away from commercial publishers, would the alternative technical and organizational supports be sufficient to manage the quantity of scholarly information being created? How far can we experiment without explicit faculty senate support for non-traditional publishing forms and venues, without a sustainable business model, without a new approach to copyright and intellectual property?

What should become of peer review? Can we speed up peer review, or make it simpler, in the realm of the Web? Must peer review really be *more* elaborate to satisfy those suspicious of new medium? Archaeologists working with ECAI, report that suspicion with the digital medium and web publication has led to overemphasis on peer review. How much should we accommodate the felt needs of various scholarly communities, for filtering and editorial control of open archives, for paper versions of journals and monographs, without surrendering a leading vision for a transformed and mutually beneficial system of scholarly communication? One project brought before eScholarship proposed a new digital journal with an accompanying print version. eScholarship has no plans to publish in print. But should a print option be foreclosed? Can there be any mass migration of scholarly journals to the new medium without some accommodation of print?

We must continue to ask ourselves the grander questions as well. What will it take to bring about a true change in standards for tenure review? Must the change come field by field, discipline by discipline? What relationship should UC/CDL establish with other major US academic libraries and publishing programs? Can we change the flow of research dollars into and within UC without completely the reassembling of the components of the current system nationally and, perhaps, internationally?

The operating assumption at CDL is that, if the challenge is to garner sufficient resources to fully exploit digital technologies and the Web in the service of research, learning and teaching, and to reliably archive the scholarly record, the solution must include broad alliances of academic institutions and scholarly societies. UC faculty and researchers have been extremely responsive to the eScholarship initiative. But perhaps more encouraging has been the extent of the collaborations, both nationally and internationally, that came with each of these eScholarship communities. As so much of the CDL's work does, those multi-institutional ties led quickly to discussions with other academic libraries involved in similar publishing experiments. Discovering that our colleagues are grappling with the same challenges is, of course, encouraging. Discovering that they were eager to find common and transportable solutions has been exhilarating. Discovering the way to strategically coordinate our efforts to create that comprehensive system for the management of digital scholarly information remains before us.

NOTES

1. Library Planning and Action Initiative Advisory Task Force: Final Report. March 1998. (Online) Available: http://www.lpai.ucop.edu/outcomes/finalrpt/[March 1, 2001].

2. A tenth campus was added to the University of California system after the launch of the CDL.

3. The CDL and UCLA Libraries have created a database of UC editors of what are considered to be 2,000 of the top journals in the sciences, social sciences, and humanities. The database contains 318 separate faculty members from UC serving in senior editorial positions (executive, managing, associate, or regional editors) on 238 of the 1,966 surveyed titles. Based on this analysis and data gathering effort, UC faculty members have significant editorial authority for 12.1% of the top scholarly journals.

4. "From the Editor: Visions and Intersections. A Conversation with Richard E. Lucier of the University of California." *D-Lib Magazine.* February 1998. (Online) Available: http://www.dlib.org/dlib/february98/02editorial.html [March 1, 2001].

5. Ginsparg, P.G. "Winners and Losers in the Global Research Village Invited contribution for Conference at UNESCO HQ," Paris, 19-23 Feb 1996. Wed 21 Feb 1996. (Online) Available: http://xxx.lanl.gov/blurb/pg96unesco.html [March 1, 2001].

6. Varian, H. Paper presented at the Scholarly Communication and Technology Conference, Emory University, Atlanta, April 1997. (Online) Available: http://arl.cni.org/scomm/scat/varian.html [March 1, 2001].

7. Lucier, R. and Ober, J. "Scholar-led Innovation in Scholarly Communication: University ePub: An Initiative in Electronic Scholarship," October 1999. (Online) Available: http://www.cdlib.org/eschol/summary.htm [March 1, 2001].

8. From the ECAI Web site at http://www.ecai.org/.

Perspectives on Scholarly Online Books: The Columbia University Online Books Evaluation Project

Mary Summerfield
Carol Mandel
Paul Kantor

SUMMARY. The Online Books Evaluation Project at Columbia University studied the potential for scholarly online books from 1995 to 1999. Issues included scholars' interest in using online books, the role they might play in scholarly life, features that scholars and librarians sought in online books, the costs of producing and owning print and online books, and potential marketplace arrangements. Scholars see potential

Mary Summerfield is Director of Business Development and Planning, University of Chicago Press, 1427 East 60th Street, Chicago, IL 60637 (E-mail: msummerfield@ pressuchicago.edu). At the time of the project, she was Project Director, Columbia University, and Coordinator of Online Books Evaluation Project.

Carol Mandel is Dean of Libraries, New York University, 70 Washington Square South, New York, NY 10012 (E-mail: carol.mandel@nyu.edu). Her responsibilities include oversight of the NYU Press. At the time of the project, she was Deputy University Librarian at Columbia University and served as Project Director, Online Books Evaluation.

Paul Kantor is Professor of Information Science, School of Communications and Information Studies, Rutgers University, 4 Huntington Street, New Brunswick, NJ 08901 (E-mail: kantor@scils.rutgers.edu). He is also Chief Scientist, Tantalus Inc., through which he served as a consultant to this project.

A grant from The Andrew W. Mellon Foundation funded this project.

[Haworth co-indexing entry note]: "Perspectives on Scholarly Online Books: The Columbia University Online Books Evaluation Project." Summerfield, Mary, Carol Mandel, and Paul Kantor. Co-published simultaneously in *Journal of Library Administration* (The Haworth Information Press, an imprint of The Haworth Press, Inc.) Vol. 35, No. 1/2, 2001, pp. 61-82; and: *Libraries and Electronic Resources: New Partnerships, New Practices, New Perspectives* (ed: Pamela L. Higgins) The Haworth Information Press, an imprint of The Haworth Press, Inc., 2001, pp. 61-82. Single or multiple copies of this article are available for a fee from The Haworth Document Delivery Service [1-800-HAWORTH, 9:00 a.m. - 5:00 p.m. (EST). E-mail address: getinfo@haworthpressinc.com].

for online books to make their research, learning, and teaching more efficient and effective. Librarians see potential to serve their scholars better. Librarians may face lower costs if they can serve their scholars with online books instead of print books. Publishers may be able to offer scholars greater opportunities to use their books while enhancing their own profitability. *[Article copies available for a fee from The Haworth Document Delivery Service: 1-800-HAWORTH. E-mail address: <getinfo@haworthpressinc.com> Website: <http://www.HaworthPress.com> © 2001 by The Haworth Press, Inc. All rights reserved.]*

KEYWORDS. Electronic publishing, evaluation, publishing economics

INTRODUCTION

From winter 1995 through autumn 1999, the Online Books Evaluation Project at Columbia University examined the potential roles of various types of online books in the scholarly world. The project analyzed (1) scholars' adoption of and reaction to online books; (2) lifecycle costs of both print and online books from publishing through maintenance in libraries; and (3) the likely implications of traditions of scholarly communications and publisher and marketplace reactions for online books.[1] Summarizing the project's key findings and drawing upon other work in this field, this article first gives our assessment of the potential for online books in teaching, learning, research, and scholarly publishing and then summarizes the project's findings.

One of the project's first and key challenges was obtaining electronic files for books from which to build the collection of scholarly online books with which we were to test the concept. In most cases, publishers did not have electronic versions of their books from which we could create an HTML version.[2] Thus, development of the collection took longer and the ultimate collection of books was smaller than planned.

A PERSPECTIVE ON THE FUTURE OF SCHOLARLY BOOKS

The findings of this project lead us to believe that electronic books, in particular online books, will develop a meaningful role in the scholarly community over the next several years. In this project,[3] distinct need for certain books, e.g., for reference or for a course reading, drew scholars to the online form of the book even at that early stage in the development of such books. In individual and group interviews, scholars expressed optimism that online books would help them to be more efficient, and possibly even more effective, in their teaching, course work, and research. They recognized that this small collection did not reflect the full potential of the online medium for delivery of scholarly works. Similarly, college and university librarians perceived that there was more to this medium than this project could demonstrate. They saw that within a few years they might be able to provide their scholars with much greater access to books via the online format, with easier access to materials that would otherwise be available only in print form, and with better access to books now available only through inter-library loan or visits to another library. Librarians anticipated that in a few years they would acquire some books in print form only, but that they would provide others, such as reference works or texts that are quickly outdated, in online format only, and yet others in both print and online format.

In a few years, (1) the book software industry will be providing stable electronic books; and (2) the hardware industry will be creating multi-functional, portable devices that make the reading and manipulation of texts on-screen satisfactory for most users of such texts. Perhaps by the end of this decade, scholars will have access to print versions of new scholarly books but electronic versions of recent reference works, text-books, scholarly monographs, and collections of essays will serve most scholars for many of their uses of these books. Publishers may decide to print with traditional offset technology only books expected to sell thousands of copies.

Students will use electronic–online, downloaded, on-disk, or e-paper[4]–versions of books for much of their course reading, for manipulating data, and for using analytic software or multi-media information within a textbook. New devices will be more compact than a laptop computer, with better screen ergonomics, and better analytical and annotational tools.

By 2010, scholars may use electronic versions of books and journals for most of their preliminary and intermediate level browsing and reading. Most scholars may seek out a portable or print copy of a book only to read from it at length.[5] Over the years as computers providing reading tools improve, fewer people will seek the print form of a scholarly book even for extensive reading.

In this vision, the design of individual electronic books and of whole collections will facilitate scholars' use of the books as well as protect copyright. In discussions about electronic scholarly materials, scholars and librarians advocated the following design features.

- Searchability across a whole subject category or a specified subset of online books.
- Inclusion of online books in a library's Web catalog with hyper-links to the books themselves.
- A stable Web address for each book or article, allowing design of user-friendly access.
- Vendors providing libraries with catalog records and standard statistics on use of online resources.
- Vendors migrating and refreshing electronic books over time so that the books continue to be accessible.
- Table of contents with a comprehensive set of chapter subheading and graphics links.
- Grouping of images as thumbnails and links of the thumbnail images to their presentation in normal size and location.
- Smooth movement among pages of a book.
- Footnote text in a block adjacent to the linked text in the book.
- Capacity to view multiple pages or pages and images simultaneously.
- Pagination consistent with that of the print book.
- Hyper-linked references if the referenced book or article is available online.
- Links to a dictionary and to other relevant reference materials, such as multilingual dictionaries, atlases, and encyclopedias.
- Pages with adjustable fonts, margins, and the like so that each reader can select the look.
- Individual's files of annotations, highlightings, and notes for each book. An instructor and the students in a class could share a set of annotations to a text.

This vision relies on the availability online of a major share of the materials that a cohort of scholars seeks. If they must go to the library and search the stacks to find most of the books and journals that they need, scholars will find less value in the online format. Students, who largely rely on textbooks, relatively recent monographs and collections of essays, and other readings placed on reserve, are likely to be earlier adopters of online books. Their materials are likely to be available electronically sooner than the backlist of scholarly books.[6] In general, advanced graduate students, researchers, and faculty are likely to adopt this format more slowly, as fewer of the books and journals that they use will be available in it in the early years. These more senior scholars will stay with print books more extensively for a longer time and will move to the online format only when it provides substantial advantages in size and currency of collection and convenience of use.

Market conditions will determine the availability of online books to individuals. Will a scholar be able to use an online book if his library has not purchased it? Will he be able to search across titles and to browse titles free–equivalent to looking at a book in the bookstore–with someone, e.g., library, department, scholar, paying only when he wants to use a book at length?

At this time, publishers see that online books may enhance their profitability in a few years. They believe that they will be able to streamline the steps from initial submission directions to authors through manuscript editing through typesetting to produce a flexible digital version that will create multiple formats. Scholarly publishers are striving to create that integrated digital process. In that world, electronic versions of new works will be available at least as soon as the print version. However, publishers and vendors will reissue older scholarly works in an online format only if they project sufficient demand to cover the costs of producing and distributing that version. A decade or so may pass before the collection of online scholarly monographs becomes large enough to induce senior scholars to change their patterns of research behavior markedly. However, such scholars may soon adopt electronic formats for journals, reference books, and new monographs, if they can access many of the works in their field in those formats.

PROJECT CONCEPTUAL FRAMEWORK

The project analyzed (1) scholars' behavior and reactions to online books, (2) lifecycle costs of traditional print books and online books for publishers and libraries, and (3) marketplace reactions to the concept of online books, in the context of relevant environmental developments. The evaluation employed a wide variety of tools, including server data, a variety of online, mailed, and hand-distributed surveys, and individual and group interviews.[7]

DEVELOPMENT AND DESIGN OF THE ONLINE BOOKS COLLECTION

The project began formal activity in January 1995. When Columbia's digital library research and development team envisioned this project, we expected to develop a custom SGML browser, as other online publishing projects were doing. However, once the project was underway, the emergent World Wide Web seemed to be the best delivery mode. Scholars would have access to the Web from university locations and many, if not most, would be able to access it soon from home via modem dial-in to campus servers, or ISPs. The Web could maximize the value of online books to scholars, as their greatest potential benefit would come with truly digital books.[8] Only this online format would allow development of truly interactive books taking advantage of current and anticipated capabilities of Web technology, such as links to other online resources, and inclusion of sound and video, data files and software for manipulating data. Perhaps only such enhanced online books would offer sufficient advantages over traditional print format that scholars would substitute them for the print format in some or all of their modes of use and for some or all classes of books.[9]

As of June 1999, the end of data gathering, the collection totaled 168 online texts, including six reference works and fifty-four classical texts in social thought. Columbia University Press, Oxford University Press, Garland Press, and Simon and Schuster Higher Education provided modern books. The contemporary works were in six subject areas: biography, literary criticism, earth and environmental science, philosophy, political science/international affairs, and social work. A few of these books were textbooks; the rest were scholarly monographs or collections of essays. Each book was in the library's collection in print form, circulating from the regular collection or reserves, or non-circulating in reference, as well as in one or more online formats.

At the outset, the project team decided that a book would be mounted with each major element as a separate file, e.g., a table of contents-title page, the introduction, each chapter, the bibliography, the index. The user could click on a chapter title in the table of contents to go to that chapter. To move among chapters the scholar returned to the table of contents and clicked on the new chapter heading.[10] Footnote numbers were hyperlinked to the footnote text; a *back* link returned the reader to the footnote location. The browser's *find* feature located words within a chapter. A pagination tool took the scholar to a known page number, e.g., from the index or from a citation. The design omitted pagination, so scholars could not cite a page number in a reference to the online book.[11]

Other digital journals and books projects also faced the challenge of deciding what features to include in a system design and under what conditions to modify that design. Substantial changes may confuse existing users of a collection. Such confusion often leads to misuse, resultant dissatisfaction, and a smaller chance that a scholar will return to the collection. On the other hand, if such modifications are true improvements, they should result in greater user satisfaction overall and more use in the end.[12]

FINDINGS OF THE ONLINE BOOKS EVALUATION PROJECT

Project Context

As anticipated, during the six years of planning and executing this project, relevant environmental factors changed substantially. Developments in the Internet and the World Wide Web, in computer literacy and access within all levels of academia, in the development of digital libraries, and in scholarly publishing are outlined below.

National Environment–Expanded Potential Access to Online Resources

Changes in the national computing environment increased the likelihood that scholars would adopt computers, the Internet, and online resources. Prominent mainstream newspapers featured computers, the Internet, and related topics daily. The price/power ratio for personal computers improved enormously, with adequate computers available for under $1,000 since 1998. However, after 1997, the typical domestic user experienced little improvement in available speed of access to the Internet (56K at best) or in prices for ISP accounts.

Penetration of personal computers and use of the Internet grew throughout American society, with over half of households owning one or more computers by mid-1999. At that time, over 100 million adults in the U.S., or about half of all adults, were using the Internet, up from 65 million a year earlier. By 1999, Americans were using email and the Web more heavily and with more sophistication.[13]

Columbia Environment–Increased Access to and Use of Computing and the Web

At Columbia University, even as it grew, the modem pool ran at near peak capacity utilization, leaving scholars often frustrated in their attempts to dial-in to the campus network for email or electronic resources.[14] Student ownership of computers grew markedly; by the end of the project, most students reported possession of a computer in their campus residences and easy access to the Web. Students living in Columbia residence halls had the luxury of Ethernet connections that made their Web connection vastly superior to that of the typical graduate student or faculty member working at home and using an ISP or other telephone link.

Scholars and Libraries–A Potentially Frustrating Relationship

As knowledge and publication of journals and books expand, scholars face increasing difficulty in locating articles and books that will be useful to their course preparation and research. Libraries struggle with the challenges of acquiring the materials that their scholars need and keeping those materials readily available for students and faculty. Limitations of the traditional library frustrate scholars. They often find that:[15]

- their libraries have not acquired the books they want to use;
- their libraries acquired these books but they are not yet on the shelf;
- these books entered circulation and are not now on the shelf and the recall process will take many days;
- the online catalog lists these books as on the shelf but they are not to be found in the library;
- these books are on reserve and, hence, available at best for a period of time too brief to allow extended reading and review;
- browsing through the stacks that might have books relevant to their work takes substantial time and can only be done during the hours that the library is open;
- the brief contents of the records in a library catalog do not reveal all of the books that may be relevant to an area of research.

Many scholars are enthusiastic about online books, which they believe will solve all of these problems, except possibly the first.

Continuing Roll-Out and Expanded Use of Electronic Scholarly Resources

Coincident with the growing penetration of the Internet and development of the Web came the early digital scholarly resources–abstracts and indices (A & I), electronic journals, and reference works. The digital A & I resources are so popular that publishers have nearly ceased production of paper versions. Electronic journals are increasing in availability and popularity over time. As time passes, more scholars are aware of what is available in electronic form, find the growing collections of value, and choose to use them.[16] As scholars become familiar with electronic versions of these two key categories of scholarly library resources, they both recommend them to their colleagues and develop expanded interest in all types of electronic resources. In the first seven months of 1999, Columbia scholars had 37 percent more accesses of the growing JSTOR collection of journal backfiles than they had in all of 1998. In the peak month, April, JSTOR use was equivalent to about one access per Columbia community member.

Reference works were clearly suited for the online format and scholars adopted their online forms quickly.[17] This project focused on other forms of scholarly books, such as collections of essays, monographs, and textbooks.

Economics of Scholarly Book Publishing and Online Books

A key facet of this project was analysis of the lifecycle costs of scholarly books in print and online format. What does it cost to publish and provide these books to scholars via libraries? Would online books be more or less costly than the traditional print format?

The online book format has developed slowly; the industry of online publishing and the terms of providing online books are still in their infancy. With technology evolving as well, the various systems for and costs of publishing, distributing, maintaining, and owning online books are early in their developmental cycles. Nor do publishers or libraries typically calculate lifecycle costs for print books. The available evidence permits order-of-magnitude comparisons of costs at this early point in the development of electronic books.

Online Books Integrated into Publishing Process

The model evolving is one in which production of online books is part of the standard publishing process.[18] Publishers or vendors will develop collections of online books that they will maintain on servers and offer as individual titles or groups of titles to libraries and individual scholars. Some publishers have begun to offer online texts in this way. NetLibrary, with a single-copy circulation model, was the first major vendor in the general library online book market.

Publishers or vendors would incur additional costs in creating a permanent URL, maintaining a server, refreshing and migrating the files, and transmitting the online books to the reader via the Web or an alternative secured Internet mode.

Print Books–Analysis of Costs to Scholarly Publishers

Exhibit 1 gives pro forma revenues and costs for five print books from a major university press and estimates of the costs of producing and maintaining online versions of those books. The publisher expected these five books to have sales of several thousand units each. Their costs were lower than those for the many scholarly books that sell fewer than 500 copies.[19]

These financial estimates projected that total sales for these five books would be 13,650 copies (3,450 cloth copies and 10,200 paper copies) at an average net price of $17. The projected surplus (total net income minus total cost) for these books was $12,668, or $0.93 per copy sold.[20]

Online Books–Modest Incremental Costs to Publishers and Vendors

Hitherto, online books have been a secondary product. Publishers and libraries have converted print books or electronic files to HTML or SGML[21] as an add-on cost to the traditional publishing process.

The University of Michigan gained extensive experience in processing existing books through its Humanities Text Initiative. The process of scanning, using optical character recognition software on the scanned texts, encoding in SGML, and proof reading cost an average of $1.51 per page. This cost omits project management and information systems.[22]

EXHIBIT 1. Scholarly Book Publishing: Projected Revenues and Costs (Sample of Books in Print and Electronic Format)

	Book 1	Book 2	Book 3	Book 4	Book 5	All 5 Books
Book Pages	296	320	300	232	280	1,428
Cloth Copies Printed (#)	1,000	500	500	1,500	400	3,900
Cloth Copies Sold (#)	900	400	450	1,350	350	3,450
% Sold of Printed Copies	90%	80%	90%	90%	88%	88%
List Price - Cloth	$45.00	$42.00	$50.00	$32.50	$49.50	$43.80
Net Margin - Cloth	80%	80%	75%	65%	80%	76%
Net Price - Cloth	$36.00	$33.60	$37.50	$21.13	$39.60	$33.29
Net Income - Cloth	**$32,400**	**$13,440**	**$16,875**	**$28,519**	**$13,860**	**$105,094**
Paper Copies Printed (#)	0	2,500	3,500	na	3,000	na
Paper Copies Sold (#)	0	2,300	3,300	1,800	2,800	10,200
% Sold of Printed Copies	na	92%	94%	nc	93%	na
List Price - Paper	na	$17.50	$15.50	$17.50	$17.50	$17.00
Net Margin - Paper	na	65%	75%	77%	80%	74%
Net Price - Paper	na	$11.38	$11.63	$13.48	$14.00	$12.62
Net Income - Paper	**$0**	**$26,163**	**$38,363**	**$24,255**	**$39,200**	**$127,980**
Total Copies Printed	1,000	3,000	4,000	na	3,400	na
Total Copies Sold	900	2,700	3,750	3,150	3,150	13,650
Total Net Income	**$32,400**	**$39,603**	**$55,238**	**$52,774**	**$53,060**	**$233,074**
COSTS						
Plant (Typesetting)	$4,903	$4,962	$5,936	$4,085	$4,089	$23,975
Paper, Printing, Binding	$3,633	$7,451	$7,887	$8,312	$8,015	$35,298
Royalty - % cloth	0%	7%	10%	7%	7%	6%
Royalty - % paper	na	7%	10%	7%	7%	8%
Royalty Amount	$0	$2,772	$5,524	$3,694	$3,714	$15,704
Others (Contributors Payments, etc.)	$0	$0	$3,600	$0	$0	$3,600
Total Cost of Sales	**$8,536**	**$15,185**	**$22,947**	**$16,091**	**$15,818**	**$78,577**
Gross Margin	**$23,864**	**$24,417**	**$32,291**	**$36,683**	**$37,242**	**$154,496**
Fixed Overhead	$11,268	$11,268	$16,179	$16,179	$11,268	$66,162
Variable Overhead	$10,692	$13,069	$18,228	$16,168	$17,509	$75,666
Total Overhead	**$21,960**	**$24,337**	**$34,407**	**$32,347**	**$28,777**	**$141,828**
Total Costs	**$30,496**	**$39,522**	**$57,354**	**$48,438**	**$44,595**	**$220,405**
Surplus (Net Income - Costs)	**$1,904**	**$80**	**-$2,116**	**$4,336**	**$8,465**	**$12,668**

Source: Major University Press. This press reports stability in these costs.

Electronic Book Production Costs

Using Print Text: ~$1.51/pg.		$447	$483	$453	$350	$423	$2,156

EXHIBIT 1 (continued)

	Book 1	Book 2	Book 3	Book 4	Book 5	All 5 Books
Using E-Files:						
HTML - ASCII pg: ~$1/pg.	$296	$320	$300	$232	$280	$1,428
HTML - Quark pg:~$2.15/pg.	$636	$688	$645	$499	$602	$3,070
Proofing & Fine-tuning, Graphics: ~$0.42/pg.	$124	$134	$126	$97	$118	$600
PostScript to Web PDF: $0.04/pg.	$12	$13	$12	$9	$11	$57
E-File Management:	$20	$20	$20	$20	$20	$100
Maintain on Server: PV $0.35/pg	$104	$112	$105	$81	$98	$500
Costs of Online Version for 30 year period (except refreshing & migrating):						
Print to SGML	$551	$595	$558	$431	$521	$2,656
ASCII to HTML	$544	$586	$551	$430	$516	$2,627
Quark to HTML	$884	$954	$896	$697	$838	$4,269
PostScript to PDF	$136	$145	$137	$110	$129	$657

In the final phase of this project, Columbia contracted out HTML coding of the books' electronic files. The digital library editing staff established standards for this coding. Some files were in ASCII format; others were in Quark. The cost of coding for ASCII files was $0.36 per 1,000 characters or an average of about $1 per page. Quark conversion cost an average of $2.15 per page. Proof reading, fine-tuning, and adding graphics averaged $0.42 per page. Managing this conversion cost about $1,000 in staff time, or about $20 per book.

The University of Pennsylvania is converting and mounting current Oxford University Press history books. Its process involves distilling PostScript files into PDF files, reassembling chapters into a single file, and using Compose to build bookmarks and links from the book index to the pages.[23] Given clean PostScript files with easily interpreted fonts, a student worker creates a final, web-ready PDF file of a 300-page book in an hour, for a cost of about $0.04 a page. A troublesome book could take five times as long, for a per page cost of $0.20 or more. These costs omit supervision or other overhead costs.

In 1999, Columbia projected the annual full cost of maintaining books on a server as about $1 per MB. Books vary in size, but with forty-four pages per MB, this is an annual cost of $0.023 per page. If a book were maintained on a server for thirty years, the present value of the cost would be about $0.35 per page, or roughly $81 to $112 for the books in our sample.[24] The cost of refreshing and migrating these books might be about the same.

As Exhibit 1 shows, the costs of the online version vary with the number of pages in the books as well as the method of conversion. They would also vary with the complexity of the books, i.e., the amount of graphics, multimedia, and links to other online resources, but we have assumed uniformity in this analysis. For these five books, the present value of the lifecycle costs of production and maintenance might be approximately as given in Table 1.

The publisher projected the weighted average net income per copy sold for these five books as about $17. The publisher would need to sell 68 to 281 of these books in online format at this average price to cover the incremental costs of producing, maintaining, refreshing, and migrating the online versions.

The anticipated mix of cloth cover and paperback copies of these titles yields this $17 net income. If the online copies sold at the cloth cover price (a weighted average of $30.46), the break-even quantity would be smaller. On the other hand, if the paperback price (a weighted average of $12.55) prevailed, it would be larger. Although these break-even quantities are a modest share of the projected sales for these five books, they are two-thirds or more of the actual sales for many specialized monographs.

The publisher or an intermediary might charge the purchaser an on-going service fee for maintaining the book online, refreshing and migrating it regularly, and the like, as netLibrary is doing. If so, they could recoup these costs over time rather than through initial sales. The vendor could charge higher rates in the early years than support actual costs (knowing that the book had greater value to the libraries while it was relatively new) and use the excess funds to fund those activities in the later years. The vendor could promise to maintain books that become stale quickly, e.g., programming titles, for only a relatively short period and then taking them down when an insufficient number of libraries were willing to support them.

TABLE 1

	Base	W/Refreshing & Migrating	Break-Even Quantity
From Print to SGML	$2,656	$3,156	186
From ASCII to HTML	$2,627	$3,127	184
From Quark to HTML	$4,269	$4,769	281
From PostScript to PDF	$657	$1,157	68

Libraries Save with Online Books

The project hypothesized that online books would have lower lifecycle costs for libraries. Two expectations backed this hypothesis: (1) print books require ever-more-expensive manpower for acquisition, processing, and circulation as well as the cost of storage space; (2) online books would use ever-less-costly computing hardware and require little staff time.

We estimated the present value of a library's lifecycle costs for both formats. Exhibit 2 lays out basic cost elements and estimates the present value of the costs at Columbia for both types of books. With a purchase price of fifty dollars for both the print book and the online book, the present value of the lifecycle stream of costs for a library is about $156 for the print copy and $127 for the online copy, for a 19 percent savings with the online version. The model assumes that libraries will buy on-line books via a system with terms negotiated with one or several publishers or intermediaries. Costs of ordering the books will be similar to those via approval plans for print books. However, the model estimates cataloging costs at the original cataloging level experienced in the Columbia experiment, rather than at the much less costly copy cataloging level that would prevail ultimately. Thus, the analysis understates potential savings.

A scholarly library incurs substantial costs for the Internet and computing infrastructure that allows it to provide electronic resources, including online books, to its scholars.[25] However, institutions incurred these costs before their libraries provided online books. As a result, one should omit these infrastructure costs from calculation of the cost of providing an online book. However, if an institution assumed unique infrastructure costs in providing online books, such an analysis should include them.

Use and User Reactions

Online Reference Works

The six reference works saw varying patterns of use, but scholars used them all more often in online form than in print form.[26] Use of the online versions of some older works aimed at a general audience declined substantially to a few hundred sessions per semester–still far more than the few uses a month that reference librarians reported for the paper versions. Use of *The Oxford English Dictionary* grew signifi-

EXHIBIT 2. Libraries' Lifecycle Costs of Book Ownership

	Print Book	Online Book
Purchase Price, Average	$50.00	$50.00
Selection	$3.59	$3.59
Processing:		
Ordering		$2.00
Locate & Handle Bibliographic Record		$5.92
Receive Physical Item	$43.67	$0.00
Payment		$2.00
Initial Physical Processing		$0.00
Cataloguing		$25.00
Storage	$4.61	$0.00
Average Cost of Circulation	$43.97	$38.43
Stack Maintenance	$5.47	
Collection Maintenance	$1.90	
Repair/Rebind	$0.28	$0.00
Replace -- New Book & Processing	$2.08	$0.00
Total	**$155.57**	**$126.94**

Selection: Estimated from share of hours spent by librarians & assistants at relevant salary and fringe rates divided by number of new items. (Assumes average librarian salary of $45,000; staff assistant salary of $22,000; and student assistant wage of $8 per hour.) Most books are purchased via approval plans, not individually selected and ordered.

Storage: Present Value of 30 years at $0.30 per year with 5% interest rate. Malcolm Getz estimated annual cost of storing one volume in off-site storage (the marginal method) as $0.30.[1]

Cost of Circulation for Print: Present Value of 30 years with 5% interest rate at $2.86 per circulation and an average of one circulation per year.

Stack Maintenance: Includes shelfreading, shifting.

Collection Maintenance: Includes searching for and tracking missing books.

Replace Print Book: 2,500 volumes lost and 116,000 purchased annually: 2.16% loss rate, assumed value replaced over 30 year period in purchase price and processing.

[1]Getz, Malcolm. "Information Storage." *Encyclopedia of Library and Information Science* 52, supplement 15 (1993), 201-39.

cantly; 1,370 individuals made nearly 29,000 hits on its Web version in spring 1999. *The OED* was the most used resource in the online collection. Use of *African-American Women, Native American Women,* and *Chaucer Name Dictionary* fluctuated from semester to semester, always in the several hundred hits or sessions range.[27]

Monographs and Humanities Texts

Use of *English Poetry Database, English Verse Drama,* and *Patrologia Latina* grew over time, but remained modest. During spring 1999, 52 to 122 individuals used each of these resources.

Hits on 54 *Past Masters* classic texts declined from 6,632 in 1996 to 3,384 in 1998 before increasing 58 percent in spring 1999. Use was largely concentrated in the titles studied in political philosophy and theory classes. From July 1996 to June 1999, one-seventh of the texts received two-thirds of the total hits.

The online collection included 36 monographic titles as of July 1997, 55 as of July 1998, 68 as of year-end 1998, and 108 as of June 1999. Faculty assigned 25 of these books in one or more courses for one or more semesters during this period.[28] These books received 3,542 hits in 1997, 4,885 hits in 1998, and 2,919 hits in the first half of 1999. In spring 1999, in 806 cases an individual used one of these titles one or more times. As some individuals used more than one online book, the total number of users was smaller.

Use of Online Books

During the course of this project, more scholars may have used these books in online format than in paper format.[29] In spring 1999, nearly three times as many scholars clicked on the average online monographic book as circulated its print version. The *Principle of Use Until Satisfaction* suggests that any encounter between a scholar and a book was equally likely to represent a complete use event. While some encounters were longer than others, in each case the user could continue until satisfied. In the use of a paper book, that use could have been as little as a glance at its title page while standing in the stacks or as much as checking it out and reading the entire book. The average number of hits per monographic online book user, per half year, hovered at four to five throughout the study. Thus, typical use of these books had depth beyond reviewing the Title Page-Table of Contents file.

Only one-fifth of the scholars using monographic online books used more than two titles during the study period. This is not surprising, given that the collection was small and lacked the critical mass of books necessary to draw scholars to an online collection extensively. The scholar users may have been satisfied with the experience of using online books, but if the online collection lacked other titles that interested them, they would have had no reason to return to it.

Online Formats Used

Surveys and interviews indicated that scholars did not simply read books online. They tended to browse online and then to print out relevant portions or to seek print copies for extended reading. Sometimes they referred to the online version to track down a quotation or a citation. Other studies have found this pattern to be common in the use of online journals as well.[30]

Format Substitution

An in-class survey, administered when an instructor assigned a book in the collection, asked which copy of a book a student used in reading the assignment. The questionnaire offered four methods of using the online book–reading online, two types of printing, and copying to disk. Over the course of the project, this survey found that a growing share of students used the online book in one or more of these ways, but few read online. By spring 1999, the last semester for this survey, 39 percent of responding students used the online book in one or more ways, the same share as used personal copies. The student's personal copy was both the most common single method of reading an assignment and the single most preferred method. By spring 1999, 43 percent preferred some form of online book use, while only a third preferred to use a personal copy.

The nature of the assignment affected the responses to these questions. If only one chapter was required reading for a course, few students would be likely to purchase a book. On the other hand, if the instructor assigned a whole book and its price were reasonable, more students would purchase it.

Cost and the Use of Books

Suppose that a scholar is familiar with online books, has easy access to them, and incurs no cost in using them. The following simple preference table illustrates the project's findings about scholars' apparent reactions to online books. One axis divides the modes of using a book into *read much of the book* and *read little of the book*. The other axis divides the cost of a paper version into *low* and *high*. If a scholar intended to read little of a book, the ability to locate things within it would be important, while comfort of reading, annotation, and the like would have less significance. In this case, the scholar would prefer an online copy provided by a library as needed at no cost to him, without regard to the price of the paper version. However, if the scholar intended to read much of the book, the inconvenience of online reading would be the dominant factor, forcing the scholar into a *buy versus borrow* decision, based on factors like the price of the book and his need for long term, easy access to it.

Scholar's Preferences for Book Access		
	Read Much	**Read Little**
Low Cost Book	Buy	Online
High Cost Book	Borrow	Online

If a library responds to its scholars' preferences, its collection of print-on-paper books should serve the substantial reading, high cost situation. At this time, the two *read little* quadrants call for the library to provide online access to books. As the readability of online books improves, and scholars' habits evolve, *read much* will shrink and *read little*–the online book-preferring situation–will steadily expand as a share of total use of scholarly books. If the library is to maintain its role as a key resource for scholarly access to books, its online holdings must expand over time to keep pace with these evolving preferences.

Librarians' Response to Online Books

In discussions from summer 1998 to fall 1999, college and university librarians expressed considerable optimism about the potential for online books in their collections. They viewed reference works as having particularly great utility in online form. They also saw value in having available online books that are in high demand, of transient topicality, or not part of their print collections. Few expected to acquire online versions of books that were in their print research collections, mainly because they could not afford to pay twice for these books.

Librarians were concerned about the evolution of the marketplace for scholarly books. How would online books be packaged and priced? What guarantees of availability in the short and long run, preservation, format refreshing and migration would publishers or vendors provide? What conditions of use would publishers and vendors seek? What would happen to *fair use?* Librarians wanted vendors to provide cataloging and usage statistics, as well as user-friendly design of both the general interface to online books and the individual books.

Potential Market Arrangements

Our findings on scholars' interests in online books and on the costs of providing online books suggest that scholarly publishers should test new models that combine print and online availability of books. With the right mix of offerings, the overall market could expand. The goal would be to increase availability of books to scholars and profitability to scholarly publishers. Mixed product models could expand research library markets, develop new academic library markets, and attract more scholars. Possible options include:[31]

- Retain and expand the research library market with:
  - A free online version, i.e., an enhanced product package, or an online version available at a small incremental price, when the library purchases the print version.
  - Modestly priced online collections offered to libraries that buy a substantial share of the titles in print version. This would likely expand sales of the print copies somewhat.
- Expand sale of scholarly monographs into the libraries in the U.S. and abroad that purchase few such books. Price online collections for sale to consortia. Make an on-demand electronic version available as an attractive alternative to interlibrary loan.
- Encourage individual scholar's purchases of monographs with:
  - Pay per electronic view. This could be attractive to scholars not having library access to print or electronic copies.
  - Online ordering of a print copy at a discount from the site of a library's online version.
  - Lowered prices for the print copies to reflect their modest marginal cost.

The processes of designing, producing, and marketing online books are in their infancy. Some scholars who have begun to author books with an online format in mind find it poses unanticipated challenges. How should primary documents be included and incorporated into the analysis? Will the text automatically update itself? Such issues do not arise in authoring traditional scholarly monographs.

Over the next several years the concept of online books will resolve itself so that scholars, authors, publishers, vendors, and libraries will be able to decide what combinations of modes and models will be most beneficial for the scholarly community as a whole, including new and seasoned authors, publishers, vendors, libraries and readers. In the final analysis, the system is one by which authors communicate to readers across spans of both space and time.[32]

The present system has evolved in a way that supports value-adding transformations at several points: the publisher adds quality and authentication; the vendor adds distributional services; the library adds organization and preservation, as well as further quality certification. With electronic books, there is no reason to sacrifice any of these values. However, the final economic driver will be the value delivered to readers, which is the ultimate quid pro quo that leads to the injection of a revenue stream into the process. As technology permits us to blend several of the traditional stages of the communication chain, ultimately economic models will more accurately reflect that value delivered to readers, and will correspond more closely to their allocation of attention to the works, whether in reading or in citation. Writers, editors, and publishers in the world of online magazines like *Salon* are already finding that they can assess specific articles, and even headlines, by logging the amount of attention that readers pay to them. The scholarly world is also very much concerned with the capture of attention, as measured by citation analysis. Thus, it is likely that scholars will introduce such analyses at several points in the chain of communication, and will eventually make them the basis for assignment of costs and prices.

NOTES

1. *The Online Books Project, Columbia University: Final Report* (available with all other project reports at http://www.columbia.edu/cu/libraries/digital/texts/about.html) details the project's results.

2. This remains a problem in 2001 as publishers and vendors seek to develop a business of online books. Commonly, publishers do not have final electronic typesetting files available for easy conversion into online books. They must either scan the print-on-paper books or rekeyboard the text.

3. Use of this collection of online books was restricted to members of the Columbia community by the need to sign-in with Columbia identification. Server data analysis provided considerable insight into how scholars used these books.

4. E-paper is a concept that researchers at MIT and at other research institutes are exploring for displaying digital images–text or graphics–temporarily. It involves elec-

trostatic charges through the material that makes up the pages and which rotates micro-balls that are white on one side and black on the other, hence producing the images.

5. Our research found that most of the use of scholarly books does not involve such extended reading.

6. Some monographs that are considered to be classics are being converted to electronic form and made available online. Questia is including such books in its subscription service, which offers students an online college library. The ACLS History E-Book Project will include several hundred key books in history in its collection. This project will license its books, both new and classic, to libraries.

7. The project research plan and the final report described these methods in detail.

8. Many projects working with existing books have used scanning and optical character recognition to index contents.

9. The project was not able to test these enhancements as we were converting existing books not creating new products. Other systems, such as PDF, have greater capabilities than they did in 1995. Publishers, vendors, and libraries would be wise to evaluate the trade-offs of the various digital book options.

10. Web enhancements over the period of the project would have allowed us to add features. However, we could not economically modify the books already in the collection. Our designers decided that consistency within the collection was more important than adding features for only the more recent books.

11. Even by the end of the project, scholars had not accepted this practice. They wanted the online books paginated as their print counterparts.

12. See Bishop, A.P, Neumann, L.J., Star, S.L., Merkel, C., Ignacio, E., and Sandusky, R.J., "Digital Libraries: Situating Use in Changing Information Infrastructure," *Journal of the American Society of Information Science* 51, no. 4 (March 2000). This reports on the NSF/DARPA/NASA Digital Libraries Initiative project at the University of Illinois. This project used a test bed of recent engineering journals.

13. Estimates by the Strategis Group reported in *The New York Times on the Web,* November 10, 1999. http://www.nytimes.com/library/tech/99/11/biztech/articles/10net. html.

14. Many Columbia scholars residing off-campus had ISP accounts as well as the ability to dial-in to Columbia directly. The online books were accessed via a sign-in with one's Columbia ID.

15. See Kantor, Paul, *Objective Performance Measures for Academic and Research Libraries,* ARL (1984).

16. Journals projects have found that breadth and depth in a collection are key to user adoption. In addition, scholars need time to become aware of the availability of these resources and to find an opportunity to use them. *Summary of SuperJournal Findings: Readers,* Draft April 26, 1999, http://www.superjournal.ac.uk/sj/findread.htm and Bishop et al (2000) discuss these issues.

17. In 1994, the text-based *Concise Columbia Electronic Encyclopedia* had over 15,000 sessions at Columbia. As more sophisticated, Web-based substitutes became available, its use dropped at an increasing rate, with sessions down to about 2,700 in 1997. Typically, use of the more sophisticated resources increased over time. Columbia scholars made nearly 50,000 hits on documents in the online *Encyclopedia Britannica* in 1998. Usage of the Columbia Web version of *The Oxford English Dictionary* nearly doubled from the first half of 1998 to the first half of 1999 to nearly 29,000 hits. The number of users of *The OED* increased by 28 percent from the last half of 1998 to the first half of 1999 to 1,370 distinct users.

18. This will likely occur somewhere between the author's creation of an electronic manuscript and the typesetter's creation of the final book file, but it might occur as part of that last step. Publishers may eliminate typesetting for a class of low demand books for which desktop publishing and on-demand printing could become standard.

19. See Summerfield, Mary, *Issues in the Economics of Scholarly Communication: A White Paper Supporting The Andrew W. Mellon Foundation-Funded Projects–The Online Books Evaluation Project and Columbia International Affairs Online,* Revised March 1998 for more detail on this analysis.

20. Net income equals net price–after discounts to vendors–times units sold. This press received free space and utilities from its parent university so this analysis does not reflect full costs.

21. If a book were marked up in SGML, the standard was to then convert it to HTML for Web viewing *on the fly.* John Price-Wilkin at the University of Michigan championed this system.

22. Personal communication from Christina Powell, Coordinator, Humanities Text Initiative, University of Michigan, July 1999. These data reflected costs for the process in use in 1998.

23. In a personal communication Roy Heinz, Director, Information Systems, University of Pennsylvania Library, provided information on their process for conversion and the costs that they were experiencing in 1999.

24. This present value estimate assumes a real cost of money of 5 percent per year as well as a thirty year time span. The later estimates of the lifecycle costs of a book for a library use these parameters as well.

25. A college or university uses these resources for many purposes beyond library services.

26. We lacked a firm count of use of reference resources that were on open shelves as scholars could access them and reshelve them at will. Reference librarians could track of use of books kept behind their service center.

27. These resources were available in two formats for which the measuring systems varied. It is impossible to know if gains in use of the browser-accessible CWeb versions, measured in hits, offset declines in use of the text-based CNet versions, measured in sessions.

28. This count is based on faculty having put a book on reserve for a course. We had no way of determining if an instructor used a book in a course but did not put it on reserve.

29. We could not track in-library use of print-on-paper books so we lack a total count of use of books in that format.

30. See *SuperJournal* (1999) and Bishop et al (2000).

31. Mandel, Carol and Summerfield, Mary, *Scholarly Monographs Online: Potentialities and Realities Suggested by the Columbia University Online Books Evaluation Project,* January 1998, (at http://www.arl.org/scomm/epub/papers/mandel.html) discussed these market models more fully.

32. Its use in the certification of young scholars as they seek to get their first positions in academia and to earn promotions and tenure complicates the decision-making and economics of the scholarly communications process. Their first books, generally revised dissertations, tend to have a narrow focus and interest to only a few scholars. Publishing such books is nearly certain to be a financially losing enterprise with current processes. Perhaps changes in technology and the expectations of academia will correct this situation.

Project Euclid
and the Role of Research Libraries
in Scholarly Publishing

Zsuzsa Koltay
H. Thomas Hickerson

SUMMARY. Project Euclid, a joint electronic journal publishing initiative of Cornell University Library and Duke University Press is discussed in the broader contexts of the changing patterns of scholarly communication and the publishing scene of mathematics. Specific aspects of the project such as partnerships and the creation of an economic model are presented as well as what it takes to be a publisher. Libraries have gained important and relevant experience through the creation and management of digital libraries, but they need to develop further skills if they want to adopt a new role in the life cycle of scholarly communication. *[Article copies available for a fee from The Haworth Document Delivery Service: 1-800-HAWORTH. E-mail address: <getinfo@haworthpressinc.com> Website: <http://www.HaworthPress.com> © 2001 by The Haworth Press, Inc. All rights reserved.]*

Zsuzsa Koltay is Coordinator of Electronic Publishing and Manager of Project Euclid, Cornell University Library, 201 Olin Library, Ithaca, NY 14853 (E-mail: zk10@cornell.edu).

H. Thomas Hickerson is Associate University Librarian for Information Technologies and Special Collections, Cornell University Library (E-mail: hth2@cornell.edu).

[Haworth co-indexing entry note]: "Project Euclid and the Role of Research Libraries in Scholarly Publishing." Koltay, Zsuzsa, and H. Thomas Hickerson. Co-published simultaneously in *Journal of Library Administration* (The Haworth Information Press, an imprint of The Haworth Press, Inc.) Vol. 35, No. 1/2, 2001, pp. 83-98; and: *Libraries and Electronic Resources: New Partnerships, New Practices, New Perspectives* (ed: Pamela L. Higgins) The Haworth Information Press, an imprint of The Haworth Press, Inc., 2001, pp. 83-98. Single or multiple copies of this article are available for a fee from The Haworth Document Delivery Service [1-800-HAWORTH, 9:00 a.m. - 5:00 p.m. (EST). E-mail address: getinfo@haworthpressinc.com].

KEYWORDS. Project Euclid, electronic publishing, research libraries, scholarly communication, scholarly publishing

PROJECT EUCLID

Project Euclid's mission is to advance the cause of effective and affordable scholarly communication in theoretical and applied mathematics and statistics by developing an infrastructure that allows responsibly priced, high-quality independent journals to create and share an online presence. A non-profit joint venture of Cornell University Library and Duke university press, whose development was funded by The Andrew W. Mellon Foundation beginning in 2000, Project Euclid is forging an alliance with journals to allow for both the continued intellectual and economic independence of its participants and a competitive edge that comes from a fully functional online publishing environment. In an era in which users are accustomed to the power and convenience of online journal aggregations, Project Euclid strives to bring this capability to a segment of scientific publishing that, by and large, has not benefited from the potentials of cooperative online publishing.

The functionality of the resulting system will span the scholarly communication process: prepublication, editing and peer reviewing, and journal publishing. The system will have the following three main modules:

- *Module 1: Preprint server to facilitate the fast dissemination of research.* Authors will upload their papers to the repository and submit papers with a simple click to particular participating journals for peer review. Those who prefer not to submit preprints to the archive can submit papers directly to participating journals. Additionally, authors can submit preprints and send them to journals that do not participate in Project Euclid.
- *Module 2: New toolkits.* Password-protected area and toolkit for editors and reviewers to streamline the peer review and editorial process. Editors can maintain a database of their reviewers, each of which will have an assigned password. Editors can post papers to the desired reviewers' password-protected areas and alert them via e-mail to read the papers. Reviewers can submit their comments and/or the marked-up papers confidentially. Editors can link the revised versions of the papers to the preprint versions if

applicable. Editors can also upload the final versions of papers and journal issues to the third module of the system.

- *Module 3: Enhancements to online journal publishing.* Journals will gain added exposure on the large Euclid site and will benefit from advanced user features that they cannot afford individually. Such features include: browsing journal by journal; flexible keyword and full-text searching (journal by journal, any combination of journals, all journals, or the whole Euclid site, including e-prints); and e-mail current awareness services. Individual journals will also provide access to their own titles. Journal editors may choose either to allow open access to the full text of articles or to limit that access to journal subscribers only. The URLs for the individual journals can be constructed to reflect the institution where the journal originates, and not the Euclid site.

Availability of the electronic journals will facilitate participation in the Open Archives Initiative (OAI).[1] We consider the OAI a significant development in scholarly communication and intend to extend its potential for cross-archive searching to both the e-prints and the journal delivery module. The OAI makes it possible for decentralized archives to develop in response to the needs and interests of specific disciplines without these activities jeopardizing the potential for broadly integrated access to information.

The OAI initiative may also prove instrumental in our efforts to enhance mutual synergies between Euclid and other math-related projects being conducted around the world. It is in our journals' best interest to be discovered by as many search engines, portals, indexing, and linking services and schemes as possible. Significant examples include NSF-funded National Science Digital Library projects and two important German projects, MathNet and Euler. Although there are different expectations and standards being implemented by these different projects, we expect that the OAI will provide a lowest common denominator for metadata discovery and sharing.

THE CONTEXT FOR PROJECT EUCLID

In 1999, Steven Rockey (Director of Cornell's Mathematics Library) conducted an exhaustive analysis of journal publishing in mathematics. At that time, *Mathematical Reviews,* the major American indexer of mathematical literature, provided cover-to-cover indexing of 544 titles that are considered high-density mathematics journals. Seventeen large publishers (including Springer-Verlag, Reed Elsevier, Academic Press, the American Mathematical Society, and the Society of Industrial and Applied Mathematics) accounted for 179 titles. The remaining 365 titles were all from publishers who produced three or fewer titles, the vast majority publishing only one title.

Very few of these independent publishers are commercial concerns; most are scholarly societies or are associated with universities. Many are mathematics departments or colleges. Research in mathematics is conducted at a wide variety of institutions, and there are many reputable local journals that are considered core publications. A number of the major journals that are essential to any mathematics collection are included in these 365 titles. *Zentralblatt MATH,* the European counterpart of *Mathematical Reviews,* presents a very similar picture.

By 2001, significant consolidation has occurred with the giant publishers Elsevier and Kluwer substantially enhancing their position in the mathematics and statistics publishing, each one now publishing more than 35 titles. Elsevier has acquired several smaller commercial publishers including Gauthier-Villars and Pergamon and has become a very significant force in the discipline. Elsevier is now poised to acquire Academic Press, an acquisition that would make them the largest publisher of mathematics and statistics. Kluwer has also substantially expanded its position both by acquiring smaller commercial publishers including Consultants Bureau and by taking control of a number of individual titles from non-commercial and commercial entities.[2]

In this era of commercial consolidation, independent journals are, more than ever, important for their role in maintaining the diversity of expression that mathematicians value so highly. These journals are also valuable for their significant quality and low prices, in many cases providing serious competition for the much more expensive commercial titles. Thus, maintaining their competitive edge and economic balance is important for the scholarly community.

The independent publishers have been slow to make the move to the online environment. Many of them have not made the transition at all; others have an online presence that was created on a shoestring and without an institutional commitment to addressing important user issues, such as searching and reference linking, or operational feasibility issues, such as metadata, authentication, electronic commerce, system development, and preservation. Although these titles are a critical part of the intellectual landscape in the field and are among the most-affordable ways to publicize mathematics research, the independent publishers need assistance in entering the world of electronic publishing. Since editors of small journals tend to value their editorial integrity very highly, they are hesitant to accept help from any source that is not considered organizationally neutral.

Although it is a scientific discipline, mathematics has not fully benefited from the scholarly communication revolution in science and technology because in several ways math faces the same issues that humanities disciplines face. These issues include: the economics of the field (unlike engineering or biomedicine, for example, mathematics has a limited financial impact); its reliance on a painstaking refereeing process that substantially changes about 70 percent of the papers by the time they are published; the emphasis on the validity of the articles, rather than the speed of communication; and the practice of referring to past research material. While certain fields of physics and computer science rely heavily on free e-print aggregations, primarily the arXiv, for communicating research results, that is not the case for mathematics. Despite a healthy growth in the number of math papers submitted to the arXiv, the Los Alamos pre-print server originally developed for physics, it still contains less than 7% of the current math publishing output.[3] An explanation for this phenomenon lies in the fact that physics has long relied on the distribution of preprints for fast communication of research results. When the arXiv was founded in 1991, it made the existing process faster and more accessible. Even if the benefits appear compelling, change comes slowly in disciplines where change means establishing a different pattern of scholarly communication. One can argue that such patterns are rooted in the sociology and culture of each discipline. The publishing scene of a discipline evolves over time to accommodate its culture, and once it has evolved, it tends to reinforce those patterns. Consequently, up to now, new publishing alternatives have been most successful when they replicate existing patterns.

Many independent mathematics and statistics journals remain unchanged at this time, although some have added electronic versions that primarily present the printed journal online in the form of HTML-based tables of contents and abstracts and the text of the articles presented via PDF, PostScript, or DVI files. Only occasionally do journals add some extra features, such as searching capabilities. Advanced features such as reference linking and user awareness services are very rare among the independent journals. Although this would be a natural benefit of the online environment, only a handful of journals include multimedia or interactive material, and their experience tends to show that there is limited demand for these capabilities. The number of freely accessible electronic-only journals is also quite limited, despite well-intentioned efforts by some in the scholarly community to reclaim the literature produced by mathematicians and to place it under the control of mathematicians. Allyn Jackson identifies several reasons that only about 35 such journals exist worldwide. Among other things, she points to the limits of volunteer labor.[4] Interestingly, *Geometry and Topology* was forced to add a print version of its electronic journal to encourage submissions from authors.[5]

While the pattern of scholarly communication in mathematics has remained largely unchanged, there have been plenty of economic changes in the field. Journal price hikes several times higher than the inflation rate have become commonplace in this discipline as well. The 35.61% rise between 1996 and 2000 that the *Library Journal* reported for mathematics and computer science is a composite number across all publishers including commercial conglomerates, university presses, scholarly societies, and independent journals.[6] Robion Kirby has collected more detailed data such as price per page for dozens of journals and publishers from 1994 to 1999.[7] The difference in per page prices between the large commercial and the independent publishers is shocking in most cases. Another economic trend is the increasing consolidation of journal ownership previously referenced. This consolidation is evident within the commercial sector, but there is also anecdotal evidence that multinational commercial publishers have attempted to buy out several of the independent journals.

This is the backdrop against which Project Euclid is developing and the factors that mold the project. Euclid's focus is helping the independent journals remain independent and competitive. Project Euclid will not abruptly challenge the prevalent patterns of authorship, publication, and use, rather it will work with the existing patterns and shape them gradually.

PUBLISHING DESIGNED TO MEET THE NEEDS
OF A DISCIPLINE:
ESSENTIAL COMPONENTS OF PROJECT EUCLID

Project Euclid is designed to be compatible with the needs, culture, sociology, economics, and scholarly communication patterns of mathematics and statistics. Thoroughly understanding and responding to these particular needs and attributes does not guarantee success, but significantly enhances the chance to attain it. It also makes our communication with the community easier and more fruitful. The significant status of the independent journals has grown out of the culture of a discipline that values decentralization and independence. We know that Project Euclid has to support and protect this independence to succeed. Therefore it is being established as a not-for-profit consortium of partners, primarily publishers of journals that are already established in the print environment. Since each journal desires considerable autonomy in making choices about many aspects of journal production and fulfillment, the system is being designed for maximum flexibility from journal look-and-feel, through file format decisions, to user authentication and pricing of pay-per-view. One of the few non-negotiable issues is the requirement that metadata be provided in a common format to support common functionality, such as cross-journals searching.

Economic Models

The economic model Project Euclid is developing is designed for maximum benefit with maximum flexibility. To achieve cost-recovery, Project Euclid will have to start producing significant revenues after its grant-funded phase, which ends in December 2002. The source of these revenues could be the publisher partners through a fee for service model. In this model each publisher would contribute its fair share towards common expenses and would keep control of its subscription base. Since a common concern of editors is the fear of loss of subscriptions for the print edition, which they still regard as their primary product, this model is reassuringly simple and promises the least amount of disruption to existing patterns and processes for the journal publishers. However, it does not take advantage of opportunities such as offering a bundled subscription to libraries, and it might also mean that some journals will be unable to afford to participate or that Project Euclid might not be able to adequately support ongoing development.

Another possible model is the aggregation model, in which Project Euclid would become a product that is licensed to libraries and other subscribers who would be the sources of revenue. In this model, the income would be divided between Project Euclid and the participating journals. The advantage of this model is that it maximizes the subscriber base for each journal and that it strengthens the individual journals' position in the tough competition for collection development funds. This model can, however, be both threatening for journals because they may feel they are giving up individual control over their subscriptions and that by forcing libraries to subscribe to a bundle, they are using the same tactics that they find reprehensible when used by commercial conglomerates.

Project Euclid has employed an outside consultant–Professor Bruce Kingma of Syracuse University, an expert in the economics of scholarly communication and digital libraries–to research and identify possibilities for an innovative economic model. Based on his research, Project Euclid will start a comprehensive discussion with its partners to define a flexible economic model combining elements of both the aggregation and fee-for-service approaches. The decision-making process will be thoroughly consultative.

Partnerships

Partnerships are essential to Project Euclid's operation. Project Euclid is a joint venture and collaboration of Cornell University Library and Duke University Press. Each brings substantial strength and experience to the project. Recently designated as a SUN [Sun Microsystems, Inc.] Center of Excellence for Digital Libraries, Cornell University Library (CUL) has been an internationally known leader in digital library development and management for more than a decade. CUL runs several 24/7 production systems that are also well supported by user services, a traditional field of expertise for libraries that has been updated for the 21st century by the addition of solid technical skills. This experience has given CUL a sound understanding of user issues and preferences. CUL is an international leader in electronic archiving research. Also, as a library, CUL has a vital interest in keeping academics in control of scholarly communication.

Duke University Press (DUP), the long-time publisher of two influential mathematics journals, contributes invaluable knowledge and expertise regarding editorial, publishing and production issues. Both its mathematics journals are online. DUP staff also bring their mastery with different versions of TeX and LaTeX (typesetting languages common to mathematical expression) to the project, as well as their experience with economic aspects of both traditional and electronic publishing.

A handful of journal publishers designated as development partners have been actively involved in the shaping of the system from the beginning. The number has been kept purposely small to make initial development more manageable, and in selecting these partners, we sought to include a good cross section of the community we are aiming to serve. Half of the publishers are in mathematics; the other half are publishing statistical journals. They represent scholarly societies, consortia, small commercial operations, and universities. They have been active participants in the process of developing specifications for the system, designing production flow, defining their specific needs, and discussing interface design. Project Euclid will also draw on their expertise and support in shaping and fine-tuning its economic model.

Another important partnership is our alliance with the Scholarly Publishing and Academic Resources Coalition (SPARC) of the Association of Research Libraries. This international network of libraries was created to support publications and projects that contribute to a more competitive marketplace in scholarly communication and publishing. Since SPARC is actively involved with others implementing new approaches to scholarly communication, it is a valuable link to libraries. SPARC's stamp of approval confirms Project Euclid's place in the affordable scholarly publishing movement.

THE LIBRARY AS PUBLISHER: THE CORNELL EXPERIENCE

The Cornell University Library is committed to maintaining a healthy diversity in academic publishing, to creating new business models for the support of publishing, and to employing new technologies to improve the dissemination and use of scholarly information. The Cornell Library has a solid foundation for this work as it is one of the most experienced libraries in creating, managing, and distributing digital information.

Beginning in 1989, the Library, in cooperation with the Xerox Corporation, began conducting research to establish methods and standards for high resolution scanning of 19th and 20th century printed texts.[8] Major compilations were created, including a collection of distinguished mathematics monographs selected by Cornell mathematicians as pivotal works from the later decades of the 19th century and early years of the 20th century. The resulting Historical Mathematics Collection continues to serve as a respected source used by scientists worldwide, and from which other libraries often seek printed copies to enhance their own holdings. Making this collection interoperable with two newer collections in Michigan and Germany is the focus of a current project funded jointly by the National Science Foundation and the Deutsche Forschungsgemeinschaft.

The Digital Access Coalition, established in 1992, provided an early model for cooperation between the Library and faculty in the production of digital resources for teaching and research.[9] Renamed the Cornell Institute for Digital Collections (CIDC) in 1997, the Institute cooperated with Cornell's Johnson Museum of Art in the high-resolution conversion of a major portion of their holdings. Today, CIDC is the home of some of the most innovative faculty-designed digital compilations and offers an internationally recognized consulting team for issues relating to the high-volume conversion of text and visual image collections. CIDC also cooperates with the Library's Preservation Department in the production of a world-renowned educational series. In response to a recent survey being conducted by the Digital Library Federation, over fifty different digital library developments were identified in the Library.

PROJECT EUCLID AND NEW ISSUES FOR LIBRARIES AS PUBLISHERS

Such extensive institutional experience in the employment of new technologies for the creation and use of digital sources and services provides a sound foundation for developing technologies necessary to the distribution of electronic publications. Nonetheless, the experience of the previous decade is markedly different from the skills, resources, and management techniques required in academic journal publishing. Becoming an active participant in the publishing of mathematics and statistics journals electronically is a substantial new institutional challenge for the Library. New issues facing Cornell staff in entering the publishing arena fall in three principal categories: managing new cooperative relationships; business, marketing, and economic models; and operational and technical challenges.

Managing New Cooperative Relationships

At Cornell, the library's relationship with the Mathematics Department has always been a particularly strong one. As noted, one of the Library's first digitization efforts focused on mathematics. Professor R. Keith Dennis has been a trusted advisor and enthusiastic supporter of our efforts. He has been particularly active in editorial and publishing roles, serving as Executive Editor of *Mathematical Reviews* between 1995 and 1998 and as Consulting Editor since 1998. He is also an editor of *Homology, Homotopy and Applications*. His knowledge of the

Library is extensive, and he is chairing the University Faculty Library Board during 2000/2001. Such guidance is essential in developing new roles and services.

When embarking on Project Euclid, the Library needed to gain broader knowledge of the mathematics and statistics publishing environment and establish critical contacts. During the summer of 1999 the Library convened a meeting at Cornell of the publishers from major scholarly societies, including the executive directors of the American Mathematical Society and the Society of Industrial and Applied Mathematics; the director of the Clay Mathematics Institute; the scientific coordinator of the European Mathematical Information Service (EMIS), the electronic information service of the European Mathematical Society; a representative of the American Statistical Association Task Force on Electronic Publishing; and several editors working at Cornell. The purpose of the meeting was to inform each other about current publishing activities and related experiences and to identify and prioritize common issues and concerns. Through attendance at major academic conferences, contacts were established with potential publishing partners, and extensive conversations followed. In order to enhance cooperation with the European mathematics community, Cornell presently serves as a mirror site for the European Mathematical Information Service (EMIS) and the Zentralblatt MATH online database.

The Duke University Press's extensive experience in the production of math journals has been invaluable and Cornell and Duke staff have contributed jointly to all aspects of Project Euclid. Through these relationships, we have built a new base of knowledge and a productive network of organizational and collegial contacts and have established necessary credibility with many of those whose cooperation and approval are essential to the success of this venture.

Business, Marketing, and Economic Models

In their support of scholarship and teaching, research libraries have played the principal role in the acquisition, organization, distribution, and use of academic publications. The available means of producing and distributing scholarly information is now expanding. Preprint servers are increasingly important in some fields. Individual faculty websites often convey valuable information. Governmental, university, and consortial sites distribute access to statistical information and research findings. Disciplinary communities are beginning to aggregate diverse categories of related information. Libraries are challenged to select and support access to these important new vehicles for scholarly communication. In spite of expanding diversity, the refereed academic journal remains the most important means of communication for most disciplines, but even these journals are changing. Many are available electronically, some only electronically. Some are free. In their electronic manifestation, some are incorporating multimedia and analytical tools unavailable in the print environment. A few are creative new collages previously unknown in the publishing world.[10] And university libraries are increasingly instrumental to these developments.

If however, research libraries seek to be viable in publishing, they must be realistic about costs and revenues. They must acknowledge indirect as well as direct costs. They often need initial subsidies and may continue to need to be subsidized. Libraries have seldom borrowed start-up funding or seek venture capital. Financial success in journal publishing is often dependent on economies of scale and on the ability to publish in fields with commercial as well as academic sales. Although university published journals do not have to generate a profit and subsidies may be justified, sound accounting practices and realistic financial projections are necessary.

In addition to systematic financial planning and business operation, effective marketing is required. Project Euclid marketing strategies include participation in academic conferences as vendors of products and services and, recruiting publishing partners and informing potential subscribers. In this competition with commercial publishers, Project Euclid must develop a clear understanding of its particular strengths and weaknesses. In this new role, we have certain financial and professional risks. We are also risking the good will and confidence established over many years by libraries everywhere.

Good ideas will not make up for bad economics. The financial failure during 2000 and 2001 of numerous new commercial ventures based on the creative potential of the Internet should make this clear. Project Euclid owes it to its partners and its institutions to make its potential liabilities clear, while at the same time, moving aggressively. The next few years will prove to be important in establishing alternative models for scholarly communication. While further commercial consolidation at this point will significantly reduce future possibilities, the development of viable alternative models could lead to a much more diverse academic publishing environment in the near future.

Operational and Technical Challenges

Cornell University Library, like most research libraries today, is generally well prepared to manage complex systems and conduct a wide range of technology-based services. Increasingly, all of these systems operate on a 24/7 basis, and our users are located around the globe. Our technical knowledge and range of experience positions us well to take on new challenges, such as Project Euclid.

However, new technical skills and familiarities have to be developed to enter into the world of digital journal publishing. Publishing systems are available out of the box but they are sometimes inflexible, frequently expensive and they do not offer the full set of features or the modularity that Project Euclid calls for. Therefore extensive modifications, development and original programming are required, resulting in custom software that must be supported over time. It is not a simple task to develop a system that supports the features required by authors, editors, and publishers and also includes the desired user functionality combined with an attractive interface and easy navigation.

Though critical to our success, the technologies employed may not prove as difficult as managing the workflow of texts and images received from numerous publishers employing a variety of procedures and software. Here, the Library's lack of experience may be most telling. Hiring staff from the publishing industry or establishing partnerships with existing publishers may prove essential to success. Cornell's partnership with the Duke University Press gives Project Euclid credibility with other publishers. Nonetheless, establishing agreement on the necessary procedures and timelines for regular and smooth interaction with a diverse group of contributing publishers is a challenge. In addition to production schedules, the subscription and security requirements of each publisher must be managed. The library's traditional service ethic and skills will no doubt enhance the level of "user help" provided. In spite of the initial challenges in developing and organizing necessary technological and operational capabilities, research libraries will prove well suited to these aspects of electronic publishing.

As a partner in Project Euclid, the Cornell Library's move into the publishing arena is a venture with explicit risks of failure. As the project is still in its start-up phase, how well we can manage these risks and how successful we are in accomplishing the project's mission will only become clear in the future. Project Euclid's timeline calls for production delivery of the development partners' dozen journals in 2001; the addition of more journals and the development of the editorial toolkit and e-print modules in 2002. In 2003 Project Euclid's cost recovery phase will begin.

The Library's Role in the Life Cycle of Scholarly Communication

The library is choosing to enter into a pursuit in which success and failure are measured in both academic and financial terms. While universities are large businesses with bottom-line accountability, most are not-for-profit in legal and financial terms or in cultural terms. While the various divisions are expected to function within an assigned budget, within the academic sector of the university the products and services we provide are expected to contribute to the education and research process and are viewed as providing intellectual and cultural benefits for society. These products are also viewed as having economic benefits for society, and some programs, such as extension services, are expected to result in immediate practical enhancements. And while cost-benefit accountability is growing in universities, most of what we do is largely assumed to be valuable and of broad societal good.

In entering publishing, libraries are adopting a new role in the life cycle of scholarly communication. They are enabling the compilation of scholarly information, supporting its distribution, and managing its availability and use. In doing so, they are responding to the immediate needs of the academic community, including authors, editors, and readers, and also seeking to fulfill our longer-term responsibility to scholarship and society by:

1. Altering a publishing environment in which consolidation has resulted in continual price increases which are disproportionate in relation to increases in the cost of production by commercial publishers and by some scholarly societies;
2. Fostering online distribution and access to scholarly information, offering the potential to increase use and usability of such information while decreasing the per user cost of use;
3. Encouraging and enabling the creation and dissemination of new forms and combinations of academic information; and
4. Conducting necessary research and development of policies, practices, and technologies necessary to preserve the availability of information produced and distributed in electronic form.

Dynamic forces are transforming libraries today. The role of libraries in the life-cycle of scholarly communication has changed. In this new paradigm, the move into electronic publishing is a natural evolution for libraries. For the Cornell University Library, Project Euclid is an important challenge in realizing our vision for the library of today and the future.

NOTES

1. "The Open Archives Initiative develops and promotes interoperability standards that aim to facilitate the efficient dissemination of content. The Open Archives Initiative has its roots in an effort to enhance access to e-print archives as a means of increasing the availability of scholarly communication. Continued support of this work remains a cornerstone of the Open Archives program. The fundamental technological framework and standards that are developing to support this work are, however, independent of both the type of content offered and the economic mechanisms surrounding that content, and promise to have much broader relevance in opening up access to a range of digital materials. As a result, the Open Archives Initiative is currently an organization and an effort explicitly in transition, and is committed to exploring and enabling this new and broader range of applications." URL: www.openarchives.org.

2. Thanks to Steven Rockey for compiling and providing this information about the publishing scene in mathematics.

3. This is a generous estimate. Mathematics publishing output is defined based on the number of records added to Mathematical Reviews: 64,598 records of research published in 1998, 62,794 published in 1999, and, at the time of research in February 2001, 45,974 published in 2000. The low number for 2000 has to do with the lag time needed to prepare reviews and to add records. Based on earlier years our conservative estimate is that at least 60,000 records will represent the year 2000 publishing output. In contrast the arXiv saw 2,621 submissions in 1998 where the primary or secondary category was mathematics. In 1999 there were 3,213 submissions, and 3,963 in 2000 (there is no lag time to allow for with the arXiv).

4. Jackson, Allyn. 2000. The Slow Revolution of the Free Electronic Journal. Notices of the AMS 47, no. 9:1053-59.

5. Kirby, Robion. 1999. Competing with the Commercial Journals. Presented at the *Future of Mathematical Communication,* Berkeley, CA.

6. Ketcham-Van Orsdel, Lee and Kathleen Born. 2000. Pushing Toward More Affordable Access. *Library Journal* 125, no. 7:47-52.

7. Kirby, Robion. 2000. Comparative Prices of Math Journals, updated January 2000. Online. Available: http://www.math.berkeley.edu/~kirby/jp00.html. March 5, 2001. Kirby, Robion. 1997. Comparative Prices of Math Journals. Online. Available: http://www.math.berkeley.edu/~kirby/journals.html. March 5, 2001.

8. Kenney, Anne and Lynne Personius. 1992. Cornell/Xerox Joint Study in Digital Preservation._ *Studies in Multimedia: state-of-the-art solutions in multimedia and hypertext.* Edited by Susan Stone and Michael Buckland. Medford, NJ: Learned Information.

9. Hickerson, H. Thomas. 1995. Digital Technologies and Networked Resources: Developing New Patterns of Collaboration. *Going Digital: Electronic Images in the Library Catalog and Beyond.* Edited by Mimi King. Chicago: Library Information Technology Association/Public Library Association/American Library Association, 35-44.

10. One example is *Ctheory Multimedia,* a semi-annual collection of electronic art and theory published electronically through the Cornell University Library. URL: ctheorymultimedia.cornell.edu.

Content Standards for Electronic Books: The OEBF Publication Structure and the Role of Public Interest Participation

Allen Renear
Gene Golovchinsky

SUMMARY. In the emerging world of electronic publishing how we create, distribute, and read books will be in a large part determined by an underlying framework of content standards that establishes the range of technological opportunities and constraints for publishing and reading systems. But efforts to develop content standards based on sound engineering models must skillfully negotiate competing and sometimes apparently irreconcilable objectives if they are to produce results relevant

Allen Renear is Associate Professor of Library and Information Science, University of Illinois at Urbana-Champaign, 501 East Daniel Street, Champaign, IL 61820 (Email: allen_renear@brown.edu).

Gene Golovchinsky is Senior Research Scientist, FX Palo Alto Laboratory, Inc., 3400 Hillview Avenue, Building 4, Palo Alto, CA 94304 (E-mail: gene@pal.xerox.com).

[Haworth co-indexing entry note]: "Content Standards for Electronic Books: The OEBF Publication Structure and the Role of Public Interest Participation." Renear, Allen, and Gene Golovchinsky. Co-published simultaneously in *Journal of Library Administration* (The Haworth Information Press, an imprint of The Haworth Press, Inc.) Vol. 35, No. 1/2, 2001, pp. 99-123; and: *Libraries and Electronic Resources: New Partnerships, New Practices, New Perspectives* (ed: Pamela L. Higgins) The Haworth Information Press, an imprint of The Haworth Press, Inc., 2001, pp. 99-123. Single or multiple copies of this article are available for a fee from The Haworth Document Delivery Service [1-800-HAWORTH, 9:00 a.m. - 5:00 p.m. (EST). E-mail address: getinfo@haworthpressinc.com].

to the rapidly changing course of technology. The Open eBook Forum's *Publication Structure,* an XML-based specification for electronic books, is an example of the sort of timely and innovative problem solving required for successful real-world standards development. As a result of this effort, the electronic book industry will not only happen sooner and on a larger scale than it would have otherwise, but the electronic books it produces will be more functional, more interoperable, and more accessible to all readers. Public interest participants have a critical role in this process. *[Article copies available for a fee from The Haworth Document Delivery Service: 1-800-HAWORTH. E-mail address: <getinfo@haworthpressinc.com> Website: <http://www.HaworthPress.com> © 2001 by The Haworth Press, Inc. All rights reserved.]*

KEYWORDS. Electronic publishing, standards, XML, ebooks, public interest, OEBF, Open eBook Forum

INTRODUCTION

Recently there has been a resurgence of commercial and journalistic commotion around the prospect of "electronic books." On the one hand it is hard not to be immediately skeptical: electronic books have been predicted, and attempted, before, with little effect. On the other hand it is undoubtedly true that the last decade has seen enormous improvements in key technologies, and, perhaps even more importantly, substantial changes in the habits and expectations of readers. There does in fact appear to be a revolution underway in how we create, manage, distribute, and read textual materials. So while it may not be clear exactly how things will play out in detail, it is now a fairly safe bet that reading will continue to become increasingly electronic, and that electronic books will have a significant role in this new world.

The *Open eBook Forum* (OEBF) has been formed to support the development of an electronic book industry. The OEBF consists of major industry participants (including companies representing publishers, distributors, software manufacturers, hardware manufacturers, and conversion and composition service bureaus) as well as other stakeholders (universities, libraries, non-profit special interest groups, and other related trade and professional organizations).[1] The goal of the OEBF is to "establish common specifications for electronic book systems, applications and products that will benefit creators of content, makers of reading systems, and, most importantly, consumers." Its first product, the *OEBF Publication Structure Specification,* a content specification, has been widely endorsed and is already in use in a number of well-known electronic book systems.

What follows is only in part a description of the origin and nature of the OEBF and the OEBF Publication Structure Specification.[2] We begin by describing how in the 1980s an approach to modeling digital documents emerged that, although it received nearly unanimous endorsement by specialists as the fundamentally correct approach and one that would yield many social and commercial advantages, nevertheless failed until very recently to be widely used–a failure that resulted in many lost opportunities. We next consider the prospects for electronic books. The problems facing the development of a flourishing industry of high-performance interoperable electronic books are varied and daunting. Given both the difficulty of these problems and the ominous experiences of the 1980s, is there any chance for developing a content specification that would put the electronic book industry on a sound engineering foundation, helping ensure that it is both a commercial success and a positive social and cultural force? The answer to that question comes in the description of the Open eBook Publication Structure, which is held up as an example of how, with sufficient ingenuity, vision, and good will, a timely practical specification can indeed successfully negotiate these hard problems.

In the "Final Word" we reflect on the lessons of this account and encourage the library community to help continue with the hard work of developing practical standards based on sound information management principles. The extent to which new developments in electronic publishing contribute to the broader public good, and benefit all members of society, depends critically on enlightened public sector participation.

AN ENGINEERING MODEL FOR DOCUMENTS

The Emergence of Content-Oriented Document Processing

Between 1960 and 1990 publishers, designers, engineers, computer scientists, and others involved in publishing and text processing learned a great deal about how documents (such as books, articles, and other printed matter) should be represented in computers. At the core of these insights was the realization that documents are best treated as *intellec-*

tual objects, that is, as structures of logical components (such as titles, headings, extracts and lists) whose identity is intrinsically connected with the kind of information they carry or with the communicative role they have, rather than as perceptual objects which consist of the graphic components (font shifts, additional white space, and arrangement on the page) specific to some particular physical rendition of that information.[3]

This view of documents, one that separates structure from presentation, which was consistent with general theories of information management and systems design, as well as implicit in many (but not all) publishing practices, became in the early 1980s the standard recommended engineering model for document processing. When systems for creating, managing, and using documents reflected this model, efficiency and additional functionality were achieved; when systems failed to reflect it, there were more likely to be additional costs, degraded performance, and less functionality.[4]

This approach to working with digital documents came about naturally. In the 1970s computer typesetters typically placed long strings of formatting codes before bits of text to achieve the intended formatting effects when the text was processed and printed. Typesetting systems designers soon realized, however, that it was far easier to simply identify text components according to the sort of editorial role they had in the document (e.g., as a title, heading, paragraph, extract, or equation) and then separately to provide a formatting definition for each type of component. This immediately simplified the construction of the input file as it was no longer necessary to enter a string of formatting commands for each text component, a time-consuming and error-prone process. It also made global changes in formatting (if the design changed, or if different products or different output devices required different design treatments) easier and less subject to error.

As this approach matured and was integrated into the overall design of typesetting and document processing systems, more and more advantages became apparent. For example, with key text components reliably identified, systems could automatically generate apparatus such as tables of contents, figures, plates, or tables; appendices of equations or formulae; or glossaries of technical terms. It was also easier to accommodate different output devices, to convert data files from one system to another, and to "repurpose" content for applications other than print publishing. When this approach was applied beyond the obvious editorial objects typical of books and articles in general to the objects particular to specialized disciplinary domains (in the sciences for instance) or to objects particular to specialist document genres (such as legal and business documents) even more advantages beyond simple formatting became available. Finally, if the documents were published electronically computer processing could take advantage of the identification of text components to provide a vast range of new functionality: intelligent navigation, advanced searching, annotation support, automated linking, content analysis, and various database-like features.

This approach to text creation, management, and typesetting quickly came to be seen as far more functional and efficient than any other, and, combined with emerging technologies of interactive networked publishing, it seemed to promise a new world of highly effective, innovative publishing. The number and variety of advantages of this approach, and its promise of new functionality, was so impressive that it was natural, at least for the philosophically inclined, to conclude that in some sense, this approach reflected what documents "really are."[5]

SGML

In a systematic implementation of the content-oriented approach, one would develop a formal description of the logical structure of documents in the document class of interest, identifying all the possible "content objects" and specifying what patterns of combinations of these are legitimate in a document. To take a simple example: a *poem* might be defined as consisting of exactly one *title* followed optionally by exactly one *author,* followed by one or more *stanzas,* each of which contains one of more metrical *lines,* with metrical lines, author, and title containing one or more alphabetic characters. This would be a simple "document grammar" for *poems.* Scientific articles, textbooks, legal documents, and technical documentation would all have their own specific document grammars. Such grammars can be formally expressed using well understood techniques from computer science and linguistics (specifically, languages for defining context free grammars) that are ideal for supporting automatic computer processing.[6] A "markup language" based on such a formal grammar could then be used to identify the text objects, with the beginning and ends of each text object indicated by "markup tags" (e.g., using the tag "delimiters" familiar from SGML applications such as HTML: <stanza> and </stanza>).

In the early 1980s an effort headed by IBM scientist Charles Goldfarb, one of the pioneers of the content object approach to text processing, produced *ISO8879: Information Processing–Text and Office Systems–Standard Generalized Markup Language* (SGML), a specification that provides a powerful computer-processible mechanism for implementing the content oriented approach. SGML is not itself a document markup language (it contains no specific markup tags), but rather it is a specification for *defining* document markup languages; it is a *meta-grammar* for document languages. Following the SGML standard, one can prepare a "Document Type Definition" (DTD) that specifies a document grammar for the document genre of interest. The DTD spells out precisely what content objects (the SGML term is "elements") may occur in the document, what markup tags will be used to represent them, how those tags can be recognized, and what (and how) other related information may also be included in the document. A DTD thus determines a markup language that can then be used to actually markup document content. (The developers of SGML wisely realized that there would be much variation and innovation–and controversy–in the development of specific markup languages, particularly as more specialist document genres were accommodated and more fine-grained element identification attempted, and so it was more important, and more practical, to standardize the way we define and communicate markup languages than to attempt to promulgate specific definitions).

The DTD and the marked up "document instance" together are used to support efficient and high function computer processing. Software applications such as formatters, editors, and retrieval systems, can read the DTD to learn about the markup language a document is written in, and then read the document and process it in accordance with the markup definitions in the DTD. Processing here includes not only formatting (the computer would parse the document into its component elements and then apply formatting rules defined for each element type) but other things as well. For instance, on the basis of a DTD, editing software could help the document creator by adding required elements automatically, prompting with alternatives where a choice must be made, and preventing the creation of forbidden patterns; retrieval software could present the user with the possible component categories and combinations for searching (allowing, for instance, a search for "Smith" within author within citation); and authentication software could verify that all the required parts of a document are in fact present.

By the mid and late 1980s, SGML was widely endorsed by many European and North American governmental agencies, professional organizations, and scholarly societies, and implemented in many large text projects. Its use was required by law for large US and Canadian technical documentation contracts (to ensure interoperability of deliverables). Quite a number of SGML document description languages were developed, of which the most sophisticated and still the most influential (apart from HTML) is that of the Text Encoding Initiative, which, in its current XML form, provides the markup foundation for many digital library projects.[7]

Adoption Failures, Browser Wars

By the mid and late 1980s it was not only clear what the appropriate engineering model for document processing systems was, but there was an accepted international standard (SGML) for building systems based on that model and considerable successful experience with that standard. It was anticipated that the text processing and desktop publishing systems of the 1980s would quickly take advantage of these proven practices that promised not only increased interoperability and functionality (including many social benefits, reducing costs and improving access to information), but commercial advantages as well.

It didn't happen–at least not on the scale expected. Outside of a few particular domains, such as large scale technical documentation, particularly for aircraft, heavy equipment and armaments, where the financial advantages were too great to be ignored, and humanities computing, where new research capabilities could be supported, there was hardly any impact. Throughout the 1980s and early 1990s word processing systems continued with their ineffective and now outdated representational strategies. They treated documents like typographical objects, rather than intellectual objects, and their users as typesetters or typists rather than as authors. In particular, word processors in the 1980s and early 1990s continued to use presentation-oriented proprietary formats with no true common interchange format (let alone an SGML format). None of the exciting new functionality materialized and the new features that were added were typically ad hoc collections of formatting gimmicks aimed at treating the author as a typesetter rather than supporting the authorial role. Worse, a profusion of incompatible file formats created huge headaches for printing and sharing files across applications.

Things were little better with publishing systems. Although descriptive markup of some sort made steady inroads, publishers resisted systematic changes and continued outmoded production practices that carried forward old inefficiencies and made it hard to take advantage of the emerging world of electronic publishing.

When HTML came on the scene in the early 1990s there was at first the appearance of a system that reflected the content oriented approach.

For one thing, HTML looked like SGML and was soon even provided with an SGML DTD. But HTML turned out to be a disappointment to SGML proponents. First, it did not really implement the content oriented approach. Instead of organizing the document content solely in terms of its logical components and separately indicating the formatting for each type, it indifferently included elements for true content objects (e.g., "<title>") with elements that were simply formatting instructions (e.g., "<b>" to format something in boldface). This resulted in a loss of interoperability and functionality, and for legions of Web developers, it promoted confusion instead of instruction on a critical point of sound information management practice. And, as a corollary, there was also a loss of accessibility. To a blind person "reading" a document with an aural browser, encountering text marked "<b>" is not helpful at all. Only when the underlying reason the text is being rendered in bold is indicated (that is, when the text is marked, e.g., "<heading>," or "<vector>") can the aural browser communicate that information to the reader.

In addition, the HTML element set was (and still is) rather impoverished. It reflected none of the vast accumulated knowledge of what sorts of elements were needed even for basic publishing, let alone for specialist publishing or for more ambitious digital functionality. And because HTML, as used in the context of the World Wide Web, had no mechanisms for extension, its users could not easily include the specialized and domain-specific elements needed to take full advantage of the content-object approach. It thus did not reflect the fundamental SGML insight that innovation was to be supported and welcomed, not preempted. This has been a problem from which we are only now beginning to free ourselves.[8]

In addition, although appropriate standardization should channel competition into productive areas, failure to fully internalize the SGML philosophy resulted in unfortunate commercial conflicts that hurt users. Consider the best-known, if seemingly trivial, skirmish in the "browser wars": the "blink" tag. Ideally, using the SGML approach, a software company could develop special processing capability which could be associated, via an explicit rule, with an element type, representing a textual content object. Note that this approach requires that (i) processing be conceptually separated from the identification of content objects, and (ii) if new content objects are defined, the definition is made available so that the presence of the element can be anticipated and gracefully accommodated by other software, even if the specialized innovative processing isn't available. In the case of the "<blink>" tag, however, both these rules were broken. A Web browser manufacturer adapted its browser to recognize the tag "<blink>" and make the tagged text blink on and off, encouraging content developers to use the tag to get this effect. This was in the first place a fundamental contradiction of the SGML principle of separating content (represented by elements) from presentation effects (maintained separately).[9] In addition, browsers from competing manufacturers, encountering the blink tag for the first time, could do nothing at all with it, since there was no formal extension of the HTML element set, and no capability by browsers to recognize extensions. There was no possibility at all of handling the new element gracefully, or of maintaining interoperability of Web pages and the general applicability of HTML development tools. As absurd and trivial as it may seem, the blink tag is a perfect example of the underlying failures to implement, even by the 1990s, what everyone knew, in 1980, was best engineering practice.

How did this happen? Why was adoption of best practice in this area so slow and imperfect? By the middle 1980s there was a sound engineering model for document processing, an (emerging) international standard to support this model, a growing number of tools, and substantial practical experience. There was indeed no doubt in anyone's mind just what "best practice" was. Moreover, best practice appeared to be in everyone's interest, at least long-term. And yet for the most part neither word processing software, desktop publishing software, publishing industry production processes, browser software, nor World Wide Web standards reflected this knowledge. The result was an unnecessary period of non-interoperable low-function systems. This has been costly, both commercially and to society and the public good. And it is still far from behind us.

There is no simple answer as to why this happened, but such best practice adoption failures are hardly unusual. Efforts to implement new technology strategies typically run up against a familiar array of real world problems and constraints that can halt, impede, or confuse even the most compelling innovations. In this case, the usual difficulties in getting end-users to change their practices, getting professionals to change entire production systems, and getting businesses to amortize investments over longer periods, proved to be too much for arguments based on merit alone.

It is against this unpromising background that any effort to develop a content specification for electronic book publishing must be evaluated.

THE PROSPECTS FOR ELECTRONIC BOOKS

How likely is it that electronic books will play an important role in our reading lives? Prior predictions of imminent inundation by electronic books have not been fulfilled, and there are no shortages of journalistic scoffers who, after examining their evaluation version of some recent product, pronounce that it will not supplant the traditional paper version in what are apparently the three critical venues for reading: "bed, beach and bath."[10]

There is no doubt that traditional books are an enormously successful and durable piece of technology. They will not easily give up any ground to challengers, and regardless of what ground they do concede, they will continue, for at least the foreseeable future, to occupy a large part of the reading landscape. Nevertheless, it does seem at least more probable than not that the next five years will see a steady increase in the importance of electronic books.

What has changed to make this prediction reasonable now? Several things.

Hardware improvements: Storage capacity, processing speed, size, weight, and general design have all seen explosive improvements. This year a PDA can already hold dozens of books. Soon it will be hundreds, and within a few years, thousands. Memory and processing speed are no longer limitations: devices grow smaller, lighter, more durable, and increasingly more pleasant to the hand and eye.

Software improvements: User interfaces, navigation techniques, information retrieval, and annotation capabilities all provide enormous new powerful functionality, and recent techniques for improving type rendering create an aesthetic reading experience nearly equal to print.

Ubiquity of reading devices: 144 million[11] people in the United States now own computers, and 35 million own laptops, all of which make reasonable electronic book platforms, particularly when functionality is more important than comfort and convenience–as it is for much business and professional reading. New laptop computers make even better platforms: they are now often lighter than 3 lbs., will soon have "instant on" responsiveness, and can hold thousands of volumes. In addition, 17.5 million PDAs are now in use, and these also make excellent electronic book readers in some circumstances. Finally a new wave of tablet devices ensures exploration of that extremely compelling form factor.

Critical mass of relevant content: Until recently electronic delivery frequently meant converting new material to digital form, or taking special measures to ensure that there was a digital version. Today not only have many retrospective conversion projects been completed, but, more importantly, text creation, even at the level of authors, is now almost wholly electronic. This ensures that commercially important content is usually already in electronic form, and, increasingly, prepared with the anticipation of electronic delivery.

Data standards and tools: The chaos of competing proprietary formats has diminished considerably over the last few years. Most importantly an acceptance of SGML/XML element sets for in-house archival formats as well as for interchange, and the development of SGML/XML software tools and expertise, has brought a considerable degree of interoperability and flexibility to the industry's available content–even though much content is still in low function, non-interoperable desktop-publishing and page description formats.

Culture of electronic reading: Despite complaints about the unpleasantness of reading on computers, the obvious truth is that in the western world many of us spend vast quantities of time doing just that. The share of reading that is electronic is large and growing. It is important not to think of "bed, bath, and beach" reading as typical. Most reading takes place in the workplace, in the offices of various businesses, professions, and bureaucracies–and this is largely reading at the computer, as any tour through a modern office building will reveal. Schools and universities are another location experiencing very rapid growth of electronic reading. Finally, the amount of time outside of school that all of us–adults, children, and teenagers–spend at the computer outside of work and school (surfing the web, reading email, shopping, listening to music, chatting, etc.) is already very large and growing. The result is that reading *already* is mostly electronic and continues to become more so, with no end to this trend in sight. The special advantages to electronic reading–fast access to many resources, following hypertext links, retrieval by key word, phrase, or more sophisticated means, navigation, integration with other activities, etc.–are familiar and valued by almost everyone.

However, while it now seems likely that electronic books will happen, in some form, fairly soon, and will continue to increase in significance, many things about just how they will happen are not clear. For instance:

- *Market segments:* What will take off first: mass market fiction? glossy magazines? high school and college textbooks? technical documentation? STM publishing? business documents? reference works? Every market segment has its partisans.
- *Form factor:* Will we read electronic books on PDA-size, book-size, or tablet-size devices? Perhaps all three? Or will specialized hardware fail to compete with the ubiquity of the laptop? Will certain devices be popular for certain genres?
- *Business models:* How will the current ecology of publishers, distributors, composition houses, content developers, software manufacturers, and hardware manufacturers change? Who will make money, and how? Who will flourish? Who will be "disintermediated"? What new players will emerge?
- *Rights infrastructure and security:* How will our approach to conceptualizing intellectual property and usage rights change? What will be the new infrastructure of security and rights conceptualization that will fit with the technological opportunities?

But most of all, and of particular interest to us, is whether electronic books will be a thriving industry with interoperable high-performance content and reading devices. Or will it succumb to the real-world constraints described in the previous section, resulting in low performance, non-interoperable books, or even new "browser wars"?

If a thriving electronic book industry is to be created, one that delivers the functionality and social value we would like to see, some of the daunting underlying problems that must be faced are:

- *Interoperability vs. functionality:* How do we ensure that content is both interoperable and yet also allow for new functionality?
- *Interoperability vs. competitive innovation:* How do we enforce interoperability, while allowing competitors to innovate?
- *Current practices vs. future opportunities:* How can we simultaneously exploit current practices (including current data formats, tools, and expertise) and yet also align the industry to take advantage of future opportunities?

What we know now, what we have learned from the experiences of the 1980s and 1990s, is that it is not enough simply to recommend best practice based on good engineering models. The world is more complicated than that. To get best results means using those models as a basis for the skillful management of competing technical objectives, and for negotiating the necessary difficult tradeoffs and compromises needed to get the best results possible within the constraints of technological, social, and commercial circumstances. That is what the OEBF Publication Structure does.

THE OPEN EBOOK FORUM
AND THE OEBF PUBLICATION STRUCTURE

History

The "Open eBook Initiative" was announced in October 1998 at US National Institute for Standards and Technology's (NIST) first *Electronic Book* conference. Following the conference, three companies (Nuvomedia, Microsoft, and Softbook) planning ebook reading systems wrote a preliminary draft proposal to initiate discussion. The following January a meeting widely attended by publishing and software manufacturing representatives was convened in San Francisco to determine the direction future work should take. At that meeting an "Authoring Group" was formed and charged with continuing the development of the specification. NIST technical manager Dr. Victor McCrary, who had been facilitating the development of the OEB Initiative, became "Facilitator" of the Authoring Group.

The work of the Authoring Group was carried out throughout the spring and early summer of 1999 and the specification was approved by the members of the OEB Initiative, after extensive review, in August. In September the specification, now titled "The OEB Publication Structure 1.0" (OEBPS 1.0) was released, and the participants in the Authoring Group received a commendation from the US Department of Commerce.

In January 2000, the informal Open eBook Initiative became the Open eBook Forum, a non-profit association of publishing industry stakeholders: hardware and software companies, publishers, authors and users of electronic books, and related organizations including universities, libraries, and the Library of Congress. The stated goals of the OEBF are:

> . . . to establish common specifications for electronic book systems, applications and products that will benefit creators of content, makers of reading systems and, most importantly, consumers, helping to catalyze the adoption of electronic books; to encourage the broad acceptance of these specifications on a worldwide basis among members of the Forum, related industries and the public; and to increase awareness and acceptance of the emerging electronic publishing industry. [http://www.openebook.org/aboutOEBF.htm]

The OEBF has broad support throughout the publishing and publishing software industry and collaborative relationships with other trade organizations, such as the American Association of Publishers. In addition to the Publication Structure Working Group, it now has active working groups in the areas of metadata, identifiers, and digital rights management, and well as a rigorous and systematic infrastructure for collecting and analyzing industry needs and ensuring that the products of its working group are coordinated and meet those needs.

There are several observations about the development of the OEBPS that provide public sector decision makers with some useful insights into both the OEBPS in particular, and into industry standards development in general. First, the development of the OEBPS specification was an open process. Any company or individual who wanted to participate in the OEB Initiative could join, and similarly all volunteers for the Authoring Group were accepted; public sector participation was eagerly sought, and continues to be so. Second, the time from conception to completion was only one year, in dramatic contrast with the far longer times characteristic of other standards organizations (NISO, ISO, ANSI, IETF, and the W3C). While this speed can ensure the timely development, it also means that it is hard for public sector organization like libraries, to respond or even to become involved, and therefore we did not have quite as much public sector participation as we wished.[12] Third, and most importantly, the public sector participation we did have, from universities, the Library of Congress, and agencies representing the disabled, was enormously valuable in ensuring that critical sections of the specification reflected engineering best practice and took long-term social benefits, for all people, into account.

Goals

The goals of OEB Publication Structure are:[13]

- *Have an immediate and direct impact on the creation of a flourishing eBook industry.* For a flourishing electronic book industry to emerge, a content standard needed to be available as soon as possible; without one there would not be the needed critical mass of content and devices.
- *Support consumer confidence in performance of devices and books.* If consumers could not rely on their devices to reliably present the books they had already purchased, or would soon purchase, they would not purchase those devices. Similarly, if consumers were not confident that books would present well on their current devices, or on the device they might purchase next year, they would not purchase those books.
- *Limit burden on content providers.* Content providers, such as publishers, had to be able to create content easily or to convert existing content. This placed a premium on being able to exploit existing data, tools, and expertise. In addition, content providers need to have predictable reading system performance; they need to be assured of reading systems' rendering capability so that they could be confident that their books would be presented exactly as they wished them to be.
- *Limit burden on reading system developers.* The software companies developing electronic book reading systems needed manageable software requirements. Devices still have limitations on processing, memory, and screen size, and the software engineering required to implement advanced formatting and browsing systems under those limitations is difficult.
- *Position industry practices to scale with emerging standards.* Consistency with the overall emerging trends and standards in publishing, and in information processing in general, was vital.
- *Support distinctive new functionality.* Digital documents and computing resources provide extraordinary new possibilities for reading and writing: enhanced navigation, retrieval, annotation, updating and currency, multimedia and interaction, and so on. These are familiar to all of us from the World Wide Web. Ebooks must deliver new features such as these to justify their claim to provide superior reading functionality.

- *Provide an aesthetically satisfying reading experience.* Although many categories of books and documents benefit immediately from enhanced navigation, searching, annotation, and interaction, for others, such as novels, aesthetic satisfaction and the recreation of the traditional sense of "being lost in the book" is more important.
- *Maintain equitable opportunities for competitive differentiation.* Chaotic competition based on proprietary formats would delay or prevent the development of ebooks, reducing interoperability, consumer confidence, and, ultimately, functionality. But removing the opportunity for competitive development and innovation would be equally damaging. Competition must be channeled into areas where it will benefit the industry, and society, the most, in the long run.
- *Support other languages and writing systems.* Inclusive multiculturalism and the global marketplace both require that the ebook industry support the world's languages and writing systems.
- *Support access by readers with disabilities.* The ebook industry should improve, not impede, access to books by people with perceptual disabilities, such as blindness.

A glance at those requirements shows that many of them pull in different directions and reflect the fundamental opposed objectives mentioned earlier: reconciling interoperability with both innovative functionality and support for competitive differentiation, and exploiting current practices while at the same time preparing for future developments. In addition there are the problems of meeting content providers' demand for high quality rendering with the reading developers' need for a manageable engineering task.

OEBPS 1.0

Because OEBPS is primarily a combination of subsets of other standards, an overview is fairly straightforward. In fact, if recourse to the alphabet soup of information processing standards and technologies is allowed the OEBPS might be simply, if telegraphically, described with this list: XML syntax for all content; arbitrary XML elements allowed (but basic HTML 4.0 subset is identified as well); a Cascading Style Sheets (CSS) subset for presentation; Dublin Core for metadata, a "package" DTD to organize the parts of a publication; and a few other miscellaneous constraints to support interoperability and compatibility with existing software tools. Or, in more detail:

- *XML Syntax:* All OEB documents and related files must meet the XML standard of "XML well-formedness"; they do not, however need to meet the higher standard of being "XML validity." Requiring well-formedness ensures that OEBPS Publications are consistent with emerging standards and can be processed by XML software. Not requiring XML validity limits the burden on content developers and allows more content to become immediately available.
- *An HTML 4.0 Subset:* OEBPS 1.0 identifies a subset of HTML 4.0 that all reading software must support; documents that only use this subject are described as OEB Basic Documents. Identifying a set of HTML 4.0 elements that content providers can be sure will be rendered appropriately by devices takes advantages of existing content, tools, and expertise. It also helps both content providers and reading system developers by making available HTML table elements for formatting tables, rather than requiring the rendering for tables, which is difficult to specify via CSS, to be explicitly defined.
- *Arbitrary XML Elements:* Arbitrary XML elements are allowed, as long as users assign a formatting rule to such elements according to the procedure described below. Allowing arbitrary XML elements makes it possible for domain-specific encoding to be included, considerably increasing functionality beyond what would be available with only HTML elements. For instance, elements for equations, personal names, chemical formulae, and such–elements that might already exist in the content providers original archival content–can be passed into the eBook version as well (rather than converted to HTML), and used there to support special viewing, navigation, or retrieval functions. In addition, requiring that a CSS rule be defined for every arbitrary XML element ensures a base level of common interoperability, avoiding the "blink tag" problem.
- *A Cascading Style Sheet Subset:* A subset of the W3C Cascading Style Sheet (CSS) language 1.0 is identified. This ensures a minimal level of predictable rendering capability for content providers. We include only a subset however, as requiring capability match-

ing the entire CSS specification would place an undue burden on reading system developers. Content providers may specify CSS rules outside the subset, or even from other rendering specification languages, but if they do, they must also provide a specification that only uses the OEB CSS subset. This has the effect of allowing innovation and high functionality where available, and yet simultaneously ensures basic interoperability.

- *The Dublin Core:* Metadata is provided via a Dublin Core element set, a simple, well-known metadata scheme. This ensures a basic level of metadata interoperability without undue burden upon content providers. (OEBPS 2.0 will have additional metadata support.)
- *An OEB "Package" DTD:* The various parts of a publication (text, images, etc.), along with metadata, "fallbacks" (see below), and other apparatus are coordinated in a *package file.*
- *Unicode Support:* OEBPS ebooks may use, and OEBPS devices must support, the UTF 8 and UTF 16 character transfer encodings, and OEBPS devices must correctly parse Unicode character encodings, although they are not required to render them. This ensures a minimal level of character and writing system support and positions the specification to require additional support in later versions.
- *Interoperability Constraints:* To ensure maximum interoperability with existing tools and Web browsers, a few other minor constraints are specified.
- *Media Fallback Rules:* OEBPS specifies the kinds of data that all conforming reading systems must be able to process. The set is currently limited to maintain a low burden on reading system developers. Content providers may, however, include data (such as multimedia data) not in the specified OEB set as long as they also provide alternative representations that are in the OEB set. Again, this allows for innovation, high functionality, and competitive differentiation in both content and reading systems, while also requiring a base level of interoperability.

Finally, although OEBPS is conceptualized as a general format for publishing content, it need not be, necessarily, the format used by the software that immediately presents the content to the human reader. The OEBPS specification anticipates the possibility that developers of reading systems will want, for various reasons (such as reducing file size, improving processing speed, indexing, and supporting digital rights management, encryption, or special functionality) to transform OEBPS content into specialized formats for use by the software that immediately presents the content.[14] OEBPS is thus an "interlingua" *into* which archival content can be converted (while retaining the original XML encoding which provides domain-specific intelligence) and *from* which specialized formats can be created for presentation on particular devices. The level of "indirection" provided by a single common interchange format allows archival formats and device formats to develop separately and in response to their own particular needs, while ensuring an efficient conversion between the two categories–avoiding the "combinatorial explosion" of required translations that would be the result if it were necessary to go directly from every possible archival input format to every possible device format without a common interchange language.

OEBPS 2.0

Under the auspices of the Open eBook Forum the OEBF Publication Structure Working Group is now working on OEBPS 2.0. This version responds to the expressed needs of the publishing and reading communities and to experiences with OEBPS 1.0. There are four main themes:

1. Increased Content Owner Control over Publication Presentation

Increased control over presentation has been clearly identified as the area where improvement would be valuable to publishers and to other content providers. Specific objectives include better layout functionality to improve precise positioning, font and typography improvements, and device-specific processing.

2. International Content

Continuing improvements in the handling of international content are necessary for the specification to adequately support publishing in world markets. This requires improved glyph resource specification (for the appearances of characters, particularly in non-roman character sets) and improved writing system features, including additional writing direction control.

3. Enhanced Navigational Structure and Linking

To support the distinctive functionality that consumers increasingly expect from electronic material, the specification's support for navigation must be improved. This includes better support for searching, indexing, hierarchical structures, intra-publication references, and inter-publication links. OEBPS will be taking advantage of recent work in the W3C XLink and XPointer working groups.

4. Metadata Modularization

The metadata features of OEBPS need substantial improvement to accommodate rapid changes in publishing metadata, digital rights management strategies, and device profiling. To handle the significant amount of work involved, OEBPS 2.0 will provide modular support for metadata, allowing a variety of metadata systems to be used and allowing metadata innovation to proceed independently under the auspices of the recently-formed OEBF Metadata Working Group.

A FINAL WORD

In the emerging world of electronic reading the nature of the reading experience will be a direct result of the underlying framework of content standards that provide the range of technological opportunities and constraints. Organizations such as the OEBF are therefore, today, developing the standards that will determine what it will be like, tomorrow, to write, publish, and read books. Such efforts are obviously very consequential projects for the library community. Equally importantly, they can play out in many different ways. This under-determination of result is in part a product of the overwhelming complexity of the problems such projects face. Today, every significant information processing standardization effort must skillfully negotiate competing and apparently irreconcilable objectives, serve a wide variety of stakeholders with many different interests, deal with unavoidable external constraints of time, history, and commercial agendas, and, finally, produce results in time to be relevant to the rapidly changing course of technology. Sometimes specifications can solve a problem by an ingenious strategy based on best practice and science, sometimes by a necessary, but, one hopes, skillful, compromise–and sometimes we must recognize that we can't solve a particular problem just yet at all, but can, perhaps, position the industry to attempt a solution later.

The OEBPS 1.0 represents a specification that faced such problems: supporting both interoperability and innovation, meeting demands of current practice while preparing to take advantage of future opportunities, balancing the preferences of one industry segment with those of another, and meshing strategies based on the long-term with the need to provide short-term guidance before opportunities were lost. Building directly on the foundation of existing W3C standards, the OEBF has done an extraordinary job at this. Because of its efforts not only will there soon be a flourishing electronic book industry, but we will have greatly improved electronic books, for all our purposes, and for everyone. But achieving such results is hard. It requires the timely and sustained application of relevant expertise, representation from a wide variety of stakeholders, and the determination to make the decisions necessary to move the process forward, and not miss opportunities–here we need to remember the lessons of the 1980s and early 1990s.

In industry standards and specification development efforts, the interest of commercial participants in building a large new industry without giving any special advantages to any particular existing business strategy is a critical, if indirect, positive force in producing timely sound standards and specifications. But the experience of the OEBF has clearly shown that in addition to these natural "invisible hand" forces created by industry participants acting in enlightened self-interest, public sector participation plays an absolutely critical role, ensuring that the results are far better than they would have been if the process were left to commercial participants alone. Public sector expertise brings to the table a broader view, a more inclusive view, and, of course, a resolute focus on the public good. And, most strikingly in the case of the OEBF, cynicism as to the impact of general arguments based solely on sound engineering practice and benefit to the public good has proven to be entirely unwarranted. In our experience sound arguments by OEBF public sector participants were not only always given full and sincere consideration, but, in fact had considerable influence in the final result, even when doing so meant additional short-term burdens for commercial participants.

In industry standardization projects, public sector participation, particularly from expert groups such as libraries, is, in fact, eagerly welcomed. The problems that need to be solved are hard, and so more expertise, with broader and different perspectives, ensures better solutions. Public sector stakeholders in the OEBF (including universities, libraries, US government agencies, agencies representing the disabled, and others) played key roles in developing the OEBPS specification, and in making it socially, as well as commercially and technologically, valuable.[15] Unfortunately, while public sector participation is routinely sought for industry standardization projects, it is not so often forthcoming. This is not surprising: participating in standards development requires allocating valuable expert staff to a very time-consuming activity, and one that usually does not have an immediate return to the local organization. Nevertheless, public sector involvement in the current publishing standards development efforts, particularly from the library community, is the only way to ensure that books, reading, and libraries, will be all they should be, and for all of us.

Further Reading: For more information about the OEBF and the OEBF Publication Structure see the OEBF website: http://www. openebook.org. For an excellent brief introduction to the OEBF Publication Structure and its component standards see Dorothea Salo's *eBook Technical FAQ: A Basic Introduction to eBooks. (http://www.impressions. com/resources_pgs/elpub_pgs/oebfaq.html).* For a library perspective on directions in electronic book technology see Thomas A. Peters' "Gutterdämmerung (twilight of the gutter margins): E-books and Libraries." *Library Hi Tech,* 19(1) 2001. For more information about the Text Encoding Initiative see the TEI website: http://www.tei-c.org.

NOTES

1. The current (May 2001) members of the OEBF are: Adobe Systems Incorporated, Aerrius.com, LLC, AlienZoo, Inc., AmazeScape.com, Amazon.com, LLC, American Foundation for the Blind, American Library Association, American Printing House for the Blind, AMS–Advanced Marketing Services, Andersen Consulting, Ansyr Technology Corporation, Apex Data Services, Aportis Technologies Corp., Association of American Publishers, Autotext A/S, Baker & Taylor/Yankee Rights Management, Barnes & Noble, Inc., Beijing Founder Electronics CO., LTD, BinaryThing. com Pty. Ltd., Book Industry Study Group, Inc., Bookface, Bookoo, Inc., Books24x7.com, Brown University (Scholarly Technology Group), Bsquare Corporation, CAS-Computed Air Services, Cast, Inc., CDI Systems Ltd., Certicom Corp., Chief Officers of State Library Agencies, Cloakware Corporation, Consolidated Graphics, Content Guard, Inc., CYTALE, Daisy Consortium, Data Conversion Laboratory, DataQuad, Inc., Digital Imaging & Technologies, Digital Owl, Inc., Earlychildhood.com, EAST Co., Ltd., e-bks, LLC, eBooks.com, Echyon Co., Ltd, Everybook, Inc., Franklin Electronic Publishers, FX Palo Alto Laboratory, Inc., Galaxy Commutech Limited, Gemstar, Genisoft Development Corporation, GlobalMentor, Inc., Gyoza Media, Har-

court Worldwide STM Group, HarperCollins Publishers, HEALTH COMMUNI-CATIONS, INC, Helsinki University of Technology, Hewlett Packard Labs, Houghton Mifflin, IBM Corporation, iBooks.com, IDG Books Worldwide, Inc., Impressions Book and Journal Services, Imprimerie Des Presses Universitaires De France, Infraworks, Interactive Composition Corporation (ICC), Intertrust Technologies, Inc., IPM-Group, IPR Systems, isSound Corporation, iUniverse.com, J. J. Keller & Associates, Inc., J. Whitaker & Sons Ltd, Knovel.com, Knowledge Engineering, Inc., Law Offices of Bruce E. Matter, Lernout & Hauspie Speech Products, Library of Congress, NLS/BPH, Lightning Source, Inc., LizardTech, Inc., Magex Ltd, MarkAny, Inc., Maryland State Department of Education/DLDS, McGraw-Hill, MediaDNA, Inc., Mibrary.com, Inc., Microsoft, MOBIPOCKET.COM, Mondadori.com, MultiReader Consortium, National Institute of Standards & Technology, Neovue, Inc., netLibrary, Inc., Nokia, NTRU Cryptosystems, Inc., Office Workstations, LTD., Overdrive, Inc., Palm, Inc., Planeta Actimedia S.A., PlazaDigital, PriceWaterhouseCoopers, Profound Learning Systems, Inc., Quark, Inc., Questia Media, Inc., Random House, Inc., Reciprocal, Inc., Recording for the Blind & Dyslexic, Red Cube, Rightscom, Ltd., RightsMarket, Inc., Royal National Institute for the Blind, RR Donnelley & Sons Company, Sagebrush Corporation, Samsung Electronics Co., LTD, SecoData Vertriebs-und Entwicklungs GmbH, Shinano Kenshi Co., Ltd., Simon & Schuster, SoftLock.com, Softwin SRL, SOMEDIA S.R.L., Stavanger University College, Stonehouse Productions, Strijelac, Ltd., Sunhawk.com, TechBooks, Telex Communications, Inc., The Cutting Corporation, The E Book Company Inc, The Hadley School for the Blind, The Software & Information Industry Association, Thomson Consumer Electronics, Time Warner, Trymedia Systems, Inc., University of Illinois at Urbana-Champaign (Graduate School of Library and Information Science), UPSO.COM, Versaware Technologies, Inc., Vetri Systems, VisuAide, Inc., Waxinfo Ltd., WebReading Limited, Werner Söderström Corporation. The current board of directors of the OEBF includes representatives from Adobe Systems Incorporated, the American Association of Publishers, the Daisy Consortium, Intertrust Technologies Inc., Microsoft Corp., Overdrive Inc., and Random House Inc.

2. There are, of course, many other important standardization issues in electronic publishing besides content standards. For instance, rights management, business models, device ergonomics, and security, to name a few that are particularly critical, and which the OEBF is also concerned with. However, content standards is an area that goes to the very heart of the reading experience, and one where timely involvement from public sector institutions, such as libraries, is needed—and can, in fact, have a major impact on what reading will be like in the next few decades.

3. The seminal early accounts are Reid 1980, Goldfarb 1981; for earlier history see Goldfarb, http://www.oasis-open.org/cover/sgmlhist0.html; for an overview see Coombs et al. 1987.

4. For an general review of this approach and its advantages, from the perspective of the mid 1980s, see Coombs et al. 1987.

5. For the resulting "text ontology" see DeRose et al. 1990 and Renear et al. 1996.

6. The mathematical technique for specifying these syntactical constraints is based on the meta-grammar formalism developed by Noam Chomsky to describe natural lan-

guages grammars; versions of this technique are now widely used in computer science to define programming languages.

7. The Text Encoding Initiative is a large international project that between 1987 and 1998, in a effort which involved nearly 200 scholars and dozens of professional organizations, libraries, archives, and other institutions, developed a modular and extensible system of SGML Document Type Definitions to support research and publishing in the humanities disciplines. These DTDs (now in XML form) are very widely used in the humanities and library communities and have influenced many other information processing standards. For more information see: http://www.tei-c.org/.

8. The W3C, under Tim Berners-Lee's direction (Berners-Lee is the inventor of HTML) has creditably been moving steadily in this direction. Format-centric elements are largely "deprecated" in recent versions of HTML, and the XML (eXtended Markup Language), a simpler and less demanding version of SGML, is specifically designed to support user-defined specialized or domain-specific elements.

9. Since this separation had not been reflected in browsers there was arguably no alternative.

10. The three "three B's" as they are called in Peters 2001, an extremely insightful article on current directions in electronic books, written from the library perspective. For one of the early classical meditations on electronic books see Yankelovich 1985; for an account of some current research directions see Schilit 1999.

11. Analysts' projections for 2001, from Intel, IDC, Dataquest, DisplaySearch, Wilt Soundview, and Bernstein Research.

12. This was only in part a result of the intensity of the effort. The OEBPS is not a new fundamental data standard, but rather an application of existing standards (which is why it describes itself not as a "standard," but a "specification"). So to a large extent the OEBPS is an application of the more arduous foundational work carried out by other organizations.

13. These are not necessarily official OEBF goals, but rather our conclusion based both on articulated objectives, and also on our observation of OEBF de facto priorities and decision-making.

14. OEBPS therefore carefully defines "Reading System" as "A combination of hardware and/or software that accepts OEB publications, and directly or indirectly makes them available to readers . . ." and "Reading Device" as "The physical platform (hardware and software) on which publications are rendered." (OEBPS 1.0 section 1.3). A Reading Device may in fact be coextensive with a Reading System, but it need not be. In any case it is the Reading *System* that is required (if it is OEBPS conformant) to correctly process OEBPS content; the behavior of the Reading Device is not directly constrained by the specification.

15. Among the important public sector contributors to OEBPS are the Library of Congress, Brown University, the Daisy Consortium (Digital Talking Book Standard), Recording for the Blind and Dyslexic, Royal National Institute for the Blind, the National Library Service for the Blind and Physically Handicapped, Project Gutenberg DE, the National Institute of Standards and Technology, and the Text Encoding Initiative. There are in addition a number of other public sector organizations in the OEBF, such as the American Library Association, and the Chief Officers of State Library Agencies, many of which participate in other OEBF working groups.

REFERENCES

Coombs, James S., Allen H. Renear and Steven J. DeRose. "Markup Systems and the Future of Scholarly Text Processing." *Communications of the Association for Computing Machinery.* 30(11) (1987): 933-47.

DeRose, Steven J., David Durand, Elli Mylonas and Allen H. Renear. "What is Text, Really?" *Journal of Computing in Higher Education,* 1(2), 1990, pp. 3-26.

Goldfarb, Charles. "A Generalized Approach to Document Markup." In *Proceedings of the ACM SIGPLAN–SIGOA Symposium on Text Manipulation.* New York: ACM, 1981, pp. 68-73.

_____. *The SGML Handbook.* Oxford: Oxford University Press, 1990.

International Organization for Standardization (ISO). *Information Processing–Text and Office Systems–Standard Generalized Markup Language (SGML),* ISO8879-1986. International Organization for Standardization (ISO), 1986.

OEBF Publication Structure 1.0, Open Electronic Book Forum, 1999. (see http://www.openebook.org).

Peters, Thomas A. "Gutterdämmerung (twilight of the gutter margins): E-books and Libraries." *Library Hi Tech,* 19(1), 2001.

Reid, Brian. "A High-Level Approach to Computer Document Formatting." In *Proceedings of the 7th Annual ACM Symposium on Programming Languages.* New York: ACM, 1980, pp. 24-30.

Renear, Allen. David Durand, and Elli Mylonas. "Refining Our Notion of What Text Really Is." *Research in Humanities Computing,* edited by Nancy Ide and Susan Hockey. Oxford: Oxford University Press, 1996, pp. 263-280. Originally presented at ACH/ALLC 1992, at Christ Church Oxford.

Salo, Dorothea. *eBook Technical FAQ: A Basic Introduction to eBooks.* http://www.impressions.com/resources_pgs/elpub_pgs/oebfaq.htmlSperberg-McQueen, C. Michael. and Lou Burnard, eds. *Guidelines for the Encoding and Interchange of Machine-Readable Texts..*Chicago and Oxford: TEI, 1990, 1993. For further updates see: http://www.tei-c.org.

Schilit, Bill N., Morgan N. Price, Gene Golovchinsky, Kei Tanaka, and Catherine C. Marshall. "As We May Read: The Reading Appliance Revolution." *IEEE Computer,* 32(1), January 1999, pp. 65-73.

Yankelovich, Nicole, Noman Meyrowitz, and Andries Van Dam. Reading and writing the electronic book. *IEEE Computer,* pp. 15-30, 18(1), October 1985.

ACCESS TO DIGITAL LIBRARY COLLECTIONS

The Open Archives Initiative: Realizing Simple and Effective Digital Library Interoperability

Hussein Suleman
Edward Fox

SUMMARY. The Open Archives Initiative (OAI) is dedicated to solving problems of digital library interoperability. Its focus has been on defining simple protocols, most recently for the exchange of metadata from archives. The OAI evolved out of a need to increase access to scholarly publications by supporting the creation of interoperable digital libraries.

Hussein Suleman is affiliated with the Computer Science Department, Virginia Polytechnic Institute and State University, 203 Craig Drive, Blacksburg, VA 24060 (E-mail: hussein@vt.edu).

Edward Fox is Professor, Computer Science Department, Virginia Polytechnic Institute and State University (E-mail: fox@vt.edu).

This material is based upon work supported by the National Science Foundation under Grant Numbers IIS-9986089, IIS-0002935, IIS-0086227, DUE-0121679, DUE-0121741, and DUE-0136690. Any opinions, findings, and conclusions or recommendations expressed in this material are those of the authors and do not necessarily reflect the views of the National Science Foundation.

[Haworth co-indexing entry note]: "The Open Archives Initiative: Realizing Simple and Effective Digital Library Interoperability." Suleman, Hussein and Edward Fox. Co-published simultaneously in *Journal of Library Administration* (The Haworth Information Press, an imprint of The Haworth Press, Inc.) Vol. 35, No. 1/2, 2001, pp. 125-145; and: *Libraries and Electronic Resources: New Partnerships, New Practices, New Perspectives* (ed: Pamela L. Higgins) The Haworth Information Press, an imprint of The Haworth Press, Inc., 2001, pp. 125-145. Single or multiple copies of this article are available for a fee from The Haworth Document Delivery Service [1-800-HAWORTH, 9:00 a.m. - 5:00 p.m. (EST). E-mail address: getinfo@haworthpressinc.com].

As a first step towards such interoperability, a metadata harvesting protocol was developed to support the streaming of metadata from one repository to another, ultimately to a provider of user services such as browsing, searching, or annotation. This article provides an overview of the mission, philosophy, and technical framework of the OAI. *[Article copies available for a fee from The Haworth Document Delivery Service: 1-800-HAWORTH. E-mail address: <getinfo@haworthpressinc.com> Website: <http://www. HaworthPress.com> © 2001 by The Haworth Press, Inc. All rights reserved.]*

KEYWORDS. Interoperability, harvesting, metadata, protocol, repository

INTRODUCTION TO THE OAI

Historical Background and Context

The World Wide Web (WWW) is frequently thought of as the technology that revolutionized computer networking by effectively breaking down the barriers between the providers of content and the users of that content. The underlying idea was not actually a novel one since the hypertext community has been investigating such avenues for decades. However, it was backed up by free, easy to utilize software that satisfied a need in the rapidly advancing networked community, and so it was immensely successful.

The WWW broke down a major barrier in making information freely accessible, but it also created information management problems for which simple solutions did not exist. One such problem is that of persistence: how can we guarantee that a digital object on the WWW will always exist? Another question has to do with authority: how much trust can we place in the authenticity of a source of digital objects? These and other concerns led some individuals and organizations to begin creating managed repositories of digital information, nowadays called Digital Libraries (DLs), with additional and specialized services to enhance the users' experience beyond what the WWW had to offer.

While the WWW thrived because of its distributed nature, most DLs tried to provide one-stop shopping for users in specific communities. As the number of DLs increased, users looking for resources found that they needed to search through many DLs before finding what they needed. Most DLs are driven by databases; thus the popular search engines do not index their contents. As a result, search engines are not of much use to users who want to perform searches across multiple DLs.

In order to address this need, different approaches were taken by various communities of users. The Z39.50 (ANSI/NISO, 1995) protocol was designed for client/server access and adapted to federated searching, whereby a system performing a search operation on multiple repositories could send the query to all of them in a standardized format and then process the returned results as appropriate. The Harvest system (Bowman et al., 1995) attempted to gather metadata from websites and create a central searchable index. The Dienst protocol from Cornell University (Davis and Lagoze, 2000) and the STARTS protocol from Stanford University (Gravano et al., 1997) both implemented variations of federated search algorithms, where queries are sent to remote sites in real-time. Kahn and Wilensky's Repository Access Protocol (Kahn and Wilensky, 1995) allowed remote access to the contents of a repository, thus facilitating search and browsing operations. These projects had varying degrees of success, in most cases limited to large or research DLs where there was a commitment to building interoperability into the systems. Smaller DLs were not prepared to make the investment in a complex protocol for interoperability, especially since the rewards were not immediately tangible.

In October 1999, a meeting of representatives of various existing archives was held in Santa Fe, New Mexico, USA, to address the concern that interoperability was beyond the reach of most DL systems. Delegates at this meeting included representatives of the Association of Research Libraries, Coalition for Networked Information, Council on Library and Information Resources, Digital Library Federation, Library of Congress, Networked Digital Library of Theses and Dissertations (NDLTD), Scholarly Publishing and Academic Resources Coalition, and various universities and research institutes. The primary focus of delegates was on facilitating the creation of a Universal Preprint Archive (van de Sompel et al., 2000)–a DL that contained all electronic pre-prints such as papers, articles, and theses. The result of this meeting, the Santa Fe Convention (van de Sompel and Lagoze, 2000), was an agreement among the parties to subscribe to a common standard for interoperability based on transfer of metadata from repositories using a minimal protocol and leveraging existing technology to achieve this.

Initial Technical Efforts

The Santa Fe Convention laid the groundwork for future efforts by defining the guiding principles of what soon was named the Open Archives Initiative (OAI) (OAI, 2001)–principles that are largely unchanged after 18 months of further discussion within an expanding community of digital librarians and users of information.

At the Santa Fe meeting, it was decided that archives would be able to exchange metadata with one another using a modified subset of the Dienst protocol. As is often the case, however, this first iteration of the interoperability protocol led to much debate over semantics and ambiguities inherent within the specifications. Early implementations for the Computer Science Teaching Center (CSTC, 2001) and the Physics Preprint Archive (arXiv, 2001) were based on subtly different interpretations of the protocol. Discussions among implementers of the protocol convinced some proponents of the Santa Fe Convention that more work was needed to make the protocol specification robust and thus truly standardized. This notion was formalized at two workshops and a technical committee meeting, which, along with a Steering Committee, guided the evolution of that initial protocol into its current incarnation.

Evaluation: Community and Technical Meetings

The OAI held two workshops in conjunction with ACM DL2000 (San Antonio, USA, June 2000) and ECDL 2000 (Lisbon, Portugal, September 2000) conferences, where the initial work was evaluated and a future course was charted for the OAI.

Unlike the inaugural meeting, these workshops were openly advertised to digital library practitioners and they drew a broad range of participants from sectors of the community ranging from publishers to researchers. It was unanimously agreed that the initial protocol needed revision and that the OAI needed to broaden its scope to serve communities beyond its initial mandate of pre-print archives. To address these issues, a technical committee was formed and tasked with revising the protocol to eliminate the shortcomings that were recognized and to meet the needs of the larger OAI community. This committee met in September in Ithaca, NY, USA to launch an intensive period of writing, implementing and testing, which culminated in the official release of the OAI Metadata Harvesting Protocol in January 2001 (Lagoze and van de Sompel, 2001). This protocol, having undergone extensive alpha testing prior to release, promises to provide a simple mechanism for DLs to interoperate effectively.

BASIC OA CONCEPTS

Repositories and Open Archives

The words "Open Archive" frequently conjure up images of information access without any associated cost or restriction. While this is a goal for many proponents of the OAI, it would place too many restrictions on DLs that wanted to conform to OAI standards. So, the OAI defines an Open Archive (OA) simply as being an archive that implements the OAI Metadata Harvesting Protocol, thus allowing remote archives to access its metadata using an "open" standard.

A "Repository" is frequently used as a synonym for an OA. In the traditional DL context, a repository is a collection of digital objects, but in the context of the OAI, it has to be network accessible and it has to support the OAI Metadata Harvesting Protocol.

Harvesting and Federation

The first crucial decision made by the OAI was the selection of a method to achieve basic interoperability among repositories, with special emphasis placed on the ability to do cross-archival searching. It is generally considered that there are two major approaches to accomplish this: harvesting and federation.

Federation refers to the case where the DL sends the search criteria to multiple remote repositories and the results are gathered, combined, and presented to the user. Harvesting is when the DL collects metadata from remote repositories, stores it locally and then performs searches on the local copy of the metadata. Figure 1 illustrates the differences in data flow.

Federation is a more expensive mode of operation in terms of network and search system constraints since each repository has to support a complex search language and fast real-time responses to queries. Harvesting requires only that individual archives be able to transfer metadata to the central DL. The frequency of queries, quantity of metadata, and availability of network resources also factor into this comparison but, in general, federation places a greater burden on the remote sites while harvesting reduces the demand on remote sites and concentrates the processing at the central DL site. Since it is more likely that providers of services, such as search engines, will expend the effort to store, index, classify, and otherwise manage searchable metadata, the

FIGURE 1. Data Flow for Federation and Harvesting

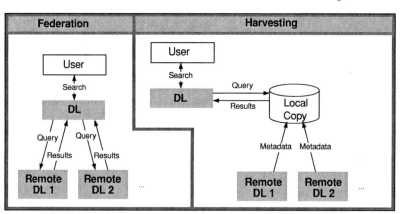

OAI opted for harvesting, primarily as a means of lowering the barrier to interoperability for providers of data.

Metadata and Data

The question of what to harvest has been a contentious issue for many, as it is not obvious whether an archive should be sharing its metadata, its digital objects, or both. There are advantages to exchanging complete digital objects since that would support operations like full-text search of text documents. However, in most instances DLs need only harvest metadata in order to provide search, classification, and related services. This approach was adopted by the OAI, with the implicit understanding that the metadata should contain pointers to the concrete renditions of digital objects.

Data and Service Providers

A data provider maintains a repository that allows external online access to its metadata through the OAI Metadata Harvesting Protocol. In the interest of brevity, "data provider" is sometimes used to refer to such repositories. A service provider is an entity that harvests metadata from data providers in order to present users with higher-level services. This distinction allows for a clean separation between the provider of data and the provider of services (as illustrated in Figure 2). This helps eliminate the current barrier to quality services that arose because of the

FIGURE 2. Layered Organization of Data Storage and Service Provision

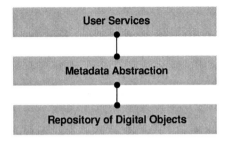

historical connection between ownership of data and provision of services. In general, archives with large quantities of content prioritize information management over the provision of user services. On the other hand, if information management is not a primary function of an archive, more effort can be devoted to service provision. The OAI attempts to clarify and separate these approaches to present users with the best of both worlds.

TECHNICAL FRAMEWORK

Underlying Technology and Standards

HTTP

In creating a protocol for interoperability, it was considered prudent to build upon the existing infrastructure provided by the WWW. Thus, the OAI Metadata Harvesting Protocol is based on HTTP (Fielding et al., 1999), closely following the model upon which HTTP is based, and leveraging its mechanisms for redirection, error handling, and parameter passing. The Metadata Harvesting Protocol is a request-response protocol–the client makes requests for data and the server returns corresponding responses.

XML

While all requests are encoded as HTTP GET or PUT operations, responses are in XML (Bray et al., 2000) so as to allow for structure within the response data. This is especially well suited to handling the case where a service provider requests structured metadata from a data repository. The frequently thorny issue of character encoding also has been deftly avoided by utilizing the support for such features in XML.

XSD and Namespaces

Data quality and correctness of implementations are crucial to the success of any new standard. To maintain such quality, automatic and manual testing can be performed on data providers to ensure conformance to the protocol. In both instances, this testing is largely driven by precise definitions of valid XML responses in the form of XML Schema Descriptions (XSD) (Fallside, 2000). While XSD is still a very young technology, it greatly enhances the ability to specify what constitutes a valid XML document. Service providers and conformance testing tools like the Repository Explorer (Suleman, 2001) use XSD tools to automatically validate XML responses from data providers.

XML tags may be grouped together by using a prefix for each group called a namespace. Namespaces are used to support the reuse of existing semantics and schemata, making validation a modular process. For example, some responses contain metadata fields embedded within a larger structure–in these cases, the metadata will use one namespace and the rest of the XML could belong to another namespace.

Figure 3 is a fragment of typical XML where namespaces are used to delineate tags from different namespaces by means of "xmlns" attributes. At the same time, the schema for each namespace is indicated with an "xsi:schemaLocation" attribute that creates a mapping from the namespace to the XSD document that can be used to validate the XML.

Dublin Core

It is compulsory that all open archives be able to generate metadata for all resources in unqualified Dublin Core (DC) (Dublin Core Metadata Initiative, 1997). This will ensure that service providers who do not understand any other metadata format will at least be able to glean the basic information about resources from their DC renditions. Dublin Core is almost never the best choice for metadata for any given repository, but its generality makes it suitable for interoperability in the context of the OAI and its application to various different types of repositories such as papers, theses, and multimedia documents. In addition to DC, repositories also may support other optional metadata formats that are better suited to represent the objects they contain. Thus,

FIGURE 3. Fragment of XML Illustrating Namespaces and Schema Locations

```
<testxml xmlns="space1" xsi:schemaLocation="space1 space1.xsd">

  <name>Joe Smith</name>
  <comment>testxml, name and comment are in the namespace space1</comment>

  <metadata xmlns="space2" xsi:schemaLocation="space2 space2.xsd">
    <date>2000-02-28</date>
    <description>
      metadata, data and description are in the namespace space2
    </description>
  </metadata>

</testxml>
```

repositories connected with NDLTD also should support MARC or a newly devised thesis metadata standard (Atkins et al., 2001).

Sets

Sets are a special construct which allow a repository to expose its internal structure to service providers. It is not compulsory for an archive to support set constructs but it provides one mechanism for selective harvesting. There are no predefined semantics for what constitutes a set, so any use of sets must be by explicit agreement between data providers and service providers. For example, in the context of NDLTD, a national archive might have sets for each region, and subsets for each university.

Records

A record is the metadata bundle that is associated with a unique identifier. Usually, records correspond to simple digital objects but this is not necessary–records also could refer to collections or sub-objects. Records are encapsulated within a special structure that includes both the metadata and a header containing special fields used to support the harvesting operation. Figure 4 displays a typical record.

OAI Metadata Harvesting Protocol

The OAI Metadata Harvesting Protocol supports 6 service requests that may be made to a repository. The protocol specifies the formats for the corresponding HTTP queries and XML responses. These service

FIGURE 4. Sample Record from the arXiv Open Archive

```
<record>
 <header>
  <identifier>oai:arXiv:alg-geom/9202004</identifier>
  <datestamp>1992-02-10</datestamp>
 </header>
 <metadata>
  <oai_dc xmlns="http://purl.org/dc/elements/1.1/">
   <title>Mirror symmetry and rational curves on quintic threefolds: a guide
          for mathematicians</title>
   <creator>Morrison, David R.</creator>
   <subject>Algebraic Geometry</subject>
   <description> We give a mathematical account of a recent string theory
                calculation which predicts the number of rational curves on
                the generic quintic threefold.</description>
   <date>1992-02-10</date>
   <type>e-print</type>
   <identifier>http://arXiv.org/abs/alg-geom/9202004</identifier>
  </oai_dc>
 </metadata>
</record>
```

requests are as follows: GetRecord, Identify, ListIdentifiers, ListMeta-dataFormats, ListRecords, and ListSets.

- GetRecord retrieves the metadata for a single object in a specified metadata format.
- Identify is a request for information about the repository as a whole. Returned is such information as the name of the repository, the version of the protocol, and the email address of the adminis-trator. There also is an extension mechanism for a repository to specify additional information by supplying its own schema.
- ListIdentifiers lists identifiers for all objects or, if specified, those within a given date range and/or within a given set.
- ListMetadataFormats will return the list of all metadata formats supported by the archive, or all the metadata formats in which a particular object may be rendered.
- ListRecords lists complete metadata for all objects or, if specified, within a given date range and/or within a given set.
- ListSets lists the sets (and subsets, recursively) contained within the repository.

Flow Control

In principle, the OAI subscribes to the philosophy that the act of a service provider harvesting a repository ought not to interfere with the regular use of the archive by users through, for example, an exist-ing WWW-based search and retrieval interface. However, some service requests have the ability to return very long response sets, e.g., ListContents. To prevent overloading, the data provider can break result sets into chunks and return one chunk per request with a token being passed to keep track of the state of the system. Other flow control mechanisms, like the ability to redirect a request or the ability to postpone a request, are inherited from the underlying HTTP protocol.

Registration Services

Registration of conformant repositories is useful within communities with shared interests. For example, NDLTD will have a listing of all its member institutions that implement the OAI protocol. Registration can be automated by using the Identify service request to return information about an archive. On a more global scale, the OAI is helping to register all repositories in order to provide a name resolution service from identifiers to repositories.

Expansion and Customization

The protocol has optional features in some strategic places to allow for future expansion. Most importantly, there is no restriction on which metadata formats may be supported as long as each one has an associated schema description. Also, the data returned by the Identify request includes optional sections for descriptions that conform to external schemata. Similarly, each record has an optional "about" section that may contain information about the metadata object, as opposed to the digital object associated with the metadata. Figure 5 displays a minimal metadata record with this optional section.

REQUIREMENTS TO BE A PROVIDER

Data Provider

Any archive that wishes to become a Data Provider must satisfy a few basic requirements. Firstly, and most importantly, the archive must have an online interface and a web server that can be used for the purposes of the protocol. Then, each record in the archive must be persistent or at least must contain a persistent identifier, each of which must be unique within the archive. It also is highly recommended that each

FIGURE 5. Minimal Metadata Record from arXiv with Optional "About" Section

```
<record>
 <header>
  <identifier>oai:arXiv:alg-geom/9202004</identifier>
  <datestamp>1992-02-10</datestamp>
 </header>
 <metadata>
  <oai_dc xmlns="http://purl.org/dc/elements/1.1/">
   <title>Mirror symmetry and rational curves on quintic threefolds: a guide
          for mathematicians</title>
   <creator>Morrison, David R.</creator>
  </oai_dc>
 </metadata>
 <about>
  <oai_dc xmlns="http://purl.org/dc/elements/1.1/">
   <creator>University Library Cataloguing Service</creator>
  </oai_dc>
 </about>
</record>
```

archive have a unique archive name embedded within its identifiers for records so that OAI records can be globally unique–the OAI protocol suggests that unique identifiers adopt the form "oai:archive_id:record_id." Finally, every record must have an associated date stamp to allow for harvesting of records within a particular date range.

Service Provider

Service providers may use the data they harvest as they wish to, within the boundaries laid out by the data providers. While the protocol does allow for an entire archive's contents to be harvested, it is expected that service providers will use date ranges to incrementally harvest new additions to a repository. This is illustrated in Figure 6.

Tools and Support

The OAI website contains links to a number of useful resources that may assist developers in making their archives compliant with the protocol. The Repository Explorer is a tool that allows a user to interactively browse through an archive using only the OAI interface, while checking the interface thoroughly for errors in encoding or protocol semantics. There also is information on joining a mailing list of developers, who are more than willing to share their code and expertise in various programming languages and on various platforms to ease the process of becoming an Open Archive. It is anticipated that an expanding library of tools will be assembled in the future to support new adopters of the technology.

FIGURE 6. Example Sequence of Requests and Responses Between Service and Data Providers

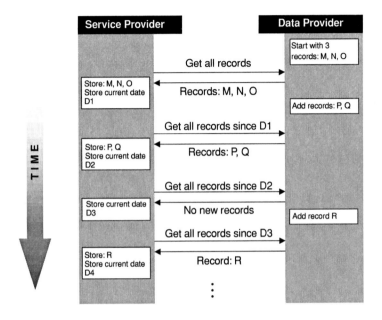

OAI SUPPORT FOR TYPICAL SERVICES

Cross-Archive Searching

The most obvious service to provide would be cross-archive searching. The service provider can harvest metadata in one or more formats from multiple remote OAs and index the data according to collection, set, or specific fields within the metadata. Such an experimental search engine has already been developed at Old Dominion University (Liu, 2001) in parallel with the development of the OAI protocol.

Reference Linking

The ability to navigate quickly from one electronic publication to another that it references is a goal of many reference-linking techniques such as SFX, developed largely at the University of Ghent (van de Sompel and Hochstenbach, 1999). OAI-accessible bibliographic metadata will greatly improve the quality and quantity of data available for constructing cross-reference databases. References could even be augmented or replaced by OAI identifiers, with an appropriate name resolution service to redirect the user to the DL that contains the referenced object.

Annotations

Since annotations are additions to existing documents, adding such a service to an existing DL usually requires the construction of a separate annotation database. In leveraging the OAI protocol, such a separate database could itself be an OA–then any entry in the OA of annotations would refer back to records in other existing OAs. A service provider would then retrieve data from both the source OA and annotation OA before displaying the metadata to the user.

Filtering

In a profile-based filtering system, users would indicate a set of interests and then all objects corresponding to those interests would be presented to them on a continuous basis. This mode of operation is perfectly suited to the OAI protocol because of the inherently incremental nature of harvesting. Thus, a filtering or routing system could use the OAI protocol to harvest new metadata and then route that as appropriate based on a set of stored profiles.

Browsing

Unlike searching, a browsing service often requires that the metadata contain fields with controlled vocabularies that can be used to build categories within which the objects may be placed. The support for arbitrary metadata formats in the OAI protocol allows embedding of categorical data into an appropriate metadata format. In addition, the requirement for strict conformance to an XML schema can ensure that a controlled vocabulary is adhered to.

EXISTING LIBRARY POLICIES FROM AN OAI PERSPECTIVE

Ownership and Dissemination Control over Digital Objects and Metadata

One of the major concerns that librarians have about this technology is its impact on ownership of digital objects and metadata. Some archives will openly share both with all and sundry while many archives will only share their metadata. There also are many archives that will share metadata for the purposes of building cross-archival search services but insist on users switching over to their website for the purpose of enforcing "brand recognition" or to request payment for resources. All of these scenarios are feasible since the OAI requires only that the metadata point to the object, and this could easily be in the form of an indirect link through the originating archive. In the case of an archive that needs to restrict access to only a specified set of service providers, that can be accomplished through the access control mechanisms built into the HTTP protocol.

Changes and Withdrawal

Besides making clear this ownership of content, most archives also reserve the right to make changes to the metadata that is associated with their digital objects. In order to propagate changes, all an archive needs to do is update the date stamp on the record so that future requests for incremental changes will result in the changed record being disseminated once again to the service provider. Service providers are expected to understand that a new record received with the same identifier as a previous one and with a later date stamp is an updated version. Deletions are handled in a similar way–if identifiers for deleted records are stored at the archive, these can be returned to service providers with a special attribute that is set to indicate that the record has been deleted at the source.

Preservation

Preservation of digital objects is a basic requirement of the OAI. Any archive subscribing to the OAI model of interoperability must maintain a stable collection of digital objects. The HTTP protocol has a feature to redirect URLs automatically–since objects are usually referred to by URLs, this HTTP feature can be exploited to preserve the integrity of metadata. Also, if it is expected that objects will change location often during their lifetime, they could be allocated persistent URLs (PURLs) or Handles instead of regular URLs. An essential aspect of any DL is the migration of content to newer archival technology–this is vital for interoperability efforts like the OAI since inaccessible content at a data provider will adversely affect every harvester of that data provider.

Uniqueness of Objects and Collections

The OAI does not require that every implementer of the harvesting protocol have a unique archive identifier. However, this is recommended so as to create a globally unique namespace for OAI identifiers. This will allow for the creation of services that are analogous to DNS name resolution–given an OAI identifier, the resolver with full knowledge of all OAs could direct a user to the archive that contains the resource.

Within an archive each record must have a unique identifier so that any single GetRecord request for metadata associated with the identifier will be unambiguous.

BUILDING OAI SUB-COMMUNITIES

Metadata Formats

Communities of archives with similar interests may benefit greatly from developing their own metadata formats or simply specifying their existing metadata formats in a form that is usable with the OAI protocol. The protocol was designed to support a much higher level of semantic interoperability than is allowed by unqualified Dublin Core, so it is expected that individual archives will choose the most appropriate format for exporting their data. For example, libraries will probably use a form of MARC encoded in XML while repositories of educational resources may wish to use IMS (IMS, 1999) instead. Thus, providers of services will be able to supply users with more information, and archives will truly be able to interoperate if they have the same underlying metadata formats.

Some representatives of pre-print archives have already begun discussion of a metadata format suited for their purposes and it is hoped that this process will be initiated within other DL communities as well.

Protocol Extensions

While the protocol as specified is useful for some purposes, there is no reason why an individual community cannot enhance or change the protocol to support additional features. These could take the form of either changes or additions and could be internal, with an external interface that conforms to the base protocol. Nobody expects that this protocol is a perfect solution to the problem–rather it is a stable and tested protocol that will be used for experimentation in research and production environments, leading to further evaluation and possibly newer versions after a sufficiently long period of time, set to be at least one year by the OAI. The encoding of a protocol version into the protocol further ensures that any future updates will not confuse service providers.

Shared Semantics

Along with shared metadata formats a community must share a common understanding of the semantics of the metadata format. Thus, for example, if a community decides to use the RFC1807 (Lasher and Cohen, 1995) metadata format, some loosely defined fields could be further restricted for the purposes of the community, thus allowing for a more tightly coupled interoperable environment. Of course, the parallel DC metadata set must still be supported so this creates the situation where an archive may export its data in a well-defined community-specific format or a loosely defined general format satisfying the general OAI community.

Case Study: Development of OAI MARC Format

In a cooperative effort between Virginia Tech's Digital Library Research Laboratory and Herbert van de Sompel at Cornell University, an XML version of the US-MARC metadata format has been specified. This mapping does not attempt to encode each MARC field into a separate XML tag, but rather encodes the fields as name/value pairs, with subfields used as required. See Figure 7 for a fragment of oai_marc XML.

The biggest challenges were in encoding of the character sets. Since the XML style recommended by the OAI is to use Unicode entities, all ANSEL characters need to be translated into Unicode before being exported. Composite characters also need to be changed since they are encoded differently in MARC and XML. Nevertheless, this MARC encoding in XML has generated much interest from librarians as a way of widely sharing catalog data because of its simplicity and the fact that any problems can be fixed at a level outside of the schema description.

Case Study: NDLTD

NDLTD, the Networked Digital Library of Theses and Dissertations, (Fox, 1999; Fox, 2001) is an international alliance of universities where

FIGURE 7. Fragment of Sample Record of XML Encoding of MARC

```
<oai_marc xmlns="http://www.openarchives.org/OIA/oai_marc" status="n" type="a"
level="m" catForm="a">
  <fixfield id="1">"tmp96303807"</fixfield>
  <fixfield id="3">"OCoLC"</fixfield>
  <fixfield id="5">"19970728102440.0"</fixfield>
  <fixfield id="8">"971114s1996 dcu f000 0 eng d"</fixfield>
  <varfield id="35" i1="" i2="">
    <subfield label="a">1258-02760</subfield>
  </varfield>
  <varfield id="40" i1="" i2="">
    <subfield label="d">GPO</subfield>
    <subfield label="d">DLC</subfield>
    <subfield label="d">MvI</subfield>
  </varfield>
  <varfield id="49" i1="" i2="">
    <subfield label="a">VPII</subfield>
  </varfield>
  <varfield id="74" i1="" i2="">
    <subfield label="a">0378-H-12</subfield>
  </varfield>
  .
  .
  .
```

students submit electronic versions of their theses and dissertations. As a preliminary step towards creating a universal catalogue of publications, the community has defined a metadata set to meet its particular needs. This metadata set is an extension of Dublin Core with one additional field for the provision of information about the type of thesis or dissertation. The fields inherited from Dublin Core are given specific semantics that will be understood by all members of the community. Also, RDF is being investigated as an encoding strategy to incorporate links and explanations of semantics into the metadata. Ultimately, this metadata format will be exported from all NDLTD sites that are accessible through the OAI Metadata Harvesting Protocol.

USAGE SCENARIOS

Dissemination of Cataloguing Information–MetaLibraries

In a library environment, cataloguing information is a vital resource that is shared among libraries. The OAI protocol provides a low barrier method of exchanging such cataloguing information without having to invest in high-end technology solutions. The existence of the oai_marc encoding further simplifies the task since there is now a standard way of transferring MARC records in XML.

While this may not appear very useful to large research and even public libraries, it can be very useful for smaller organizations that operate libraries. It provides a means for these smaller libraries to share their metadata with larger and peer institutions. Conceptually, it should even be possible for an appropriate organization to make available a "metalibrary" catalogue that describes every book in every OAI accessible library.

Name Authority Systems

The authoritativeness of names is always a problem when dealing with large quantities of data that contain references to individuals. One solution is to maintain a central (or distributed) database of names (personal and institutional) and then use links to this in each metadata item. NDLTD has adopted this approach and is currently working with OCLC (OCLC, 2001) to set up such a system. While name information is not usually considered to be metadata, the OAI protocol can be used for name lookups by issuing GetRecord requests with the name identifier as the parameter. This is being pursued actively and illustrates a scenario where the OAI protocol can be used for simple metadata access by identifier.

Case Study: NDLTD-Search and Classification for ETDs

NDLTD comprises a number of research universities with collections of electronic theses and dissertations. These collections are, however, managed as independent projects, very loosely linked. As an initial attempt to offer a cross-archive search service, Powell and Fox (Powell and Fox, 1998) created a federated search system. This suffered from the problem of scalability since each new archive could introduce new search semantics that would need to be integrated into the rest of the system. Also, there was no easy means of integrating the results from different systems into a single result list.

As an alternative approach, Virginia Tech is working with VTLS (VTLS, 2001) to offer a cross-archive search system based on their Virtua software. This project will use the OAI protocol to transfer metadata from individual ETD repositories into a central NDLTD collection that will be fed into Virtua and Virginia Tech's research system, MARIAN (France, 2001). In this instance, OAI technology is bridging the gaps among various different archives to increase the visibility of scholarly publications.

CONCLUSION

The Open Archives Initiative has provided the community of electronic libraries with a simple but extensible protocol to facilitate interoperability. But why do we need interoperability? The short answer is that there are very few digital libraries that have both extensive collections and effective services. Some contain lots of data. Others provide lots of services. In either case, users do not easily find the resources related to their particular information need. Through OAI we can turn these problems into advantages by helping both data providers and service providers do a better job at their specialties, while streamlining the data provider to service provider connection. By building interoperable DLs, we can provide users with the best of both worlds, making searching of DLs a feasible notion without compromising on the quality of information management that sets digital libraries apart from the mass of data on the WWW.

BIBLIOGRAPHY

ANSI/NISO. 1995. Information Retrieval (Z39.50): Application Service Definition and Protocol Specification (ANSI/NISO Z39.50-1995). Bethesda, MD: NISO Press.

arXiv.org. 2001. *arXiv.org e-Print archive.* <http://www.arXiv.org>.

Atkins, Anthony, Thorsten Bahne, Nune Freire, and Sarantos Kapidakis. 2001. *Interoperability Metadata Standard for Electronic Theses and Dissertations (draft).* Available http://www.ndltd.org/standards/metadata/.

Bowman, C. M., P. B. Danzig, D. R. Hardy, U. Manber, and M. F. Schwartz. 1995. The Harvest Information Discovery and Access System. *Computer Networks and ISDN Systems,* 28, 119-125.

Bray, T., J. Paoli, C. M. Sperberg-McQueen, and Eve Maler, eds. 2000. *Extensible Markup Language (XML) 1.0 (Second Edition).* W3C. Available http://www. w3.org/TR/2000/REC-xml-20001006.

CSTC. 2001. *Computer Science Teaching Center Website.* <http://www.cstc.org>.

Davis, James R., and Carl Lagoze. 2000. NCSTRL: Design and Deployment of a Globally Distributed Digital Library. *JASIS,* 51(3), 273-280.

Dublin Core Metadata Initiative. 1997. *Dublin Core Metadata Element Set Version 1.1: Reference Description.* Available http://www.dublincore.org/documents/dces/.

Fallside, David C., ed. 2000. *XML Schema.* W3C. Available http://www.w3.org/ XML/Schema.

Fielding, R., J. Gettys, J. Mogul, H. Frystyk, L. Masinter, P. Leach, and T. Berners-Lee. 1999. *Hypertext Transfer Protocol–HTTP 1.1 (RFC 2616).* Available ftp://ftp.isi. edu/in-notes/rfc2616.txt.

Fox, Edward A. 1999. Networked Digital Library of Theses and Dissertations. *Proceedings of DLW15,* July 1999. Nara, Japan: ULIS. Available http://www.ndltd. org/pubs/dlw15.doc.

Fox, Edward A. 2001. *Networked Digital Library of Theses and Dissertations.* <http://www.ndltd.org>.

France, Robert K. 2001. *MARIAN Digital Library Information System.* <http://www.dlib.vt.edu/products/marian.html>.

Gravano, L., K. Chang, H. Garcia-Molina, C. Lagoze, and A. Paepcke. 1997. *STARTS: Stanford Protocol Proposal for Internet Retrieval and Search.* Available http://www-db.stanford.edu/~gravano/starts.html.

IMS Global Learning Consortium, Inc. 1999. *IMS Learning Resource Meta-data Information Model.* Available http://www.imsproject.org/metadata/mdinfov1p1.html.

Kahn, Robert and Robert Wilensky. 1995. *A Framework for Distributed Digital Object Services.* Available http://www.cnri.reston.va.us/k-w.html.

Lagoze, Carl and Herbert van de Sompel. 2001. *The Open Archives Initiative Protocol for Metadata Harvesting.* Available http://www.openarchives.org/OAI/openarchivesprotocol.htm.

Lasher, R., and D. Cohen. 1995. *A Format for Bibliographic Records (RFC1807).* Available http://info.internet.isi.edu:80/in-notes/rfc/files/rfc1807.txt.

Liu, Xiaoming. 2001. *ARC: Cross Archive Searching Service.* <http://arc.cs.odu.edu>.

OCLC, Inc. 2001. *Online Computer Library Center Website.* <http://www.oclc.org>.

Open Archives Initiative. 2001. *Open Archives Initiative Website.* <http://www.openarchives.org>.

Powell, James and Edward A. Fox. 1998. Multilingual Federated Searching Across Heterogeneous Collections. *D-Lib Magazine*, 4(8). Available http://www.dlib.org/dlib/september98/powell/09powell.html.

Suleman, Hussein. 2001. *OAI Repository Explorer.* <http://purl.org/net/oai_explorer>.

Van de Sompel, Herbert, Thomas Krichel, Michael L. Nelson and others. 2000. The UPS Prototype: An Experimental End-User Service across E-Print Archives. *D-Lib Magazine*, 6(2). Available http://www.dlib.org/dlib/february00/vandesompel-ups/02vandesompel-ups.html.

Van de Sompel, Herbert and Carl Lagoze. 2000. The Santa Fe Convention of the Open Archives Initiative. *D-Lib Magazine*, 6(2). Available http://www.dlib.org/dlib/february00/vandesompel-oai/02vandesompel-oai.html.

Van de Sompel, Herbert and Patrick Hochstenbach. 1999. Reference Linking in a Hybrid Library Environment. *D-Lib Magazine*, 5(4). Available http://www.dlib.org/dlib/april99/van_de_sompel/04van_de_sompel-pt1.html.

VTLS. 2001. *VTLS Website.* <http://www.vtls.com>.

GLOBAL CONSORTIAL ACTIVITIES

International Library Consortia:
Positive Starts, Promising Futures

Arnold Hirshon

SUMMARY. Library consortia have grown substantially over the past ten years, both within North America and globally. As this resurgent consortial movement has begun to mature, and as publishers and vendors have begun to adapt to consortial purchasing models, consortia have expanded their agendas for action. The movement to globalize consortia is traced (including the development and current work of the International Coalition of Library Consortia–ICOLC). A methodology is explored to classify library consortia by articulating the key factors that affect and distinguish consortia as organizations within three major areas: strategic, tactical, and practical (or managerial) concerns. Common consortial values

Arnold Hirshon is Executive Director of NELINET, Inc., 153 Cordaville Road, Suite 200, Southborough, MA 01772 (E-mail: ahirshon@nelinet.net).

The author is indebted to Tom Sanville of OhioLINK, who provided the original core list of library consortia included in the Appendix. The author added to the Sanville list not only other consortia listed on the ICOLC public web site http://www.library.yale.edu/consortia/compiled by Ann Okerson, but also lists compiled by the author himself from New England and other regions of the United States and other parts of the world.

[Haworth co-indexing entry note]: "International Library Consortia: Positive Starts, Promising Futures." Hirshon, Arnold. Co-published simultaneously in *Journal of Library Administration* (The Haworth Information Press, an imprint of The Haworth Press, Inc.) Vol. 35, No. 1/2, 2001, pp. 147-166; and: *Libraries and Electronic Resources: New Partnerships, New Practices, New Perspectives* (ed: Pamela L. Higgins) The Haworth Information Press, an imprint of The Haworth Press, Inc., 2001, pp. 147-166. Single or multiple copies of this article are available for a fee from The Haworth Document Delivery Service [1-800-HAWORTH, 9:00 a.m. - 5:00 p.m. (EST). E-mail address: getinfo@haworthpressinc.com].

147

are examined, and a list of known international library consortia appears in the appendix. *[Article copies available for a fee from The Haworth Document Delivery Service: 1-800-HAWORTH. E-mail address: <getinfo@haworth pressinc.com> Website: <http://www.HaworthPress.com> © 2001 by The Haworth Press, Inc. All rights reserved.]*

KEYWORDS. Library consortia, international librarianship

The growth of library consortia has been substantial over the past ten years, both within North America and globally. The articles that follow feature some of the major consortial programs being developed throughout the world. These articles reveal that there is much that the North American community can learn and gain from the experiences of other consortia internationally.

Although library networks and consortia have been around for many decades, the recent burgeoning growth of, and interest in consortia was definitely affected by one major change: the advent of widespread licensing of electronic information resources. It was in large part the outgrowth of this phenomenon that galvanized the international consortium community. However, as this resurgent consortial movement has begun to mature, and as publishers and vendors have begun to adapt to consortial purchasing models, even consortia that only formed within the last decade have begun to expand their agenda for action to seek new ways to work with and for their member libraries.

THE GLOBALIZATION OF CONSORTIA: THE DEVELOPMENT OF ICOLC

Given the rapid development of consortia, it is not surprising that consortium leaders and directors have found it desirable to organize their activities and to share ideas to improve their management and coordination of their programs and services. One of the most significant recent developments in the growth of consortia has been the formation in the mid-1990s of an informal discussion group of consortium managers. The group, which first met in 1996 as an adjunct to other professional library meetings, was the brainchild of Tom Sanville, the Executive Director of OhioLINK. The group first formed as the "Consortium of Consortia" (or COC), and under that name the group held its first independent meeting in St. Louis in February 1997. The major purpose of that meeting was for consortium leaders to hear and respond to presentations from publishers and vendors about new electronic resource products. As a result of the intense questioning that occurred, these sessions were quickly dubbed as "grill sessions." Meeting twice annually, the COC group grilled over fifty publishers and vendors between 1997 and 2001.

Beginning in 1997, the group took a major step. In October 1997 there appeared a publication developed by a consortium of university libraries in the Netherlands and Germany entitled "Dutch-German Library Joint Licensing Principles and Guidelines" (October 1997) (available at http://cwis.kub.nl/~dbi/english/license/licprinc.htm). That statement was written by Hans Geleijnse (then at the University of Tilburg, Netherlands, and now the European University Institute in Florence, Italy), Elmar Mittler (of the Niedersächsische Staats-und Universitätsbibliothek Göttingen, Germany), and John Gilbert (Netherlands Association of University Libraries, Royal Library and Library of the Royal Academy of Sciences, Netherlands).

Inspired by this document, a quartet of four active COC participants decided to craft a statement of principles that would build upon the Dutch-German statement, but which would reflect the concerns of the North American library community. This draft was prepared by Arnold Hirshon, Tom Sanville, David Kohl, and Ann Okerson, and circulated among COC members for initial comment. Eventually the document was published as the "Statement of Current Perspective and Preferred Practices for the Selection and Purchase of Electronic Information" (March 1998) (available at http://www.library.yale.edu/consortia/statement.html).

During the early stages of development of the statement concerning electronic information there was a fortuitous turn of events. Arnold Hirshon was scheduled to be on business in Amsterdam, and contacted the authors of the Dutch-German statement to see if there would be some interest in developing a single statement that could be endorsed by both the North American and Dutch groups. A meeting was arranged in The Hague, with the Dutch-German statement authors in attendance, along with Fred Friend from the United Kingdom. Out of that meeting grew not only the agreement upon a single statement, but also a more profound longer-term agreement: to turn the nascent COC into an international organization. After much debate, all parties settled upon a new name: the International Coalition of Library Consortia (ICOLC).[1]

GLOBALIZATION CONTINUES: ICOLC TODAY

While ICOLC today remains an informal group–it is not incorporated, it charges no dues, and it has no bylaws–what started as small, informal meetings has grown significantly in just a few years. The purpose remains to keep its members informed about new electronic information resources, pricing practices of electronic providers and vendors, and other issues of importance to consortia directors and governing boards. The Coalition also meets with the information provider community, creating a forum for discussion about product offerings and issues of mutual concern.

Although it is an informal organization, through volunteer efforts ICOLC has managed to expand its reach. There is a public web site maintained by Ann Okerson at Yale University (http://www.library.yale.edu/consortia/), and a listserv (consort@ohiolink.edu). ICOLC issued additional guidelines and statements of principle, including "Guidelines for Statistical Measures of Usage of Web-based Indexed, Abstracted, and Full Text Resources" (November 1998) (available at http://www.library.yale.edu/consortia/webstats.html) and "Guidelines for Technical Issues in Request for Proposal (RFP) Requirements and Contract Negotiations" (January 1999) (available at http://www.library.yale.edu/consortia/techreq.html). All of these guidelines have been frequently cited, and at their presentations to ICOLC and in the literature, vendors and publishers have often addressed the ability of their products to meet or exceed the ICOLC guidelines.

The twice per year meetings of the Coalition also continue to be very successful, attracting over 100 attendees per meeting. (Attendance is capped to ensure a high quality of dialog among the participants). Attendance is increasingly international in scope. The North American spring 2001 meeting ICOLC, held in Newport RI, attracted not only representatives from consortia in the United States and Canada, but also from consortia in Australia, Belgium, Greece, Hungary, South Africa, Turkey, and the United Kingdom. In all, about 20% of the attendees were from outside of the United States.

In addition to the North American ICOLC meetings, there have also been two European ICOLC meetings (in 1999 and 2000). Attendees at the most recent meeting in December 2000 in Berlin came from nineteen countries: Austria, Belgium, Canada, Denmark, Estonia, Finland, France, Germany, Greece, Hungary, Italy, the Netherlands, Norway, Spain, Sweden, Switzerland, Turkey, the United Kingdom, and the United States.

Given the success of ICOLC, it is interesting to ponder how many consortia there are today worldwide. In a list of consortia maintained by Tom Sanville, he records 154 different consortia in twenty-six countries. To that list the author was able to add 89 more consortia. (This expanded list appears as an appendix to this article.) Of the 243 consortia on the expanded list, 30% are located outside of the United States.

In all likelihood, even this expanded list only scratches the surface. For example, there are two countries that report having consortia but no one from the country is subscribed on the ICOLC listserv (Poland and Scotland). Conversely, there are three countries with at least one subscriber on the ICOLC listserv but no consortium listed for the country (Austria, Hungary, and Japan). Nonetheless, for the most part, on an international level the distribution is relatively even between the percentage of ICOLC subscribers from a country and the percentage of all consortia represented by that country. Even in the United States (for which the author assumes he has more complete information) there remain a significant number of consortia that are not represented on the ICOLC listserv.

If the list in the appendix is a conservative one, why is this so? In part because there is no consistent standard as to what constitutes a consortium. Not only is the categorization or classification of consortia not a science, it is not even an art.

CLASSIFICATION OF CONSORTIA

To this point there has been no formal way to categorize or classify consortia. Previous efforts (by this author and by others)[2] failed to encompass the rich diversity of differences in the reasons consortia form or how they organize themselves. While classification of North American consortia would be difficult enough (and would require at least a three-dimensional matrix to describe the consortia comprehensively), the task of categorizing consortia internationally would be impossible.

A far more valuable exercise than classifying consortia is to understand the key factors that affect why and how consortia are built and managed. This process can provide a model that can be generalized for all types of consortia, and provide an understanding of what is appropriate in terms of sponsorship, governance, staffing, funding, and other management issues. The general model also holds true regardless of the size of a consortium or its location around the world. Ultimately, it is important to understand these factors because the ability of a consortium to advance its agenda rests upon the decisions it makes in these areas.

There are at least three levels of concern that any organization considers as it starts to come together.

- *Strategic.* The strategic level encompasses issues such as the consortium's mission, sponsorship, and funding, membership composition, and the geographic boundaries within which it will operate.
- *Tactical.* The tactical level defines the programs, services, and enabling technologies of the consortium.
- *Practical.* The practical level involves issues such as the governance structures, staffing, and fee and payment structure for the consortium.

The combination of the decisions a consortium makes about its organization at these three levels ultimately will determine not only what it will do, but also how the consortium will conduct its business.

At the strategic level, the key issue the consortium must consider is its mission and the vision. For example, initially some consortia formed primarily to secure a better purchase price for electronic resources (a "buying club"). However, over time the most successful consortia have begun to broaden their agendas, and to build upon their early success negotiating electronic resources to go on to create other programs of common interest, such as research projects, educational programs, joint fund-raising or lobbying, or technology sharing. The funding and governance structure of the consortium also can have an important effect on the negotiating power of a consortium to secure an effective electronic resource offer (both in terms of the price of the product as well as the terms and conditions of the license). For example, a government-funded program (whether funded by a state or by a country) often has not only more financial resources that command the attention of publishers and vendors, but sometimes can also invoke the clout of the government to secure terms that might otherwise be unavailable to an independent self-sustaining organization.

It is for this reason that it is important to recognize at the strategic level that the patterns of development and growth that are appropriate to one country may not be applicable for another. For example, there are some countries with very well-developed library programs, while other countries may not have a strong infrastructure upon which to rely. Similarly, there are countries with formal national information policies, while others work more on a regional basis. These institutional differences can make an enormous difference, not only in how and why a consortium forms, but in its ability to negotiate with electronic resource publishers on behalf of the consortium's members.

Another key strategic issue is the composition of the membership. When negotiating a license, will the consortium purchase the product by or for all members of the consortium, or will each member of the consortium ultimately act independently on each offer? Clearly, the ability to secure good offers will depend not only upon the size of the consortium, but also upon the willingness of the membership to rally around the offer once it is on the table.

The tactical decisions a consortium reaches will heavily influence the state of development of the information services it provides. If the consortium chooses to limit its action agenda solely to negotiating licenses for electronic resources, its complexity of operations will obviously be much smaller than if the group must provide support for operations such as union catalogs, inter-library loan programs, educational or consulting services, collection analysis to create common core electronic collections, or digital library or preservation programs. Finally, there are the practical concerns. The governance structure a consortium chooses will ultimately have an effect on its ability to secure effective electronic resource licenses. A loose-knit consortium with only volunteer help and no formal elected board may be able to secure some licenses, but is unlikely to sustain this effort on a regular basis. Although such volunteer organizations are less expensive and empower the membership, paid staff can provide not only organizational stability but also people to accomplish the work that the overworked staff of each of the member libraries could not accomplish on its own. Unless the consortium is a government agency, to sustain the organization generally requires some type of dues or fee structure. The consortium must then decide whether all libraries will receive a large assessment to pay for common support of all programs, or a lower common set of dues but with transactional fees based upon actual use of each service.

CONSORTIAL SUCCESS:
COMMON PURPOSE, COMMON VALUES

All of these strategic, tactical, and practical issues must be considered as a consortium develops and begins to work together. The decisions that the consortium makes will determine where the organization may be classified. However, what ultimately brings any consortium together is that the group shares certain values. The most successful consortia are those that have a sustained record of accomplishment, and that are seen by their individual library members as being essential to their own growth and survival. These are the consortia that not only have built an admirable record of securing electronic resources at effective prices and with superior terms and conditions, but also that help their members to cooperate on a more strategic level. To accomplish this, the members must share some common values, such as the following:

- A sense of democracy, with all members actively engaged in setting and changing the agenda for action.
- A high level of quality of service. If a consortium fails to provide well-regarded service then its members will look elsewhere for support.
- Strong communication among the members.
- A contribution by all members, each according to its own ability. Obviously a small public library does not contribute at the same level that a major research library would, but ultimately a sense of fairness is critical for most consortia to maintain themselves.

Regardless of the country of origin, collectively, these values stress the importance of the community sharing a strong sense of collaboration. Each member of the consortium must work for the benefit of the common good so that members equitably share the burdens. This must be at all levels: sharing information, ideas and resources, and purchasing power. At times there may be tensions within the organization (such as between the larger and smaller members of the consortium), but on the whole, consortia do come together because they want to share.

With so much work to be done, and with so many choices for each consortium to make, the task may seem daunting. Yet, it is clear from the developments of recent years that libraries have recognized that they can and should do more together than any of them can do alone. As more consortia begin to emerge internationally, it is vital that consortia develop new models customized to meet the special needs of each country or region. The consortial movement has already become a global phenomenon, and it has been highly rewarding to see how consortia in different countries not only tackle their own problems, but have also been able to come together to tackle problems globally. For example, through the Open Society Institute's eiFL[3] program, multinational efforts are underway to aid the ability of nations in transition to secure electronic resources at realistic prices. Through ICOLC, nations are coming together to articulate to the information community guidelines on the economics and value of electronic resources. Perhaps most importantly, organizations such as these are providing forums (both electronic and in-person) for those interested in consortium management to network and share ideas. As libraries continue to face many significant challenges ahead, there is every reason to expect that through the continued growth of consortia, libraries globally will have a critical ally in solving the problems that they face.

NOTES

1. Information about the ICOLC may be found at (http://www.library.yale.edu/consortia).

2. For example, see: Hirshon, Arnold. "Jam Tomorrow, Jam Yesterday, but Never Jam Today: Some Modest Proposals for Venturing Through the Looking-glass of Scholarly Communication." 34 *Serials Librarian* (New York: The Haworth Press, Inc., 1998): 65-87. Hirshon, Arnold. "Libraries, Consortia, and Change Management." *Journal of Academic Librarianship* (March 1999): 124-126. Hirshon, Arnold and McFadden, Barbara Allen. "Hanging Together to Avoid Hanging Separately: Opportunities for Libraries and Consortia." *Information Technology and Libraries* (March 1998): 36-44.

3. eIFL is a joint project of the Open Society Institute (OSI) and EBSCO that began in 2000. The program provides over 2,000 institutions in 39 countries in transition access to EBSCO online services. During 2000, over 2,215,000 searches were performed under this program. It is also anticipated that up to 10 more countries will join the consortium in 2001. In the year 2000, the OSI paid the full subscription fee for all participating countries. In the year 2001, individual countries or their consortia are responsible for covering their subscription fees (Source: http://www.osi.hu/cpd/spf/59_'01.html#eifl).

APPENDIX. List of Library Consortia

Australia	Commonwealth Scientific and Industrial Research Organisation (CSIRO)
Australia	Council of Australian State Libraries (CASL)
Australia	Council of Australian University Librarians (CAUL)
Australia	National Library of Australia (NLA)
Australia	Queensland University Libraries Office of Cooperation
Australia	UNILINC Limited
Belgium	Flemish Research Libraries Council (VOWB, Vlaams Overlegorgaan inzake Wetenschappelijk Bibliotheekwerk)
Canada	British Columbia Electronic Library Network
Canada	Canadian Association of Research Libraries
Canada	Canadian National Site Licensing Project
Canada	Consortium Of Ontario Libraries (COOL)
Canada	Council of Atlantic University Librarians (Conseil des directeur (trice)s de bibliothèques des universités de l'Atlantique) (CAUL-CDBUA)
Canada	Council of Federal Libraries Consortium
Canada	Council of Prairie and Pacific University Libraries (COPPUL)
Canada	CREPUQ (Sub-Committee on Libraries of the Conference of Rectors and Principals of Universities in Quebec)
Canada	Electronic Library Network, British Columbia (ELN)
Canada	Health Knowledge Network
Canada	Health Science Information Consortium of Toronto
Canada	Manitoba Library Consortium Inc. (MLCI)
Canada	NEOS Library Consortium (Alberta)

Canada	Novanet
Canada	Ontario Colleges Consortium
Canada	Ontario Council of University Libraries (OCUL)
Canada	The Alberta Library
Canada	TriUniversity Group of Libraries
China	China Academic Library & Information System (CALIS)
Denmark	Danish Electronic Research Library (DEF)
Denmark	Danish National Library Authority
Denmark	Ligue des Bibliothèques Européennes de Recherche (LIBER)
Estonia	Estonian Libraries Network Consortium (ELNET)
Finland	FinELib
France	COUPERIN
Germany	Free University of Berlin
Germany	Friedrich-Althoff-Konsortium (FAK)
Germany	Gemeinsamer BibliotheksVerbund (GBV)
Germany	He-BIS Konsortium
Greece	Hellenic Academic Libraries LINK (HEAL-LINK)
Hong Kong	Collaborative Collection Development Steering Committee (CCDSC) [Hong Kong Universities]
Ireland	Dundalk Institute of Technology
Israel	Center for Digital Information Services
Israel	MALMAD: Israel Center for Digital Information Services
Italy	Coordinamento Interuniversitario Basi dati & Editoria in Rete (CIBER)
Italy	Italian National Forum on Electronic Resources (INFER)
Multinational	eiFL Soros Open Society Institute

APPENDIX (continued)

Multinational	IberoAmerican Science and Technology Education Consortium (ISTEC)
Multinational	Standing Conference of National and University Libraries (UK and Ireland)
Multinational	United Nations System Consortium
Netherlands	Netherlands Association of University Libraries, Royal Library, and Library of the Royal Academy of Sciences (UKB)
New Zealand	Committee of New Zealand University Librarians
Norway	Riksbibliotekjenesten (RBT)
Poland	Poznan Foundation of Scientific Libraries
Scotland	Scottish Confederation of University and Research Libraries (SCURL)
South Africa	Cape Library Cooperative (CALICO)
South Africa	Coalition of South African Library Consortia
South Africa	Gauteng and Environs Library Consortium (GAELIC)
South Korea	KERIS (KERIS-LINK)
South Korea	Korea Research Information Center (KRIC)
South Korea	The Association of College Libraries in Chollabuk Do (ACLC)
Spain	Consorci de Biblioteques Universitaries de Catalunya–University Library Consortium of Catalonia (CBUC)
Spain	Spanish University Library Network (REBIUN)
Sweden	Swedish University and Research Libraries(BIBSAM)
Sweden	The Royal Library's Department for National Co-ordination and Development (BIBSAM)
Switzerland	Consortium of Swiss Academic Libraries
Switzerland	Informationsverbund Deutschschweiz (IDS)
Switzerland	Réseau des Bibliothèques Romandes et Tessinoises (RERO)

Taiwan	CONsortium on Core Electronic Resources in Taiwan (CONCERT)
Turkey	Anatolian University Library Consortium (ANKOS)
United Kingdom	CHEST (Combined Higher Education Software Team)
United Kingdom	Consortium of Academic Libraries in Manchester
United Kingdom	Consortium of University Research Libraries (CURL)
United Kingdom	Joint Information Systems Committee (JISC)
United Kingdom	Research Councils Libraries & Information Consortium (RESCOLINC)
United Kingdom	Southern Universities Purchasing Consortium (SUPC)
United Kingdom	Standing Conference of National and University Libraries (SCONUL)
US: Alabama	Alabama Virtual Library
US: Alabama	Network of Alabama Academic Libraries (NAAL)
US: Alaska	Alaska State Library
US: Arizona	Arizona Health Information Network (AZHIN)
US: Arizona	Arizona University Libraries Consortium (AULC)
US: Arkansas	ARKLink (Consortium of Arkansas Academic Libraries)
US: California	California Digital Library (an initiative of the University of California)
US: California	CSU-SEIR (California State University Software and E-Information Resources)
US: California	Library of California (LOC)
US: California	Southern California Electronic Library Consortium (SCELC)
US: California	Statewide California Electronic Library Consortium
US: Colorado	Colorado Alliance of Research Libraries
US: Colorado	Colorado State Library

APPENDIX (continued)

US: Connecticut	Bibliomation, Inc.
US: Connecticut	Capital Area Health Consortium
US: Connecticut	Capitol Region Library Council
US: Connecticut	Connecticut Digital Library
US: Connecticut	Council of Connecticut Academic Library Directors (CCALD)
US: Connecticut	CTW Library Consortium
US: Connecticut	Hartford Consortium for Higher Education
US: Connecticut	Libraries Online. Inc. (LION)
US: Connecticut	Northwestern Connecticut Health Science Libraries
US: Connecticut	Southern Connecticut Library Council
US: Connecticut	Western Connecticut Library Council. Inc.
US: Florida	Florida Center for Library Automation (FCLA)
US: Florida	Northeast Florida Library Information Network (NEFLIN)
US: Florida	Southeast Florida Library Information Network (SEFLIN)
US: Florida	Southwest Florida Library Network
US: Florida	Tampa Bay Library Consortium
US: Georgia	Georgia Library Learning Online (GALILEO)
US: Georgia	Georgia Online Database (BOLD)
US: Idaho	Idaho State Library
US: Illinois	Chicago Library System (CLS)
US: Illinois	Cooperative Computer Services (CCS)
US: Illinois	ILCSO (Illinois Libraries Computer Sytems Organization)
US: Illinois	Illinet
US: Illinois	Illinois Cooperative Collection Management Program (CCMP)
US: Illinois	Illinois Digital Academic Library (IDAL)

US: Illinois	Illinois Libraries Computer Systems Organization (ILCSO)
US: Illinois	Illinois State Library
US: Indiana	INdiana COoperative Library Services Authority (INCOLSA)
US: Kentucky	Kentucky Virtual Library
US: Louisiana	Louisiana Library Network (LOUIS)
US: Maine	Colby/Bates/Bowdoin Consortium
US: Maine	Health Science Libraries & Information Consortium of Maine
US: Maine	Health Science Library Information Consortium (HSLIC)
US: Maine	Maine Info Net Consortium
US: Maine	Maine State Library
US: Maryland	University System of Maryland LIMS (USM/LIMS)
US: Massachusetts	Automated Bristol Library Exchange. (ABLE)
US: Massachusetts	Boston Biomedical Library Consortium (BBLC)
US: Massachusetts	Boston Massachusetts Regional Library System (BMRLS)
US: Massachusetts	C/W MARS–Central/Western Mass Automated Resource Sharing
US: Massachusetts	Cape Libraries Automated Materials Sharing (CLAMS)
US: Massachusetts	Central Massachusetts Consortium of Health Related Libraries (CMCHRL)
US: Massachusetts	Central Massachusetts Regional Library System (CMRLS)
US: Massachusetts	Cooperating Libraries Automated Network (CLAN)
US: Massachusetts	Cooperating Libraries of Greater Springfield (CLGS)

APPENDIX (continued)

US: Massachusetts	Fenway Libraries Online (FLO) US: Massachusetts Fenway Library Consortium (FLC)
US: Massachusetts	Massachusetts Board of Library Commissioners (MBLC)
US: Massachusetts	Massachusetts Conference of Chief Librarians of Public Higher Education Institutions (MCCLPHEI)
US: Massachusetts	Massachusetts Health Sciences Libraries Network (MAHSLIN)
US: Massachusetts	Metro Boston Regional Library Network (MBLN)
US: Massachusetts	Metrowest Massachusetts Regional Library System (MMRLS)
US: Massachusetts	Minuteman Library Network
US: Massachusetts	Northeast Massachusetts Regional Library System (NMRLS)
US: Massachusetts	Northeastern Consortium of Colleges & Universities In Massachusetts (NECCUM)
US: Massachusetts	SAILS, Inc. and Southeastern Automated Libraries, Inc, (SEAL)
US: Massachusetts	Southeastern Massachusetts Consortium of Health Science Libraries (SEMCO)
US: Massachusetts	Southeastern Massachusetts Library System (SEMLS)
US: Massachusetts	Western Massachusetts Health Information Consortium
US: Massachusetts	Western Massachusetts Regional Library System (WMRLS)
US: Massachusetts	Worcester Area Cooperating Libraries (WACL)
US: Michigan	DALNET (Detroit Area)
US: Michigan	Michigan Library Consortium (MLC)
US: Minnesota	MINITEX
US: Minnesota	Minnesota Library Information Network (MnLINK)

US: Minnesota	MnSCU/PALS
US: Mississippi	Mississippi Alliance for Gaining New Opportunities through Library Information Access (MAGNOLIA)
US: Missouri	Missouri Library Network Corporation (MLNC)
US: Missouri	Missouri Research and Education Network (MOREnet)
US: Missouri	Missouri Research Consortium of Libraries (MIRACL)
US: Missouri	MOBIUS: A Consortium of Missouri Libraries
US: Missouri	University of Missouri Shared System (MERLIN)
US: Multistate	Academic Business Libraries Directors
US: Multistate	Amigos Bibliographic Council, Inc.
US: Multistate	Associated Colleges of the South
US: Multistate	Association of South East Research Libraries (ASERL)
US: Multistate	Bibliograpical Center for Research (BCR)
US: Multistate	Big 12 Plus Library Consortium
US: Multistate	Black Gold Cooperative Library System
US: Multistate	Boston Library Consortium
US: Multistate	CAPCON Library Network
US: Multistate	Chesapeake Information and Research Library Alliance (CIRLA)
US: Multistate	College Center for Library Automation (CCLA)
US: Multistate	Committee on Institutional Cooperation (CIC) [Big 10 Universities]
US: Multistate	Cooperative Computer Services
US: Multistate	Council of State Library Agencies, Northeast (COSLINEL)
US: Multistate	Federal Library Information Network (FEDLINK)
US: Multistate	Health Science Libraries of New Hampshire & Vermont

APPENDIX (continued)

US: Multistate	National Network of Libraries of Medicine/New England Region
US: Multistate	NELINET, Inc.
US: Multistate	New England Consortium Coalition.Org (NECCO)
US: Multistate	New England Land Grant University Libraries
US: Multistate	New England Law Library Consortium (NELLCO)
US: Multistate	North Atlantic Health Sciences Libraries, Inc. (NAHSL)
US: Multistate	North Of Boston Library Exchange, Inc. (NOBLE)
US: Multistate	NorthEast Research Libraries Consortium (NERL)
US: Multistate	Northeastern Consortium for Health Information (NECHI)
US: Multistate	Northwest Association of Private Colleges and Universities (NAPCU)
US: Multistate	Solinet
US: Multistate	The Adventist Library Information Cooperative (ALICE)
US: Multistate	The Appalachian Library Information Cooperative (ALICE)
US: Nebraska	NEBASE
US: Nevada	Nevada Council of Academic Libraries
US: Nevada	Nevada Council of Academic Libraries (NCAL)
US: New Hampshire	Librarians of The Upper Valley, Coop (LUV Coop)
US: New Hampshire	New Hampshire College & University Council (NHCUC)
US: New Hampshire	New Hampshire State Library
US: New Jersey	VALE Virtual Library Environment of New Jersey
US: New Mexico	Alliance for Innovation in Science and Technology Information (formerly Library Services Alliance of New Mexico)
US: New York	Long Island Library Resources Council (LILRC)

US: New York	Medical Library Center of New York
US: New York	New York 3Rs Directors Organization (NYTRO)
US: New York	New York Comprehensive Research Libraries (NYCRL)
US: New York	New York Consortium of Consortia
US: New York	New York Office of General Services
US: New York	New York State Library (NYSL)
US: New York	North Suburban Library System
US: New York	Nylink
US: New York	Partners in Information and Innovation-Independent Higher Education (Pi2)
US: New York	Public Library System Directors Organization (PULISDO)
US: New York	State University of New York University Centers
US: New York	SUNY Connect (State University of New York)
US: New York	WALDO
US: New York	Westchester Academic Library Directors Organization (WALDO)
US: New York	Western New York Consortium (WNY)
US: North Carolina	Appalachian College Association
US: North Carolina	NC LIVE (North Carolina Libraries for Virtual Education)
US: North Carolina	Triangle Research Libraries Network (TRLN)
US: North Carolina	University of North Carolina System (LILAC)
US: Ohio	Ohio Library and Information Network (OhioLINK)
US: Ohio	Ohio Public Library Information Network (OPLIN)
US: Ohio	OhioNET
US: Ohio	Southwestern Ohio Council for Higher Education (SOCHE)
US: Oregon	Orbis

APPENDIX (continued)

US: Oregon	Portland Area Library System (PORTALS)
US: Pennsylvania	Keystone Library Network (KLN)
US: Pennsylvania	PALINET
US: Pennsylvania	Pennsylvania Academic Library Consortium Inc. (PALCI)
US: Rhode Island	Association of Rhode Island Health Sciences Libraries (ARIHSL)
US: Rhode Island	Consortium of Rhode Island Academic & Research Libraries (CRIARL)
US: Rhode Island	Higher Education Library Information Network (HELIN)
US: Rhode Island	Rhode Island State Library
US: Tennessee	Nashville Area Library Alliance (NALA)
US: Tennessee	TENN-SHARE
US: Texas	Texas State Library and Archives Commission
US: Texas	TexShare
US: Texas	University of Texas System Knowledge Management Center (UTS KMC)
US: Utah	Utah Academic Library Consortium
US: Vermont	Vermont Resource Sharing Network
US: Virginia	Virtual Library of Virginia (VIVA)
US: Washington	Washington Research Library Consortium (WRLC)
US: Washington	Washington State Cooperative Library Project
US: Washington	Washington State Libraries Statewide Database Licensing Project
US: West Virginia	West Virginia Public and Private Academic Library System
US: Wisconsin	Southeastern Wisconsin Information Technology Exchange (SWITCH)
US: Wisconsin	WILS

Licensing Experiences in the Netherlands

Hans Geleijnse

SUMMARY. The licensing strategy of university libraries in the Netherlands is closely connected with university policies to develop document servers and to make research publications available on the Web. National agreements have been made with major publishers, such as Elsevier Science and Kluwer Academic, to provide access to a wide range of scientific information and to experiment with new ways of providing information and new business models. *[Article copies available for a fee from The Haworth Document Delivery Service: 1-800-HAWORTH. E-mail address: <getinfo@haworthpressinc.com> Website: <http://www.HaworthPress.com> © 2001 by The Haworth Press, Inc. All rights reserved.]*

KEYWORDS. Licensing strategy, document servers, business models, the Netherlands

In the world of libraries, publishers and scholarly information the Netherlands plays an important role due to a set of unique circumstances, which includes:

- thirteen universities, supported by a well-developed national library and IT infrastructure;

Hans Geleijnse is Director of Information Service and Systems, European University Institute, Florence, Italy (E-mail: hans.geleijnse@iue.it).

[Haworth co-indexing entry note]: "Licensing Experiences in the Netherlands." Geleijnse, Hans. Co-published simultaneously in *Journal of Library Administration* (The Haworth Information Press, an imprint of The Haworth Press, Inc.) Vol. 35, No. 1/2, 2001, pp. 167-173; and: *Libraries and Electronic Resources: New Partnerships, New Practices, New Perspectives* (ed: Pamela L. Higgins) The Haworth Information Press, an imprint of The Haworth Press, Inc., 2001, pp. 167-173. Single or multiple copies of this article are available for a fee from The Haworth Document Delivery Service [1-800-HAWORTH, 9:00 a.m. - 5:00 p.m. (EST). E-mail address: getinfo@haworthpressinc.com].

- a pro-active national library: de Koninklijke Bibliotheek in The Hague;
- a library automation company, Pica, created by a number of Dutch University Libraries, which has expanded to other European countries and was recently acquired by OCLC;
- the two largest publishers in the world: Elsevier Science and Kluwer;
- one of the largest subscription agents: Swets Blackwell.

Although this context has provided opportunities for co-operation and new initiatives in the area of digital library development, it has also been a theatre of discussion and discrepancies among the various players. Some years ago, Dutch libraries took a firm stand against the intended merger of Elsevier and Kluwer. Press releases from the Dutch libraries criticizing the continuous price increases of scholarly journals and announcing massive cancellations if this development would continue initiated a lively debate in Dutch newspapers and magazines (http://www.uba.uva.nl/en/projects/journals-pricing-ukb/policy.html).

As the librarian at Tilburg University in 1993, I negotiated the first site license agreement with Elsevier Science for all Elsevier journals to which the university subscribed. This was a significant step in the development of the digital library at Tilburg, although in retrospect, we were ignorant about many licensing aspects and not well focused on issues such as digital archiving and use in perpetuity. Many more bilateral agreements followed, and similar developments were initiated at many other institutions.

In spite of these bilateral agreements and much positive experience with the use of electronic information, it has been very difficult to arrive at national license agreements in the Netherlands due to the following issues:

- the discrepancy between the license agreements offered by the publishers and the "Licensing Principles" developed by Dutch and German libraries and launched in October 1997 (http://cwis.kub. nl/~dbi/english/license/licprinc.htm)
- the continuous price increases of printed journals, at outrageous percentages of between 12% and 20%, and the significant surcharge publishers wanted to add for electronic access
- the difficulties libraries faced in agreeing on terms, conditions, and strategy

- the problems librarians faced in institutions where important collections were managed and financed by the academic departments.

In spite of these differences, representatives of the Dutch universities and the Dutch publishers managed to solve most disagreements on licensing issues in 1998 and to allow experiments with electronic document delivery based on electronic journals.

In Spring 1999, the UKB, the umbrella body for all Dutch university libraries, de Koninklijke Bibliotheek and the library of the Koninklijke Academie van Wetenschappen, observed that while various publishers' licensing conditions had improved, the key issues related to pricing still applied.

The joint Dutch libraries concluded that they would have to continue a very rigorous cancellation policy if the current "journals crisis" were to continue. They also decided to have more fundamental discussions with the major STM publishers on the changing environment and the challenges of Internet publishing.

The libraries appointed a small negotiating team that developed a policy paper and started high-level discussions with eight publishers.

It was stressed that all Dutch universities were or soon would be engaged in supporting electronic publishing by their own researchers and in the development of document servers and open archives. These initiatives would stimulate fast, cheap and convenient access to the scientific output of the universities and facilitate scientific communication.

This development created the need to reconsider current business models in the relationship between universities, libraries and publishers. Publishers were long accustomed to dealing with universities and libraries as their customers and as consumers of "their information." The development of university-based document servers underscored the position of the universities as suppliers of information The universities emphasized that they would be prepared to pay a reasonable price for any real value the publishers might add to the electronic information that was or would become available on the Internet. An important first result of this approach was an agreement between the Dutch universities and Elsevier Science, signed in June 2000.

The press release announcing this development stressed that

in addition to the provision of Elsevier's scientific information, the purpose of the agreement is to work together to experiment with ways of providing scientific information through the use of information and communication technology. Universities are develop-

ing document servers on which scientists can make their working papers available. This may lead to changes in the distribution and business models that form the basis of scientific publishing. Experimenting with such changes also forms part of the agreement. It was agreed that the members of the UKB will, for a period of five years, have access to the full text of all Elsevier Science primary publications. (http://www.kub.nl/~dbi/english/license/es-ukb-p.htm)

Under this arrangement, the universities agreed to pay annually (for five years) a fixed low percentage for continued print subscription plus electronic access to all Elsevier titles. The percentage is in addition to the costs of the subscription package in the base year 2000.

In May 2001 a similar agreement was made with Kluwer Academic, and agreements with other publishers are also expected.

As a result of these agreements,

- all journals of the two most important publishers will become available in electronic form for all university students, professors and researchers, which will contribute to a better user service and to a better visibility for these journals.
- the price increases have been put under control. It is obvious that publishers cannot continue with double digit price increases if they would like to stay in business.
- the agreements create a stable situation in the relationship between libraries and publishers for five years which is very important in this transitional phase, allowing both parties to move toward new models and a new relationship.

However, an obvious consequence of a five-year agreement is that a part of the university budgets has been fixed and must be reserved to pay these major publishers.

This approach can only be justified if it is embedded in a broader library, or rather, university strategy.

LIBRARY STRATEGY AND CO-OPERATION WITH PUBLISHERS AND AGENTS

Perhaps even more important than the licensing agreements is the development of joint projects to explore new distribution and business models. The starting point for the Dutch university libraries is the need to serve new innovative ways of teaching, learning and research, making full use of new information technologies. All university libraries are currently engaged in the support of electronic publishing by researchers and students, and all are committed to the creation of document servers and open archives.

The libraries believe that currently many established journals are still needed for instruction and research–but not at any price. A key question is whether the experienced publishers can play a role in the selection, validation, certification and dissemination process in the future.

In general, all Dutch universities are determined to make their output available electronically, but are still prepared to pay publishers for added value.

Current experiments with respect to changes in the distribution and business models will clarify the path to pursue in the future. Two university based projects are relevant in this respect. The Roquade project–co-ordinated by the University of Delft, the University of Utrecht and the Royal Academy of Sciences–involves creating an infrastructure for organising, co-ordinating, supporting and facilitating the digital publishing process for individual authors as well as for structured editorial boards. Additionally, Roquade will also work together with learned societies and scientific publishers who seek to improve the process of scientific communication (http://www.roquade.nl).

The ARNO project–initiated by Tilburg University, the University of Twente and the University of Amsterdam–aims to develop and implement university document servers to make available the scientific output of the participating institutions. The infrastructure that will be developed should offer a good basis for the organisation of peer review, practised by scientists independently or outsourced to existing publishers. Key is that the scientific output from the universities needs to connect seamlessly to the digital learning environments (http:www.uba.uva.nl/en/projects.arno). There will be a close co-operation between these two projects.

UNIVERSITY STRATEGY WITH RESPECT TO PUBLISHING

The Dutch university libraries understand that their strategic plans should be embedded seamlessly in the university strategy with respect to publishing, quality control of research output, creation of learning environments. Librarians have stimulated the discussion, facilitated the access to information and electronic publishing by researchers, but the key to the future of scholarly publishing is in the hands of the authors and their employers.

The experiences in the Netherlands over the last few years have identified the following elements as critical to a successful university strategy with respect to electronic information and publishing:

1. core journals should be made available electronically through fair license agreements with publishers. The move to "electronic only" should be made as soon as practicable. Guarantees of digital archiving and preservation are imperative for decisions to cancel the print version, and some large national libraries, such as the Koninklijke Bibliotheek of the Netherlands, are currently demonstrating a strong commitment to address this issue by building up digital archives of electronic journals, theses and other electronic resources;
2. unreasonable price increases should be made public, faculty informed, and the cancellation of subscriptions stimulated if there is no proper balance between quality, relevance, use, and price;
3 support electronic publishing by university researchers and encourage the development of distributed document servers and open archives;
4 facilitate discussions on copyright and copyright transfer within the academic institution;
5. intensify international co-operation among universities with respect to these issues;
6. explore new ways of co-operation between universities, libraries, publishers and agents and continue to experiment with new business models.

University leaders are now committed to fostering new university strategies with respect to publishing and information provision. This is an important development, but the implication may be that future strategic decisions will no longer be taken by librarians, but by university leaders. Librarians will continue to take new joint international initiatives in the area of publishing and should see that they provide the university leaders with relevant information for high level strategic decisions.

FUTURE DEVELOPMENTS

Universities and libraries in the Netherlands have developed a rather balanced policy with respect to the changes in the area of scholarly scientific communication. New ways are being explored to improve the easy access to research publications and teaching materials that have been produced by public funding without eliminating the value that can be added by responsible publishers. It will be a great challenge to develop new business models and to determine whether there still will be a role for the current players. Experiments in the Netherlands will be important to monitor in this regard.

The Role of CAUL
(Council of Australian Libraries)
in Consortial Purchasing

Diane Costello

SUMMARY. The Council of Australian University Librarians, constituted in 1965 for the purposes of cooperative action and the sharing of information, assumed the role of consortial purchasing agent in 1996 on behalf of its members and associate organisations in Australia and New Zealand. This role continues to grow in tandem with the burgeoning of electronic publication and the acceptance of publishers of the advantages of dealing with consortia. The needs of the Australian university community overlap significantly with consortia in North America and Europe, but important differences are highlighted. *[Article copies available for a fee from The Haworth Document Delivery Service: 1-800-HAWORTH. E-mail address: <getinfo@haworthpressinc.com> Website: <http://www.HaworthPress.com> © 2001 by The Haworth Press, Inc. All rights reserved.]*

KEYWORDS. Consortia, electronic journals, acquisitions, university libraries

Diane Costello is Executive Officer, Council of Australian University Librarians (CAUL), P.O. Box 169, Australian National University, Canberra A.C.T. 2600, Australia (E-mail: diane.costello@anu.edu).

[Haworth co-indexing entry note]: "The Role of CAUL (Council of Australian Libraries) in Consortial Purchasing." Costello, Diane. Co-published simultaneously in *Journal of Library Administration* (The Haworth Information Press, an imprint of The Haworth Press, Inc.) Vol. 35, No. 1/2, 2001, pp. 175-179; and: *Libraries and Electronic Resources: New Partnerships, New Practices, New Perspectives* (ed: Pamela L. Higgins) The Haworth Information Press, an imprint of The Haworth Press, Inc., 2001, pp. 175-179. Single or multiple copies of this article are available for a fee from The Haworth Document Delivery Service [1-800-HAWORTH, 9:00 a.m. - 5:00 p.m. (EST). E-mail address: getinfo@haworthpressinc.com].

The Council of Australian University Librarians (CAUL) comprises the library directors of the 38 universities who are members of the AVCC (Australian Vice-Chancellors' Committee–the council of Australia's university presidents). CAUL was formally constituted in 1965, and opened a permanent office in Canberra in May 1995. As stated in its mission, CAUL is dedicated to improving access by the staff and students of Australian universities to the scholarly information resources that are fundamental to the advancement of teaching, learning and research. Through an expanding program of information dissemination, coordination and consortial acquisition of electronic information services, it offers members tangible evidence of the benefits of working together.[1]

Consortial acquisitions have become a major part of the office activities, although its beginning was essentially serendipitous. Trials of a range of new electronic services were conducted from 1994-6 under the auspices of the AVCC Datasets Working Group, funded by the Federal Government to, inter alia:

- enhance best practice in the use of available information resources;
- increase the cost effectiveness of access to information by sharing infrastructure costs and negotiating consortium prices.

Following the trials, members called for the central coordination of subscriptions to these new services. The CAUL Office was the obvious choice for this task.

For the purposes of consortial purchasing, CAUL also represents fourteen other higher education and government research organisations in Australia, New Zealand and Fiji under the CEIRC (CAUL Electronic Information Resources Committee) external participation program (http://www.caul.edu.au/datasets/ceirctor.htm#external). In June 1998, a half-time staff member was appointed to assist the Executive Officer specifically with the administration related to the program, e.g., collating responses and questions from members, keeping track of due dates of responses to offers and invoice payments, and handling all financial transactions related to subscriptions.

WHAT HAS CAUL BEEN ABLE TO ACCOMPLISH?

CAUL has completed agreements for 32 products on behalf of its members and CEIRC associates. Some were finalised only after a very lengthy negotiation process, and consequent changes to access conditions and pricing models.

Many more products have been investigated over the past 6 years, but were not taken up consortially for various reasons, the most common of which is the ultimate cost. Many are under current investigation (http://www.caul.edu.au/datasets/).

CAUL has endeavoured to find cost-sharing models which suit the different needs of the 38 CAUL universities, whose interests take priority over any other CEIRC participants. In the *Current Contents* model, now in its third year, the 35 subscribers are divided into four tiers according to FTE. ISI provides a data price, and interface prices are supplied separately by ISI, Gale, Ovid and SilverPlatter. The first half of the data cost is divided evenly among subscribers; the second half is divided according to the tiers; a top tier institution pays nearly twice as much as a bottom tier. Each subscriber chooses and pays for its selected interface. This model works well for a broad-based product which is affordable by most institutions.

Another experimental model involved an offer from Bell & Howell where a minimum contribution was required from each participant, and a minimum total was required from all participants for the *ProQuest5000* collection of full-text datasets. CAUL facilitated a "bidding" process whereby each potential participant nominated how much it was prepared to pay. The 40 participants bid either at, above or below their current expenditure on ProQuest databases in approximately equal numbers.

A third model involved *MathSciNet* whose pricing model allows new subscribers to be brought in at marginal cost. The CAUL approach is to reduce the cost for current subscribers by adding a premium to that marginal cost for new subscribers and sharing the "income" among the current subscribers.

ISSUES AND CHALLENGES FACED BY CAUL

The Australian university system is not like the American system, and negotiations often begin with the education of the publishers and their agents.

- Only one institution is entirely privately funded, and in a relatively low-taxed environment, government funding for universities (and subsequently their libraries) has declined in real terms.

- Only 16 universities are essentially single-campus, while many of the rest have campuses outside the same metropolitan area. Yet all the universities, and their libraries, operate with a single administration and a single budget, and most with one Class B IP address.[2] Pricing models which count the number of "sites" are rarely affordable and rarely accepted.
- Each university teaches a wide variety of courses in multiple disciplines at multiple levels. All offer PhDs in some, if not all, disciplines. FTE numbers range from 1,557 to 32,388 with the average around 14,000. Medicine and law are not independent schools within the university but "faculties" just like arts, science and commerce.

There is a wide disparity in collection size and collection budget. CAUL's goal is to make each agreement advantageous to large and small–this is a challenge. The current-spend model is great for small institutions, and of little or no advantage to large ones unless there is some cost-shifting within the group. The current spend model is adequate in the transition period while publishers work out their ongoing costs, however it is not sustainable and doesn't allow for changes in budgets or priorities or changes of disciplines.

The vagaries of monetary exchange rates create significant levels of budget uncertainty when 80-90% of acquisitions are sourced from Europe and North America. In October 1996, the exchange rate was AUD 1.0 = USD 0.8055 falling to as low as USD 0.5125 in November 2000. Pricing based on USD, including FTE-based, is a constant challenge.

Very few publishers have offices in Australia, so the decision-makers are usually located in the USA. Even when there are regional agents, they may be as far afield as Singapore, California and Bristol (UK). Time and again we have proved that face-to-face communication can shorten negotiations by months, if not years. In most cases, visits to Australia by the decision-makers are tied to the two main trade shows at the VALA (Victorian Association of Library Automation) and Online conferences. These are held biennially, but in alternate years, in Melbourne and Sydney respectively.

Since 1996, CAUL has finalised 32 agreements, 18 for full-text products, four for factual databases and the rest for bibliographic databases. Half the consortial subscriptions commenced in 2000 or later, reflecting the burgeoning of available electronic products, and the increasing willingness of publishers to deal with consortia. For 15 products, the billing is handled centrally via CAUL, often an indicator of whether or not the publisher has a local office or representing agent. The average number of participants in each agreement is 20, with the highest number (40) subscribing to ProQuest5000.

There are certainly significant financial benefits available to libraries from participation in consortial purchasing, either direct reductions in price or, more commonly, broader content for around the same price. Less direct benefits fall into the category of information flow–information for buyers about the product, terms and conditions, pricing, and information for the sellers about the subscriber, contact details, IP ranges and subscription preferences. Member libraries regularly direct vendors to CAUL, not primarily, I believe, to negotiate better pricing, but rather to spread the load of accumulating all the details associated with access to the product concerned.

In the past, libraries had only to decide on the content and price, now they also need to know licence conditions, interface options, access to back-files and archives, links to other full-text and bibliographic databases and trial access to the product. The information required to make such decisions is collected, collated and made available centrally, added to by the members themselves through questions to vendors via CAUL and through discussion on CAUL's *datasets* list.

Member libraries have different product requirements and different budgetary cycles. They are keen to increase access to full-text, but many prefer the option of title-level selection rather than packaged publisher products. There is no universally preferred time for considering new offers, undertaking product trials, finalising commitments. Various discussions to date about a structured process for soliciting and reviewing new products have resulted in the status quo, that is ad hoc initiation of the process by members or by vendors.

We will move where the industry moves, we will develop guidelines rather than rules, we will retain our flexibility and when we reach a critical mass in any area of consortial management we will decide whether to expand our operations or to outsource it. Share the information, spread the load–this is what CAUL does.

NOTES

1. More, better, cheaper: the impossible dream, by Diane Costello. *Information Technology and Libraries* v.18 n.3 Sept 1999 154-160.

2. It is often not possible to limit access to a department or faculty, or even building, simply by IP address. We prefer to use the university's Class B address (555.555.*.*).

The UK's National Electronic Site Licensing Initiative (NESLI)

Hazel Woodward

SUMMARY. In 1998 the UK created the National Electronic Site Licensing Initiative (NESLI) to increase and improve access to electronic journals and to negotiate license agreements on behalf of academic libraries. The use of a model license agreement and the success of site licensing is discussed. Highlights from an interim evaluation by the Joint Information Systems Committee (JISC) are noted and key issues and questions arising from the evaluation are identified. *[Article copies available for a fee from The Haworth Document Delivery Service: 1-800-HAWORTH. E-mail address: <getinfo@haworthpressinc.com> Website: <http://www.HaworthPress. com> © 2001 by The Haworth Press, Inc. All rights reserved.]*

KEYWORDS. Consortia, site licensing, e-resources, NESLI, usage statistics, ICOLC, JISC

The UK's National Site Licensing Initiative (NESLI)[1] began in 1998. In its first phase, it is a three year project funded by the Joint Informa-

---

Hazel Woodward is University Librarian and Director, Cranfield University Press, Cranfield University, Cranfield, Bedfordshire, MK43 OAL, England (E-mail: h.woodward@ cranfield.ac.uk).

[Haworth co-indexing entry note]: "The UK's National Electronic Site Licensing Initiative (NESLI)." Woodward, Hazel. Co-published simultaneously in *Journal of Library Administration* (The Haworth Information Press, an imprint of The Haworth Press, Inc.) Vol. 35, No. 1/2, 2001, pp. 181-186; and: *Libraries and Electronic Resources: New Partnerships, New Practices, New Perspectives* (ed: Pamela L. Higgins) The Haworth Information Press, an imprint of The Haworth Press, Inc., 2001, pp. 181-186. Single or multiple copies of this article are available for a fee from The Haworth Document Delivery Service [1-800-HAWORTH, 9:00 a.m. - 5:00 p.m. (EST). E-mail address: getinfo@haworthpressinc.com].

181

tion Systems Committee (JISC)[2]–the body which oversees the information systems and technology requirements of the UK's higher and further education funding councils. The major aims of NESLI are:

- to increase and improve access to electronic journals (e-journals)
- to negotiate value for money deals for e-journals

HOW DOES NESLI WORK?

NESLI might best be described as a "loose" consortia of academic libraries. The NESLI consortia originally consisted of over 180 UK higher education libraries. However, from 2001, the consortia has expanded to include all further education libraries, bringing the total number of potential members to over 300. Negotiation with publishers to date have been carried out on behalf of approximately 120 higher education institutions, but this number is set to increase significantly as further education institutions are included in the negotiations. However, it is important to note that agreements are brokered on an individual library "opt-in" basis. Currently, some 50 institutions have signed up to one or more of the NESLI offers and 70 have expressed an interest and participated in trials of one or more agreements.

The strategic aims of NESLI are set by and for librarians through the NESLI Steering Group, comprised of eight senior academic librarians and three JISC support staff. The initiative forms part of the wider JISC Distributed National Electronic Resource (DNER) strategy[3] which is a managed learning environment for accessing quality assured, electronic information resources, available from a wide variety of sources. These resources include scholarly journals, monographs, textbooks, abstracts, manuscripts, maps, music scores, still images, geospatial images, as well as moving picture and sound collections. Since its inception in 1996 the DNER has established considerable pace and momentum with the creation of a DNER programme management team, and award of some $20,000,000 in funding for projects and services in tailoring services for use in learning and teaching.

The day-to-day operations of NESLI are undertaken by the Managing Agent. The Managing Agent–a consortium of the University of Manchester and Swets and Zeitlinger–was appointed in May 1998, after open European procurement. The role of the Managing Agent is to: negotiate value for money licenses with scholarly publishers; handle subscriptions to e-journals; provide a single interface for access to e-journals; address the technical issues surrounding authentication; and encourage the widespread acceptance of a standard Model Site License which is based on the Publishers Association/JISC Model License.[4]

Following initial negotiations by the Managing Agent with publishers–which can be lengthy and involve a number of meetings–offers are considered by the Steering Group. They are evaluated and assessed using a software package specially commissioned by NESLI from the Library and Information Statistical Unit based at Loughborough University. The software is a modelling programme which runs each offer through a range of different types of library budgets representing small, medium and large academic institutions in order to assess the economic outcomes. After this process, it is certainly not unknown for initial offers to be returned to the publisher by the Steering Group for further negotiation!

Assessing the value for money of each offer has proved much more difficult and complex than was first envisaged by the Steering Group. In many cases value for money has been dependant upon the size of the individual institution and the number of journals already subscribed to in print format. In addition, the financial outcome for individual institutions frequently depends on whether they are prepared to cancel printed journals and move to electronic-only provision. If such a decision is taken then savings can certainly be made.

It has also proved difficult to compare offers from each publisher. If there has been one constant in NESLI deals it is that each publisher has produced a different economic model for its offer! The spreadsheet used by the Steering Group to compare the financial basis of each deal grows larger by the day and includes such factors as:

- individual titles or all titles
- electronic only or combined with print
- content fee
- platform fee
- national entry fee
- cross access
- discount on print
- cancellations allowed
- minimum spend/number of sites
- length of agreement

Once the Steering Group is convinced that the best possible agreement has been negotiated with the publisher, the Managing Agent sends out information to the community via an email list. Each institution has a nominated NESLI representative whose task it is to receive and disseminate information about offers to colleagues within their own institution. Each offer is then evaluated according to local circumstances and orders placed as appropriate.

The Managing Agent produces a regular, electronic *NESLI Newsletter* and convenes a NESLI Advisory Group, comprising representatives from the library, intermediary and publishing communities.

WHAT HAS BEEN ACHIEVED SO FAR?

By February 2001, institutions had been offered e-journal agreements from 17 publishers: American Chemical Society; Association of Computing Machinery; Blackwell Publishers; Blackwell Science/Munksgaard; CABI Publishing; CRC Press; Elsevier Science; Internet Archaeology; Kluwer Academic; Mary Ann Liebert; MCB University Press; MIT Press; National Research Council, Canada; Oxford University Press; Project MUSE; and Sage Publications. Offers from the American Physical Society, John Wiley and Springer Verlag are currently being considered by the Steering Group. In addition, the Managing Agent is in active negotiation with many other journal publishers–including some of the major international scholarly publishers not listed above.

Further areas where significant progress has been made are, firstly, the adoption of the Model License by publishers. Unsurprisingly, the most contentious clause in the license relates to electronic interlibrary loan provision. Nevertheless, the vast majority of publishers offering NESLI deals have agreed to use the Model License. A second area concerns use/usage statistics for both libraries and publishers. Reports which have been identified as most useful include: data organised by publisher and then alphabetically by journal title showing hits at table of contents, abstract and full-text levels; and all journals sorted by number of full text accesses. The NESLI Steering Group also has representatives on another JISC/Publishers Association committee, whose aim is to produce guidelines for use statistics for e-journals. This committee is working in close collaboration with the International Coalition of Library Consortia (ICOLC) working group which is currently updating the *ICOLC Guidelines for Statistical Measures of Usage of Web-Based Indexed, Abstracted and Full Text Resources,*[5] as well as the Association of Research Libraries E-Metrics initiative.

Other NESLI initiatives under active development include the provision of MARC records and negotiations with a range of publishers to develop subject clusters of e-journals. Trial MARC records have been available from the Managing Agent since November 1999 and work is ongoing on the first of the subject clusters–political science–building on the success of the Electronic Libraries Programme SuperJournal Project in this area.[6]

WHERE DO WE GO FROM HERE?

Towards the end of 2000 the JISC commissioned an interim evaluation of NESLI by HUSAT, an Institute based at Loughborough University, specialising in research and consultancy in the human factors aspects of advanced technology. Feedback from this interim evaluation demonstrates that librarians are convinced that the UK higher and further education community stands to benefit from single national negotiation for e-journals. What is also clear is that publishers feel that they too stand to benefit from single national negotiations for e-journals. The cost of handling multiple negotiations is eliminated, there is potential to develop a bigger share of the journals marketplace, and publishers participating in NESLI have a direct connection to (and therefore an ability to influence) national policy on electronic information resources.

There is little doubt that NESLI is gathering momentum–as demonstrated by the number of publishers currently in negotiation with the Managing Agent and the number of libraries accepting the offers. However, the Steering Group is under no illusions that NESLI has got it all right. The interim evaluation makes it clear that various stakeholders have concerns about the current and future impact of the NESLI model. Some librarians and publishers are concerned that NESLI has created a virtual monopoly, both as regards the access front-end (SwetsNet) and as regards the source through which they must acquire their electronic subscriptions. Subscription agents articulate similar concerns arguing that separating the role of negotiation with publishers from the role of supplying the service could overcome this problem.

These specific issues and a range of wider questions relating to the dissemination of journal content are currently being addressed by the Steering Group as the first phase of NESLI comes to an end in 2001. A draft *JISC 3-Year Collection Strategy for the DNER* has recently been issued and this identifies eight key collecting areas as priorities–journals, books, discovery tools, geospatial resources, images, learning materials, moving pictures and sound, and primary research data. Working Groups have been set up to oversee each of these collecting areas and NESLI will migrate to the Journals Working Group.

In the meantime, the NESLI Steering Group is having discussions with a wide range of e-journal stakeholders. Questions being addressed include: How long will libraries be prepared to pay for dual (print and electronic) delivery? In the short term, do libraries wish to "cherry pick" individual journal titles from publishers lists or are they prepared to pay a small premium to acquire the entire journal output of a publisher? How quickly (or not) will e-journals become the main vehicle of journal information provision? What are the economic consequences for libraries and publishers of a large scale move to "pay per view"? What about archiving? Will the concept of the journal issue survive in the medium to long term?

New economic models for the delivery of journal content clearly need to be tested and NESLI believes that it can be a major catalyst in this process. To this end, the Steering Group will be continuing discussions with a range of stakeholders on how the new NESLI contract will be framed and how the various activities might be undertaken to provide best service and value-for-money to the academic community. Priorities for the coming year will be to undertake renewals of existing offers, negotiate new offers with a number of targeted publishers, and to migrate negotiations for databases and datesets to the new Journals Working Group.

NOTES

1. NESLI: www.nesli.ac.uk/.
2. JISC: www.jisc.ac.uk/.
3. DNER Strategy document: www.jisc.ac.uk/pub99/dner_vision.html.
4. Model NESLI Site License: www.nesli.ac.uk/ModelLicence8a.html.
5. ICOLC Guidelines: www.library.yale.edu/consortia/webstats.html.
6. SuperJournal project: www. Superjournal.ac.uk/sj/.

The Canadian National Site Licensing Project

Deb deBruijn

SUMMARY. In January 2000, a consortium of 64 universities in Canada signed a historic inter-institutional agreement that launched the Canadian National Site Licensing Project (CNSLP), a three-year pilot project aimed at bolstering the research and innovation capacity of the country's universities. CNSLP tests the feasibility of licensing, on a national scale, electronic versions of scholarly publications; in its initial phases the project is focused on full-text electronic journals and research databases in science, engineering, health and environmental disciplines. This article provides an overview of the CNSLP initiative, summarizes organizational and licensing accomplishments to date, and offers preliminary observations on challenges and opportunities for subsequent phases of the project. *[Article copies available for a fee from The Haworth Document Delivery Service: 1-800-HAWORTH. E-mail address: <getinfo@haworthpressinc.com> Website: <http://www.HaworthPress.com> © 2001 by The Haworth Press, Inc. All rights reserved.]*

KEYWORDS. Consortia, consortium, Canada, academic libraries, site licensing, electronic journals, CNSLP

Deb deBruijn is Executive Director, Canadian National Site Licensing Project, University of Ottawa Library Network, 65 University Street, P.O. Box 450, Stn. A, Ottawa, Ontario, Canada K1N 6N5 (E-mail: debruijn@uottawa.ca).

[Haworth co-indexing entry note]: "The Canadian National Site Licensing Project." deBruijn, Deb. Co-published simultaneously in *Journal of Library Administration* (The Haworth Information Press, an imprint of The Haworth Press, Inc.) Vol. 35, No. 1/2, 2001, pp. 187-193; and: *Libraries and Electronic Resources: New Partnerships, New Practices, New Perspectives* (ed: Pamela L. Higgins) The Haworth Information Press, an imprint of The Haworth Press, Inc., 2001, pp. 187-193. Single or multiple copies of this article are available for a fee from The Haworth Document Delivery Service [1-800-HAWORTH, 9:00 a.m. - 5:00 p.m. (EST). E-mail address: getinfo@haworthpressinc.com].

OVERVIEW

In January 2000, a consortium of 64 universities in Canada signed an historic inter-institutional agreement that launched the Canadian National Site Licensing Project (CNSLP), a three-year pilot project aimed at bolstering the research and innovation capacity of the country's universities. CNSLP tests the feasibility of licensing, on a national scale, electronic versions of scholarly publications, and in its initial phases is focused on full-text electronic journals and research databases in science, engineering, health and environmental disciplines.

The objectives of CNSLP are three-fold:

* *Capacity building:* to increase the quantity, breadth and depth of published scholarly content available to academic researchers throughout Canada, thereby building a rich and multidisciplinary milieu to underpin world-class research;
* *Transforming the content environment:* to speed the transition from print-based to digital and value-added forms of scholarly content, thereby maximizing the use and utility of that content for researchers;
* *Influencing the marketplace:* to leverage Canadian universities' buying power and influence in the international scholarly publishing marketplace, achieving advantageous terms and conditions for usage and developing new business and service models.

By applying an innovative cost-sharing model based on the research intensity of participating institutions, CNSLP amassed Cdn$30 million from university and provincial government sources. The project secured an additional Cdn$20 million from the Canada Foundation for Innovation[1] by demonstrating that systematic access to published research constitutes an integral component of Canada's research infrastructure. Following the three-year pilot phase, the initiative will continue with funding commitments from participant institutions.

WHY A NATIONAL STRATEGY?

The benefits of collaborative licensing of information resources have been demonstrated in Canada at the provincial and regional levels, most commonly through consortia of academic libraries within the same educational/political jurisdictions.[2] However, the relatively small size of the Canadian academic community, low per-capita level of research funds available, and volatility of currency exchange rates continue to disadvantage Canadian scholars and institutions, in terms of their influence and buying power in the international marketplace. For Canada to improve its capacity for research output in this environment, innovative strategies that work across jurisdictions are critical. New organizational, business and scholarly communication models must be developed over the long term to meet researchers' information needs, even as practical and transitional strategies for securing electronic journals and databases are implemented in the short term.

CNSLP represents such strategies. The project brings together universities in Canada across ten provinces, two official languages (French and English), and diverse degree and program offerings, and puts in place a national foundation for acquiring scholarly research content in digital formats. The 64 institutions that currently participate in CNSLP include all research universities offering degrees at the Masters and Doctoral level as well as the vast majority of institutions offering Baccalaureate degrees, and represent over 650,000 full-time equivalent faculty, graduate students and undergraduates.[3] The CNSLP model is inclusive; that is, participant universities are committed to licensing a broad portfolio of research content from multiple vendors, with resources acquired available equally to all participants. It is anticipated that additional institutions, such as two-and four-year colleges, will be invited to join the project as implementation proceeds.

ORGANIZATIONAL MILESTONES

In its first year of operation, CNSLP established a national governance and management structure, with stakeholder representation from university libraries, administrators, researchers, and associations. Key committees include a Steering Committee, responsible for project direction, policy development, and resource allocation; a Negotiations Resource Team, responsible for development of the license procurement process, vendor proposal evaluation, and recommendation of contract terms to the Steering Committee; and an Evaluation Task Group, charged with developing means to track and assess the project's impact.

The University of Ottawa, Canada's largest bilingual university, was designated as agent for the consortium and CNSLP's administrative headquarters. CNSLP staff include a full-time executive director and part-time administrative assistant; two additional staff positions (technical manager and communications director) will be filled in 2001. Specialized legal, translation and procurement services have been secured through the use of contract personnel.

LICENSE PROCUREMENT PROCESS AND RESULTS

In March 2000, the Steering Committee approved a formal license procurement process, driven by two requirements: (a) to secure the best value of electronic content within the budget available, and (b) to ensure a fair opportunity for vendors. The process was designed to break new ground with scholarly publishers, introduce as much competition as possible among vendors, and "push the envelope" on emerging service and business issues in the networked environment. At the same time, the process had to comply with interprovincial and international trade regulations, navigate the complexities posed by a diverse range of publishers, electronic products, and researcher/library requirements, and demonstrate sound decision-making that could stand up to scrutiny by CNSLP participants, funders, and vendors.

The license procurement process consisted of three components:

- an open call to vendors through a Pre-Qualification Bid, to elicit general content, functionality, technical and pricing information from vendors;
- a detailed Request for Proposal (RFP) issued to vendors who met the pre-qualification criteria;
- negotiations with vendors in ranked order according to results of the RFP evaluation.

A draft CNSLP model license agreement, developed by the Negotiations Resource Team and endorsed by the Steering Committee, was an important part of the RFP. This document was based on an international model developed for academic consortia by John Cox Associates[4] and revised to reflect CNSLP's operating principles and organizational structure as well as the Canadian legal context. Inclusion of the draft model license agreement with the RFP requirements allowed CNSLP to evaluate bidders on how closely they would comply with terms and conditions advantageous to Canadian universities, to anticipate potentially complex license issues, and to shorten the negotiations period following RFP evaluation.

Altogether, 42 vendors submitted pre-qualification bids. A priority group of 23 full-text and sole-source content providers were identified and invited to respond to the RFP; CNSLP received proposals from 21 of the 23 invited bidders by the September 14, 2000 closing date. One vendor subsequently withdrew its proposal, leaving CNSLP with 20 bids for evaluation.

Vendor proposals were scored and evaluated according to a formal methodology specified in the RFP. This proved to be an excellent way for CNSLP to take a large number of technical and customer support dimensions into account, and to ensure due diligence in the assessment of vendors as full service, and not merely content, providers. Scoring criteria included vendor capability, technical support, content and interface, licensing approach, usage information reporting capabilities, and annual price increase limits. An additional dimension–institutional demand for the products/services–was derived from ranking surveys submitted by participant libraries. These rankings were factored into the evaluation following scoring of the other RFP criteria.

Finally, financial information was folded into the evaluation. A *value proposition* for each bid was devised, by dividing the proposed 3-year price of the product by the number of articles to be provided (including backfile coverage as well as the current-year offering), and divided again by the total score from the RFP evaluation. This resulted in a ratio for each bidder that allowed comparison across products, and identified those proposals that represented the highest value for each CNSLP purchasing dollar.

An intensive period of negotiations with vendors, in the order of their value proposition, took place from November 2000 to January 2001. By February 2001, CNSLP had issued letters of intent to seven vendors,[5] resulting in access for participants to over 700 full-text journals, two reviewing journals, and three citation indexes, pending finalization of license agreements. All retained vendors agreed to sign the CNSLP model license agreement, offer three-year agreements priced in Canadian dollars, and unbundle their pricing models so as to offer electronic access to their full content suite through CNSLP, with no obligation on the part of participating institutions to maintain print subscriptions.

PRELIMINARY OBSERVATIONS AND LESSONS LEARNED

As a pilot project, the CNSLP is by nature pragmatic and iterative. The project is deliberately focused in its initial scope to allow all parties to gain experience, explore critical issues, apply lessons learned, and develop the means to extend the initiative over time.

Working on a national scale has involved significant challenges in terms of product evaluation, decision-making, accountability and communication far beyond the challenges facing smaller or more homogenous groups of institutions. Clearly, the results of this effort must be of sufficient magnitude and benefit to warrant the time, complexity and cost of the process.

Early indicators of CNSLP's results are highly encouraging in this regard. First of all, creating a large, inclusive group of participating institutions who were willing to commit funds to a national process proved singularly effective in attracting significant new funds from federal and provincial sources, and in positioning academic libraries as strategic partners in the national agenda of strengthening Canada's research capacity. The formal procurement process adopted by CNSLP, coupled with an unprecedented opportunity for publishers to expand their markets, created a competitive environment among vendors that proved advantageous to the academic sector. Scholarly publishers, who traditionally may have little incentive to compete, found that CNSLP's highly-structured procurement process was anything but "business as usual." Instead, vendors were required to demonstrate both superior quality of service (including content, access, support, account management, and contractual terms and conditions), as well as aggressive and strategic pricing, if they were to win the right to enter into negotiations with CNSLP. At the same time, the stability and predictability the consortium could offer in the way of high-volume, multi-year agreements served to mitigate risks for vendors and universities. As a result, vendors were able to trim their pricing margins, make strategic shifts in their business and service models, and align their contractual terms and conditions with CNSLP requirements.

A pilot project can be expected to raise more questions and issues than answers, and within the complex world of scholarly publishing and communication, CNSLP will be no exception. To be sure, CNSLP faces major technological, financial, organizational and political challenges in its subsequent phases, that are related both to the national scale of the operation as well as to local issues of implementation and integration within its member universities. On one hand, CNSLP is a pragmatic and transitional approach to the current environment, leveling the playing field for researchers across the country and speeding the take-up of digital forms of scholarly content. More significantly, however, "proof of concept" of the pilot project may lie in the active collaboration among scientists, administrators, librarians, publishers, aggregators and granting agencies that is required to reshape scholarly communication processes in our networked future.

NOTES

1. See: www.innovation.ca.
2. In Canada, responsibility for education and university funding falls under provincial government jurisdiction.
3. A list of participating institutions may be found at: www.uottawa.ca/library/cnslp/docs/CNSLP_participants_may00.pdf.
4. See: www.licensingmodels.com.
5. Vendors/products retained by CNSLP through this process include Academic Press IDEAL, American Chemical Society Web Editions, American Mathematical Society MathSciNet, ISI Web of Science, Institute of Physics Publishing Journals, Royal Society of Chemistry Electronic Journals, and Springer-Verlag LINK.

TRANSFORMING TEACHING AND LEARNING

Library Services Today and Tomorrow: Lessons from iLumina, a Digital Library for Creating and Sharing Teaching Resources

David McArthur

Bill Graves

Sarah Giersch

SUMMARY. This article is based on the emerging experience associated with a digital library of instructional resources, iLumina, in which the contributors of resources and the users of those resources are the

David McArthur is Senior Consultant, Eduprise Inc., 2000 Perimeter Park Drive, Suite 160, Morrisville, NC 27560 (E-mail: dmcarthur@eduprise.com).

Bill Graves is Chairman and Founder, Eduprise Inc. (E-mail: wgraves@eduprise.com).

Sarah Giersch is Consultant, Eduprise Inc. (E-mail: sgiersch@eduprise.com).

This work, still in a preliminary phase, was funded as part of the NSF DLI-Phase 2, grant #0002935.

[Haworth co-indexing entry note]: "Library Services Today and Tomorrow: Lessons from iLumina, a Digital Library for Creating and Sharing Teaching Resources." McArthur, David, Bill Graves, and Sarah Giersch. Co-published simultaneously in *Journal of Library Administration* (The Haworth Information Press, an imprint of The Haworth Press, Inc.) Vol. 35, No. 1/2, 2001, pp. 195-217; and: *Libraries and Electronic Resources: New Partnerships, New Practices, New Perspectives* (ed: Pamela L. Higgins) The Haworth Information Press, an imprint of The Haworth Press, Inc., 2001, pp. 195-217. Single or multiple copies of this article are available for a fee from The Haworth Document Delivery Service [1-800-HAWORTH, 9:00 a.m. - 5:00 p.m. (EST). E-mail address: getinfo@haworthpressinc.com].

same–an open community of instructors in science, mathematics, engineering, and technology. Moreover, it is not the resources, most of which will be distributed across the Internet, but metadata about the resources that is the focus of the central iLumina repository and its support services for resource contributors and users. The distributed iLumina library is a community-sharing library for repurposing and adding value to potentially useful, mostly non-commercial instructional resources that are typically more granular in nature than commercially developed course materials. The experience of developing iLumina is raising a range of issues that have nothing to do with the place and time characteristics of the instructional context in which iLumina instructional resources are created or used. The issues instead have their locus in the democratization of both the professional roles of librarians and the quality assurance mechanisms associated with traditional peer review. *[Article copies available for a fee from The Haworth Document Delivery Service: 1-800-HAWORTH. E-mail address: <getinfo@haworthpressinc.com> Website: <http://www.HaworthPress.com> © 2001 by The Haworth Press, Inc. All rights reserved.]*

KEYWORDS. Digital libraries, library automation, metadata, standards, interoperability, user issues, reusable software, distributed systems

INTRODUCTION: THE E-LEARNING CONTEXT

The Internet changes everything. Indeed. But purposeful, enterprise change in higher education is difficult to achieve when, in the general absence of change management processes, the rapid pace of technological change too often leads to random acts of progress. Consider the use of the Internet in instruction–*e-learning*. Anyplace-anytime (virtual) technologies are increasingly used to remove friction from the instructional process, both for learners and instructors. The resulting convenience can even be used to replace traditional classroom instruction with *virtual* (anyplace-anytime) instruction–the most place-and time-independent form of distance education (Graves, 2000). But convenient instruction, whether virtual or traditional, is not necessarily quality instruction. The most important metric for the quality of instruction should focus on learning outcomes. Yet many instructors are worrying instead about the ownership of the online course materials they develop, as though course materials determine the quality and value of the courses they teach, a premise worthy of a brief counterargument below and a reference to a more detailed analysis elsewhere (see Twigg (2000) for ideas on course ownership).

If course materials were the primary basis for quality in instruction, then there likely would be no instructor in the instructional compact between student and institution. Traditional institutions presumably would not have organized courses around the classroom model of instruction. Instead, they would have avoided classroom construction in favor of sending the student to a special library/bookstore for access to a course-based self-study environment comprised of (1) notes, materials, and syllabi developed by the faculty expert(s) responsible for the student's course and (2) commercial textbooks, other commercially published instructional materials, and non-commercial, informally published materials selected by, but not developed by, those faculty expert(s). In this model, there either would be no instructors or instructors would have little contact with their students. But there has been important and direct instructor/student contact in the traditional classroom model of instruction.

Examining the overall roles of the instructor in traditional instruction will shed light on the roles of the instructor in e-learning–and on the functions of instructor-developed shareable instructional resources. Consider the roles sketched in Table 1.

Using the Internet in instruction does not generally eliminate the instructor's obligation to spend time on these four roles. Concerning, for instance, the third item above, by tapping the power of the Internet as a revolution in human communication, e-learning provides new and convenient ways to accomplish many of the learning goals associated with organizing discussions by replacing or supplementing the classroom as the locus for interactive, collaborative learning among students and instructors. And, in the case of virtual instruction in which there is no classroom as a safety net for that interaction, the effective practice of encouraging and enabling interactive, collaborative learning is arguably the most important contribution of the instructor to the quality of instruction.

Similarly, e-learning does not eliminate the other responsibilities in the above list, but it can change the way those responsibilities are fulfilled. In this regard, the first item on the instructor's selection and refinement of instructional resources deserves reflection. But first note in the context of instructional resources that the four primary responsibilities do not include either (1) publishing a commercially viable textbook or other course materials or (2) developing or using non-commercial in-

TABLE 1. Roles in Traditional and Traditional Instruction and E-Learning

Instructors:

1. select and supplement/interpret a "published" expression of the course's knowledge base–a published expression that is typically developed and copyrighted by others;

2. guide and sequence students' self-study-by advising, tutoring, and developing a syllabus to assign readings, papers, projects, learningware, tests, and so on;

3. organize and facilitate discussions and other group activities to encourage collaborative, interactive learning in the context of creating and sustaining a learning community specific to a course or a collection of related courses; and

4. critique, measure (grade), and report their students' progress within an institutional or inter-institutional process that allows the appropriate institution(s) to award credentials certifying students' individual accomplishments.

structional materials designed for external use on a broad inter-institutional scale. Few instructors have ever been involved in such activities. Does the Internet change this? No to the first activity, and yes to the second.

No, the Internet is not likely to change substantively the percentage of instructors who commercially "publish" comprehensive instructional materials. Yet the Internet will become a native medium for developing *learningware* as a superior digital replacement for the textbook. (Learningware is a software application informed by research in learning theory to provide structured opportunities for active and even interactive learning.) Learningware allows active decision-making via simulations with parameters under the control of the learner(s), opportunities to create and/or interpret data, tutorial opportunities to react to spoken words or visual cues presented in a multimedia format, and so on. The development of learningware will require much more than subject matter expertise. So in parallel to the current relationship between instructors and textbooks, a few instructors will successfully participate in the development of commercially viable learningware, most likely as subject matter experts working with companies in the learningware business and their corps of technologists, graphics and animation experts, learning theorists, instructional designers, market researchers, and business experts.

Yes, the Internet is likely to change substantively the percentage of instructors who develop or use non-commercial instructional materials designed to encourage external use on a broad national or global inter-institutional scale. These materials will be digital, but unlike learningware, generally will not be designed as self-study materials covering the entirety of a course's knowledge base. They will include photos, graphs, animations, tools, and what many today are calling learning objects–mini-learningware applications covering or illuminating one specific item in the course syllabus. The Internet, as a revolution in resource sharing, permits the sharing of non-commercial digital instructional materials on a scale heretofore unprecedented, and this paper provides a glimpse into one such project, iLumina, and the issues that it is raising.

In pre-Internet terms, trying to share and maintain these non-commercial, informal instructional materials and tools beyond local boundaries or beyond a small grant-funded consortium created too much maintenance friction to justify the effort. Librarians occasionally could provide help in storing and indexing locally developed non-commercial course materials for intra-institutional use, but they could provide little help with such activities on an inter-institutional scale. But now that the Internet enables the inter-institutional sharing and maintenance of non-commercial instructional materials that are not professionally indexed, librarians' indexing and retrieval skills and perspectives are needed to support indexing and other aspects of the searching, retrieving, and updating processes that will fall to the faculty creators and users of such materials. So the Internet changes everything, not in this case by absolute disintermediation but by shifting the locus of mediation from librarians to instructors–a process of democratization. And in a similar manner, the organic, bottom-up inter-institutional sharing of instructor-created non-commercial instructional materials may democratize the review process, shifting its weight away from professionally organized reviews toward more spontaneous user reviews–other instructors as "consumers" utilizing variations of the review models made familiar by the likes of Amazon.com, e-Bay, and Zagat.com.

As in any revolution, democratization of indexing responsibilities and review responsibilities can be chaotic and unsuccessful in the absence of change management. That's why our description of iLumina, will purposefully raise issues that require the collaboration of instructors and librarians if the inter-institutional sharing of instructor-created non-commercial instructional materials and tools is to succeed. We will describe metadata protocols that support instructional communities wishing to index or retrieve non-commercial instructional materials in a way that can tame the wild, wild Web. Unlike the transition from commercial textbooks to commercial learningware, in which professionals will continue to index course materials and peer review will precede "publication" to the Web, the creation and maintenance of vast, distributed digital libraries of non-commercial instructional materials will require new approaches to indexing, reviewing, and adding value to such materials. Librarians will have to assist instructors in searching for and selecting these non-commercial instructional resources and, so, should strive to disintermediate their assistance by first contributing to instructor developers' ability to index such resources during the processes of development and use.

To set the stage for a discussion of these issues, which will occupy the second-half of this article, in the first sections we review in some depth the structure and organization of iLumina, our digital library.

A SKETCH OF iLUMINA

iLumina is a digital library of undergraduate teaching materials in science, mathematics, technology and engineering (SMETE) education that is being developed by Eduprise, The University of North Carolina at Wilmington (UNCW), Georgia State University, Grand Valley State, and Virginia Tech. Our experience suggests that faculty across the country have already created a wealth of digital resources for teaching–often small in scale, such as a well-crafted image–and are willing to share them. But they lack a repository where they can submit their materials, find related ones (without having to reinvent them), create new content (either individually or through collaboration), and, collectively, improve both the quantity and quality of digital teaching resources. iLumina will try to provide such a repository, and related user services.

ORGANIZATION OF iLUMINA:
COMPONENTS AND COMMUNITY ROLES

At least three architectural, descriptive and functional features distinguish iLumina from related digital library projects:

- *Partly distributed, partly centralized federation.* Viewed broadly, each digital library resource associated with iLumina has two components: the resource content itself and the metadata that describe the resource (see Figure 1 [A]). iLumina will actually be a library of *only the metadata* for each resource (Figure 1 [B]), while the content itself will be housed in various distributed content re-positories (Figure 1 [C]). iLumina will expect project partners that own these component repositories to manage their content, ensur-ing that all resources are preserved and that links remain valid and up-to-date. Component repositories can also offer their own user-services, in addition to providing data for iLumina. However, iLumina's main role will be to make the content of the federated repositories available through a centralized Web-based interface that includes a collection of user services which rely on a founda-tion of rich standardized metadata (Figure 1 [D]).

- *Resources described using IMS metadata.* Metadata descriptions can range from very informal notes, such as readers' opinions of books on Amazon.com, to the highly authoritative and standard-ized cataloging descriptions created by publishers and cataloging librarians (Dempsey and Heery, 1998; Gilliland-Swetland, 1998). The metadata structure for iLumina's digital resources permits de-scriptions at both ends of this spectrum. Furthermore, iLumina will need to describe, in a uniform way, large digital resources and small, chemistry and mathematics content, and simple pictures as well as complex simulations. To meet these expressive challenges, we have derived iLumina's metadata from the IMS (Instructional Management System) metadata specifications,[1] one of several ar-eas in learning in which the consortium is active (IMS, 2001).

- *Tools and supports for resource contributors as well as consum-ers.* The driving vision of iLumina is to provide a platform of con-tent and services that will dramatically improve the ability of fac-ulty to create, exchange and use educational materials, across a wide range of science, math and engineering disciplines. These re-sources will frequently be learning fragments, even single images, rather than large course segments. iLumina must therefore provide tools and services that motivate educators to create new resources from these pieces and submit them to the library, as well as offer a diverse collection of materials to the end-user communities that consume these resources.

ACQUISITION OF RESOURCES IN iLUMINA

Many bricks-and-mortar bookstores and libraries, and most online databases and digital libraries, emphasize the services and tools they provide their end-users–the consumers of their content. However, in the

FIGURE 1. Overview of iLumina Digital Library Components, Acquisition Processes and End-User Services

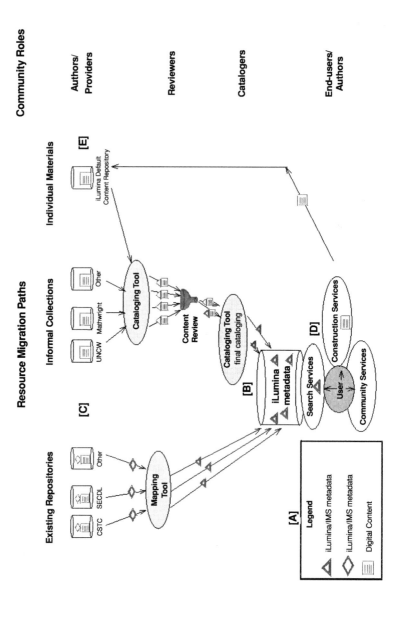

community-sharing model adopted by iLumina, end-users that consume library resources and educators that contribute and share them are one and the same. iLumina, therefore will provide many acquisition services as well as end-user tools.

Collections and Content: Multiple Migration Routes into iLumina

The general sequence of activities applied to digital resources that are submitted to iLumina is sketched graphically in Figure 1 and outlined in more detail in Table 2. The activities represent only a part of the full life cycle of a resource in a digital library; they do not include usage, preservation or archival services, but rather emphasize the initial acquisition processes.

Viewed broadly, Table 2 says that every entry in the centralized iLumina library must be a complete IMS metadata record, its associated

TABLE 2. Overview of iLumina Submission Process

1. Author/provider creates a piece of digital content

2. Author/provider uses a Web-based *cataloging tool* to create initial metadata, including title, a unique link (URI) to the location of the resource content, and several other basic elements that describe the resource content, then attaches the metadata to the resource content, and submits the pair (collectively, the resource) to iLumina

3. iLumina *catalogers*, also using the cataloging tool, augment initial or author metadata, adding elements such as technical format and educational resource-type, and save the record

4. iLumina *editors* send the resource, including metadata, out for peer review

5. *Reviewers* provide content review for the resource, again using a version of the cataloging tool to augment the metadata record with review information

6. The resource is either accepted into iLumina or rejected (if rejected, the author may modify and resubmit, along with the original metadata record)

7. Accepted resources are subjected to a *final cataloging*, further enhancing the metadata

8. The metadata record for an accepted resource is *added* to iLumina; at this time it is accessible to *end-users* who browse or search the library

9. If the resource content associated with a submitted and accepted resource is **not** already resident in a repository, it is placed in the *iLumina default content repository* (Figure 1 [E]); otherwise, iLumina does nothing further with the content itself, and it remains in its original, distributed repository

Note: This Table references the basic tools and community members involved in the submission process, as well as the general submission activities themselves.

resource content must have been reviewed for quality, and the resource content must be maintained in a distributed repository that is referenced in the resource metadata. However, because the resources in iLumina will come through one of several different migration routes (see paths diagrammed in Figure 1), this sequence of activities will be tailored, to reflect the needs of the different routes. Specifically:

1. *Existing repositories.* These materials already have metadata and have undergone review; the content of the resources is also already housed in a repository. Consequently, the path to add them to iLumina is simple: the metadata needs only to be translated by a *mapping tool* from its original format to the IMS-based metadata used by iLumina. Partners currently contributing previously-reviewed materials are the Computer Science Teaching Center (CSTC; http://www.cstc.org), and the ACM SIGGRAPH Education Committee's Digital Library (SECDL; http://www.education. siggraph.org). iLumina represents an additional distribution channel for such repositories.

2. *Informal collections.* As with formal existing repositories, the content of these collections will be maintained in their own content repositories. However we do not assume their materials will have been reviewed; iLumina will mange this process. Currently, most of these informal collections will come from faculty at UNC Wilmington, although developers from the CCP (http://www.math. duke.edu/education/ccp/) and Mathwright (http://www.mathwright. com) projects will also contribute. The resources in such collections may or may not already have metadata. In the case of our current partners, UNCW's collection does have metadata, which has been created "from scratch" using metadata cataloging tools that comply with the iLumina metadata specification; this metadata will not need additional transformation using a mapping tool. Other informal collections, however, may require mapping, or may need a full range of cataloging as well as review activities.

3. *Individual materials.* Finally, iLumina will encourage faculty authors of digital content and course materials to contribute their resources to iLumina. In some cases, such individuals will come to iLumina to submit their materials; however, in other cases iLumina might proactively seek their contributions. We assume resources provided by individual authors are likely to require the full range of acquisition activities, including metadata cataloging, review and management of their digital content in the default iLumina repository, as outlined in Table 1 and Figure 1 [E].

Tools for Adding Resources to iLumina

Since resources come to iLumina through various migration routes, and at differing degrees of readiness for inclusion in the library, it might seem that an extensive range of tools and services would be needed to create rich iLumina metadata records. However, as the preceding discussion suggests, a single common Web-based iLumina cataloging tool can underpin several of the author submission, cataloging and reviewing activities that collectively build these metadata. This is possible because all these activities create descriptions of a submitted resource in terms of iLumina's uniform IMS-based metadata specification. It is therefore relatively easy for a single flexible tool to be reconfigured to expose different metadata elements–and elicit input of their values–at different times.

In iLumina we will use such a flexible cataloging tool to get library community members to contribute metadata for the elements they should know best in the production-cycle of digital library content. For example, authors or creators will provide a title and description when a resource is submitted; reviewers can insert peer assessments; catalogers will add discipline-level classifications and perhaps a range of technical information; and elements such as submission date can be set automatically.

USE OF RESOURCES IN *iLUMINA*

iLumina's metadata will support end-user services, much as they underpin the acquisition tools used to catalog and review digital resources submitted to the library. Consider the basic user services of search and retrieval. This is a two-stage process, reflecting the library's partly distributed and partly centralized architecture:

- *Search.* End-users initiate searches of iLumina resources from a single centralized Web site. Queries are matched against all the metadata records that are contained in the iLumina library. Matching records are reported to users in the form of Web pages of results that will look similar to the lists returned by standard search engines–although the descriptions of each iLumina "hit" will be much richer than typical search results, since they will include all relevant resource metadata. All dialogue in this first-stage search takes place strictly between the end user (client) and the iLumina

metadata repository; only in stage-two retrieval do the distributed content repositories become involved.
* *Retrieval.* When users find a resource they want to retrieve, by reviewing its metadata description, they can request that iLumina retrieve the resource content. iLumina will honor the request by using the unique link to the content (the URI) embedded in the metadata to locate the resource, and then download the resource from the distributed content repository where it resides. Since the initial version of iLumina will include only free digital content, library users will be able to download digital copies of resources and reuse them without constraints–at least for personal, non-commercial purposes. In the future, as we begin to address subtle intellectual property-rights issues, this protocol may become complex, possibly resembling an e-commerce transaction more than a free download.

This two-stage search-and-retrieval process promises several benefits for end-users. The rich, uniform descriptions of iLumina resources can, at a minimum, improve the library users' ability to discover valuable digital resources. Even though searches and browsing through resources will be conducted centrally, through iLumina's Web front-end, users will, in effect, be exploring a federated collection of repositories. Each repository may have its own interface; iLumina users, however, will not need to learn these differing front-ends in detail (unless they choose to). Similarly, by standardizing metadata conventions, users will need to learn only one language for describing resources in the federation, relying on iLumina's automated harvesting and mapping of metadata from the distributed repositories to translate between the different terminologies. This should reduce the cognitive demands on users.

Extending iLumina Library Services

iLumina's standardized metadata not only support broad and powerful search engines, but can also be the basis for a "second tier" of user services in the library. We are still designing some of these; consequently we will only illustrate a few of the many possibilities (see McArthur et al. (2001) for more details and examples).

* *Directory and browsing services.* Many search services provide more than a simple query form for users. Yahoo, for example, also

presents its databases through structured directories that organize resources in a hierarchical collection of categories. This structure actually derives from the metadata that Yahoo wraps around each resource it catalogs. Our IMS-based metadata can be used to build a similar directory-oriented and browsable interface for iLumina end-users. For example, if a user wants to browse resources by subject, the controlled vocabularies (such as The Library of Congress Subject Headings) that are values for iLumina metadata elements would provide appropriate directory structures to guide browsing through a hierarchy of disciplines.

- *Flexible access to reviewed resources.* As noted, resources will be reviewed before admitted into iLumina. At this time, our reviewing procedures are not yet firmly established. However, we are seriously considering very open policies–for example, admitting all resources meet very minimal standards, or perhaps even including unreviewed or "rejected" materials. One reason for considering such policies is that peer reviews (or at least summaries of them) are represented in iLumina metadata. This can allow iLumina to, in effect, defer review policies to end-users. If users, for example, want to see only reviewed materials, they can instruct iLumina's search services to filter-out unreviewed resources, or ones that have poor reviews, before returning results.

- *Integrating formal reviews and informal ratings.* Representing reviews in metadata can benefit iLumina users in several additional ways. One is that end-users themselves can become reviewers. To implement this, we are planning to use the IMS "annotation" metadata element to allow users of iLumina resources to rate and comment on them–in effect, providing a "non-authoritative" (Amazon-style) level of reviews of library materials, to complement formal peer reviews.[2] Such ratings become, in effect, a user service provided not by iLumina staff, but by the user community itself.

- *Connecting library users.* Metadata are mostly viewed as a means to connect library users to the resources they need. However, the previous examples suggest they can also help connect users to one another. For instance, a library user might not only be able to gather information about the subject or technical format of a learning resource, but also learn about who has downloaded it, and how they rated it (for users who permit the sharing of such personal information). This is the foundation of several community-based tools iLumina is planning to offer. For one, the forums that our company, Eduprise, builds into online courses for clients (Graves,

1998; Hale & Nicolet, 1999) also provide an ideal medium for discussions among faculty who have connected to one another through iLumina resources. The online forums enable them, among other things, to collaborate on new materials, or to discuss effective classroom uses of online content. In this way, our community-based tools can at least begin to help digital libraries fulfill some of the important (but recently, it seems, very overlooked) social functions of their bricks-and-mortar counterparts.

LIBRARY SERVICES AND ADMINISTRATION ISSUES FOR iLUMINA

iLumina, like many digital library projects, is relatively new; consequently, we have little data on which to build solid claims about the future organization and structure of libraries. However, we believe iLumina does provide a distinctive perspective on several library service- and administrative-related issues relevant to libraries as they confront the digital age. The viewpoint is interesting not just because iLumina is a digital library, but also because it is a grassroots community, where, like the many burgeoning open-source exchanges, the producers of content or resources and the consumers are one and the same. In the following sections, we draw on these characteristics of iLumina to address three topics of broad importance to libraries, whether they are traditional organizations transitioning to (partially) digital ones, or ones born digital. All of the discussion is speculative. Nevertheless, we hope it can stimulate some "out of the box" thinking that libraries will need to engage in as they rethink their tools, services, functions and missions, in this time of disruptive technology and rapid organizational change.

DIGITAL LIBRARIES AND DISINTERMEDIATION

The digital revolution has spawned all sorts of speculations about the future of the academe and its allied institutions. One common view is that digital libraries–and the increasing use of network technologies in non-digital libraries–will make most human roles in library services unnecessary, or, to use an awkward but increasingly popular term, libraries will be "disintermediated."

Middlemen are, indeed, disappearing in virtually all sectors of the economy. Factories that once employed thousands can now turn out more steel than ever before, staffed with only a handful of employees. Staid investment firms are losing many of their clients to online broker- ages that put traders in direct contact with volumes of market informa- tion. And academic librarians have discovered that faculty and students prefer to conduct searches at terminals–often foregoing conversations with skilled professionals, even though they usually yield better results in less time.

One of the most well-known recent examples of disintermediation is Napster, a peer-to-peer exchange that puts consumers who want songs in direct contact with suppliers who already have them online (see Ta- ble 3), completely bypassing all middlemen (including musicians, pub- lishers and other copyright owners). The Napster model is not only technically simple to implement, but also has applications in many busi- nesses and areas where sharing is central, from movie trading to collab- orative research.

Not surprisingly, one such area is the research library. Daniel Chudnov (2000), among others, envisions a Napster-variant called Docster, which adapts the model of file sharing for use in interlibrary lending. A re- searcher looking for a (digital) article, for example, could use his Docster client to connect to his university Docster server, which in turn would search for the article through linked servers until it finds one that knows of a faculty member who has the article, at which point that fac- ulty member's Docster client would send a copy of the article back to the first researcher. Chudnov not only sketches this process, but also notes that the role of the library (servers) is minimal–and rightly won- ders why the researchers wouldn't create a work-around and bypass the libraries altogether.

But forgetting all the copyright problems (which Chudnov, in fact, does address), while this might happen in online libraries that house al- ready-published materials–well known by title, reviewed by peers, and produced and marketed by publishers–it cannot work in grassroots digi- tal libraries such as iLumina. The problem is not technical in nature, since it is no harder to connect the hard drives of faculty members to one another than it is to link together the machines of music aficionados. Rather, the difficulty is that the content in iLumina simply cannot be found by title. Users come to Napster knowing exactly what they want, thanks in part (as the recording industry insistently points out) to the ef- forts of music companies to find and promote works of high-quality art- ists. On the other hand, users come to iLumina knowing generally the kinds of digital resources they want, but rarely who might have created them, and almost never what they are called (if they have a title at all).

TABLE 3. Napster in a Nutshell

1. Download and install the Napster client application
   - This is the simple interface through which Napster members find songs stored on other "peer" machines

2. Create an account and select files and folders for sharing
   - This establishes a directory of MP3 songs that others can access on your machine

3. Start Searching
   - Think of a song title
   - Enter it on your Napster client utility
   - Napster connects you to a centralized Napster index server that keeps track of all clients now online
   - Your system queries the index server for clients that have, in their shared MP3 directories, the song you requested
   - The server replies and your Napster client build a list of these peer systems in its results window

4. Download selected files
   - In your results window click on the files (titles) that you want, then choose "download"
   - Your Napster attempts to create a direct connection to the host system and download the file

(Adapted from Napster for Windows: Getting Started http://www.napster.com/help/win/gettingstarted/)

All this means that the descriptive metadata associated with iLumina resources can play a critical role in search and retrieval (whereas, as Chudnov notes: "Funny how Napster doesn't care about dublin core or MARC"). But that, in turn, means that iLumina, although a fully digital library, could require more careful manual cataloging and resource management than many traditional libraries–not less. And this will require the expert touch of librarians along with some reviewing, editing, and marketing functions, at the very least (see Table 1 for a brief description of iLumina's diverse library roles). In many respects this is more than librarians do now, since traditionally they rely on publishers to carry out some of these activities. Now digital libraries like iLumina, as well as many eprint repositories, such as arXiv.org (Ginsparg, 1994) and CogPrints (Harnad, 2001), will have to adopt several of the editorial roles, and in doing so blur the traditionally clear boundaries between libraries and publishers.

In short, the example of iLumina suggests that digital libraries might indeed disintermediate some library services, say, by putting all simple search and retrieval directly in the hands of users. However, at least repositories with a significant grassroots component probably will add human mediation in other areas. History tells us this is not surprising. It was always thus with new technologies, in work, in education, in libraries: change, even radical change, does not necessarily reduce the number of people or mediating agents involved, but it does change what they do.

DIGITAL LIBRARIES AND SELECTION OF RESOURCES

Along with aggregation and creation of collections, selection or gatekeeping of resources has long been viewed as one of the core functions of public and research libraries. Digital libraries, especially of the grassroots variety, may generally change the activities of library staff. But will forces of the digital age increase or decrease the importance of this particular service: is library selection ripe for disintermediation?

Opinions differ. On the one hand, it is widely acknowledged that selection has been largely ceded to publishers (see Gilreath, 2000); this pattern is likely to continue if digital libraries are largely populated by ebooks provided by traditional vendors and new companies such as netLibrary. However, today such formally vetted resources are a small fraction of digital materials: most resources on the Web, for example, are self-published, and have never been subjected to review. For that reason, some argue that selection of resources and related gatekeeper functions might be an even more important role for libraries in the future than in the past.

iLumina suggests an eclectic selection process, one that neither completely delegates gatekeeping to external agencies, nor manages it centrally within the library. According to our formative model, the iLumina librarians will impose standards for acquisition, but the aggregate selection procedures could involve several library community members, whose diverse roles would depend largely on which of the three migration paths (existing repositories, informal collections, or individual materials) a given resource followed to enter iLumina (see Figure 1):

- *Existing federated repositories.* Because grassroots materials have no formal publishers, iLumina will have to manage review–hence selection. iLumina is planning to define the general parameters for review and inclusion. But we will distribute the processes of selection, and the details of implementing selection policies, to iLumina's federated partners, currently including CSTC and SECDL, as noted above. These partner repositories have already established selection procedures. Viewing them as "trusted" sources of content, we will not insist that they standardize on a single iLumina-wide selection policy. This means that selection in iLumina will not only be a distributed process, but also that it will encompass multiple different selection policies, since some of our partners, present and future, will admit liberally to their collections, while others may be very exclusive.

- *Informal collections and individuals.* For those resources iLumina obtains from informal collections and individual faculty, rather than from existing repositories, we are, as discussed, planning to implement a very open review and selection process, admitting all resources that meet very minimal standards, or perhaps even including unreviewed or "rejected" materials. In effect, this means we are off-loading at least a part of the selection policy to end-users themselves. Whether this shift in responsibility will be effective and desired by iLumina users is an empirical question on which we now have very little data. Part of the answer may depend on how well users can learn to use (metadata-driven) library personalization tools, such as user-rating schemes, to shoulder their new part of this responsibility–or on how easy it is to divest it, should they choose to do so (for example, by turning on a filter that would hide unreviewed iLumina content). Still, the increasing popularity of personalized information services on the Web (myYahoo, myMoreover, my-whatever), suggests that information-content providers, including libraries, will generally have to adapt their selection policies in the future, substantially liberalizing them so that they can share this role with their communities of users.

- *Community-based reviews and selection.* Digital library users can exercise their expanding review and selection responsibilities through individual tools that enable them to personalize their "views" of content to their preferences. But increasingly, users of information-rich Web sites are exerting their influence in a more communal way. Earlier we noted how iLumina will use its IMS-based metadata to enable users to become reviewers and raters of library resources and to share these comments with other users, as part of the visible resource metadata. Some online news and information sites, such as SlashDot (see Table 4), already take this idea much further, to the point where elaborate community review processes, in effect, determine the editorial and selection policies of the site. These sites are, in a sense, "self-organizing," devolving more content decisions to the distributed user community and reserving fewer to a centralized acquisitions staff (Hafner, 2001). Technically, it would not be hard to implement this scheme for digital libraries, or even for traditional libraries that have a vibrant user community that is motivated to discuss all this online. A tougher problem is to decide how far to push this decentralization and how to implement effective policies consistent with this shift (SlashDot's FAQ indicates its originators continue to tinker with policy changes). But perhaps the most difficult challenge of all will be to motivate library users to care as much about the content and directions of their digital repositories as SlashDot users care about their news for nerds. Without that commitment, an online community will likely turn into a ghost town. On the other hand, a dedicated community can become a powerful way to democratize decision-making in resource selection and review, as well as in other library services.

In general the iLumina model again suggests that grassroots libraries (or the parts of libraries that have grassroots content) will not only change the roles of library staff, but will also blur the roles played by official staff and those performed by other members of the library community–especially as collaborative network technologies make it easier to put together federations of distributed repositories and to connect diverse library users and contributors into a shared hub of discussion and decision-making.

DIGITAL LIBRARIES AS COMMUNITY COORDINATORS

Viewed broadly, iLumina suggests an almost complete reversal of the widespread view that digital technologies will automate library functions and disintermediate library staff. If anything they are likely, at least for grassroots libraries, to bring more role-players into the mix. But what is left for core library staff to do, if members of the user and contributor community are now taking over some of their traditional activities?

One answer is that they can play various roles that fall under the umbrella title of community coordinators. This topic is worthy of much discussion and extended experimentation: these are early days, and ef-

TABLE 4. SlashDot and Selection Policies

SlashDot, (http://www.slashdot.com) is a popular online source of "news for nerds." It publishes stories on high-tech topics, but far more of the site's content (and value) comes from users' comments. A story on, say, the Microsoft anti-trust trial might be posted at 10:30; by noon it could have over 200 comments attached. These comments are threaded, rated, and those scoring below a threshold set by the user will not be visible. Some of these comments come with the names of contributors; others are from "Anonymous Coward." Contributors can not only comment on stories, but also can submit their own, though no one is guaranteed that their submissions will be accepted.

To make all this work, SlashDot has evolved a very elaborate scheme, where not only the stories are rated, but so are the comments, and so, therefore, are the reviewers themselves (one metric is called "karma"). Good karma and performance enables a reviewer to gain more privileges in SlashDot, such as moderating discussions. These powers extend to actually determining the stories that appear on SlashDot-in effect, dictating its editorial or selection policies.

Very little decision-making at SlashDot, therefore, is centralized. Says Jeff Bates of SlashDot: "the site carries far more articles about civil liberties than it did two years ago. It's not a decision we made by sitting down in a smoky room and saying, 'All right, we're going to be all about civil liberties now,' " Mr. Bates said. "But we all agreed, in some kind of Jungian collective unconscious way, that that topic was a big deal." (Hafner, 2001).

fective policies for the community-sharing of library responsibilities are likely to evolve slowly, through painstaking trial-and-error. A few possibilities, just by way of illustration, include:

- *Infrastructure and standards.* At the technical level, a digital library will need staff to manage the physical infrastructure, ensure resource preservation, and provide a common and standardized platform for the community collaborative-construction of knowledge. Librarians may also retain a gatekeeper responsibility; not necessarily to select resources for the libraries collections, but to filter users' ideas concerning library content and interfaces, and to identify candidate new library tools and services. All this will probably become more important as federated partners and end-users increasingly provide library services and even content themselves. To make these diverse pieces and partners work together, the library will need to establish centralized interoperability standards, such as the IMS metadata specifications. One model for this can be found in the NSF's National Science, Mathematics, Engineering and Technology Education Digital Library

Initiative (NSDL, 2000), which separates the library's Core Integration System (CIS) from Services and Collections. Traditional library staff are likely to be key role players in the CIS; Services and Collections may be controlled by other library community members.

- *Mentoring and training.* There is much anecdotal evidence that users will need to acquire many new skills if they are to carry out or share in library roles that used to be played almost exclusively by library professionals. To take a simple example, students, and even faculty, often have poor search and retrieval habits–and these are among the most elementary of digital-library behaviors. Instead of encouraging users to let librarians do this for them, a strategy which has largely not succeeded in the past, why not *mentor* and *train* users to do this effectively themselves? This is analogous to the strategy our company, Eduprise, has implemented in the e-learning sector. Among other things, we help faculty who are skilled at face-to-face teaching transition their expertise into Web-enhanced or fully online courses. Someone needs to train library users through similar transformations, especially as they adopt ever-more library roles and responsibilities.

- *Models and design.* Libraries, whether traditional or digital, or hybrid, comprise a rather complex chain of activities–from acquisition, to collection management, to archival processes–that collectively yield valuable services for users. At present, digital libraries have incorporated only a very few of these, such as search and retrieval. Many of the less obvious services of traditional libraries have not been deeply investigated yet by the digital library community (a community that is, in the main, stronger on the "digital" than they are on the "library"). Archival and preservation services, for example, have not been considered carefully at all. Traditional libraries can provide important models for these and other services, and research librarians can be valuable sources of expertise in designing the digital versions of such services–or new services that capture all the valuable functionality of a library, whether wholly digital, or only partially so.

CONCLUSIONS

We have argued that the Internet changes everything, at least when it comes to information and knowledge-intensive enterprises, especially those that are more social and collaborative than individual in nature. For this reason, networked technologies are likely to be a stimulus for dramatic, even disruptive changes in libraries. iLumina suggests several possible trends. Libraries may be disintermediated. Even when mediating agents continue to play roles in library services, these may be very different in the future. As digital learning objects become easier and easier to create and share, libraries increasingly may become repositories for informal, grassroots materials, where the end-users that consume library resources and educators that contribute and share them are the one and the same. And these library community members could take over some functions that previously were owned by professional librarians. In this way, decision-making in libraries may be significantly democratized. But professional librarians, who might offload such roles, could beneficially take on various new guiding and governing responsibilities.

Viewed as predictions about the future of libraries, digital or otherwise, most of these trends are likely to be wrong, even though they reflect patterns of change that are already clearly evolving in other areas of e-learning and e-commerce. But we do not see these lessons from iLumina as predictions, any more than we see iLumina itself as a prediction about digital libraries. Rather, they are better viewed as design options for creating new libraries and for reconstructing traditional ones. Some will succeed; some will fail. A main goal for library development, therefore, should not only be to fashion more innovative design possibilities–iLumina embodies a scant few–but also to subject these alternatives to extensive testing and refinement. Tomorrow's libraries will not just happen; they will need to be invented through experiments conducted by all members of the library community.

NOTES

1. For all practical purposes our metadata schema derives equally from the IEEE LOM 3.5 metadata specification [http://ltsc.ieee.org/doc/wg12/scheme.html], which differs only in small ways from the IMS specification.

2. The Instructional Architect project (Recker and Wiley, to appear) is planning a similar digital library service; the term "non-authoritative metadata" originates with them.

REFERENCES

Chudnov, D. "Docster: Instant document delivery." *The Shy Librarian*, April 2000. <http://shylibrarian.com/ebooks/articles/docster.htm>.

Dempsey, L., and Heery, P. "Metadata: a current review of practice and issues." *Journal of Documentation* 54, 2, (1998): 145-172.

Gilliland-Swetland, A. "Defining Metadata." In M. Baca, ed. *Introduction to Metadata: Pathways to Digital Information*. Los Angeles: Getty Information Institute, 1998.

Gilreath, C. Digital Libraries of the 21st Century. Academic Libraries of the 21st Century, 2000. <http://library.tamu.edu/21stcentury/>.

Ginsparg, P. "First steps towards electronic research communication." *Computers in Physics* 8, no. 4 (1994): 390-6. <http://arXiv.org/blurb/blurb.ps.gz>.

Graves, W. "Learning as an Expedition, Technology as a Unifying Tool." *Syllabus*, August 1998.

Graves, W. "Framework for an Enterprise-Learning Strategy." EDUCAUSE Conference, 2000. <http://www.educause.edu/ir/library/pdf/NLI0014.pdf>.

Hafner, K. "Web Sites Begin to Get Organized, on Their Own." *New York Times*, January 18, 2001.

Hale, K. and Nicolet, T. "Moving Beyond the Walls: Creating a New Pedagogy with Discussion Forums" EDUCAUSE Conference, 1999. <http://www.eduprise.com/public/resources.nsf/6d303110d7730de4052564ab005719d1/02f508f9dc0072458525683900 5c637c>.

Harnad, S. CogPrints Project page, 2001. <http://www.ukoln.ac.uk/services/elib/projects/cogprints/>.

IMS. The IMS Global Learning Consortium, 2000. <http://www.imsproject.org>.

NSDL. National Science, Mathematics, Engineering and Technology Education Digital Library, 2000. <http://www.ehr.nsf.gov/ehr/due/programs/nsdl/>.

McArthur, D. et. al. "Towards a Sharable Digital Library of Reusable Teaching Resources: Roles for Rich Metadata." Submitted to *Journal on Educational Resources in Computing*, 2001.

Recker, M., and Wiley, D. (2001) "A non-authoritative educational metadata ontology for filtering and recommending learning objects." *Interactive Learning Environments: Special issue on metadata*, pp. 1-17.

Twigg, C. "Who Owns Online Courses and Course Materials? Intellectual Property Policies for a New Learning Environment. Pew Symposia in Learning and Technology." 2000. <http://www.center.rpi.edu/PewSym/mono2.html>.

Index

Page numbers followed by "n." indicate notes; page numbers followed by "fig." indicate figures; and tables and exhibits are also indicated.

Integrating Total Quality Management in a Library Setting, edited by Susan Jurow, MLS, and Susan B. Barnard, MLS (Vol. 18, No. 1/2, 1993). *"Especially valuable are the librarian experiences that directly relate to real concerns about TQM. Recommended for all professional reading collections." (Library Journal)*

Leadership in Academic Libraries: Proceedings of the W. Porter Kellam Conference, The University of Georgia, May 7, 1991, edited by William Gray Potter (Vol. 17, No. 4, 1993). *"Will be of interest to those concerned with the history of American academic libraries." (Australian Library Review)*

Collection Assessment and Acquisitions Budgets, edited by Sul H. Lee (Vol. 17, No. 2, 1993). *Contains timely information about the assessment of academic library collections and the relationship of collection assessment to acquisition budgets.*

Developing Library Staff for the 21st Century, edited by Maureen Sullivan (Vol. 17, No. 1, 1992). *"I found myself enthralled with this highly readable publication. It is one of those rare compilations that manages to successfully integrate current general management operational thinking in the context of academic library management." (Bimonthly Review of Law Books)*

Vendor Evaluation and Acquisition Budgets, edited by Sul H. Lee (Vol. 16, No. 3, 1992). *"The title doesn't do justice to the true scope of this excellent collection of papers delivered at the sixth annual conference on library acquisitions sponsored by the University of Oklahoma Libraries." (Kent K. Hendrickson, BS, MALS, Dean of Libraries, University of Nebraska-Lincoln) Find insightful discussions on the impact of rising costs on library budgets and management in this groundbreaking book.*

The Management of Library and Information Studies Education, edited by Herman L. Totten, PhD, MLS (Vol. 16, No. 1/2, 1992). *"Offers something of interest to everyone connected with LIS education–the undergraduate contemplating a master's degree, the doctoral student struggling with courses and career choices, the new faculty member aghast at conflicting responsibilities, the experienced but stressed LIS professor, and directors of LIS Schools." (Education Libraries)*

Library Management in the Information Technology Environment: Issues, Policies, and Practice for Administrators, edited by Brice G. Hobrock, PhD, MLS (Vol. 15, No. 3/4, 1992). *"A road map to identify some of the alternative routes to the electronic library." (Stephen Rollins, Associate Dean for Library Services, General Library, University of New Mexico)*

Managing Technical Services in the 90's, edited by Drew Racine (Vol. 15, No. 1/2, 1991). *"Presents an eclectic overview of the challenges currently facing all library technical services efforts. . . . Recommended to library administrators and interested practitioners." (Library Journal)*

Budgets for Acquisitions: Strategies for Serials, Monographs, and Electronic Formats, edited by Sul H. Lee (Vol. 14, No. 3, 1991). *"Much more than a series of handy tips for the careful shopper. This [book] is a most useful one–well-informed, thought-provoking, and authoritative." (Australian Library Review)*

Creative Planning for Library Administration: Leadership for the Future, edited by Kent Hendrickson, MALS (Vol. 14, No. 2, 1991). *"Provides some essential information on the planning process, and the mix of opinions and methodologies, as well as examples relevant to every library manager, resulting in a very readable foray into a topic too long avoided by many of us." (Canadian Library Journal)*

Strategic Planning in Higher Education: Implementing New Roles for the Academic Library, edited by James F. Williams, II, MLS (Vol. 13, No. 3/4, 1991). *"A welcome addition to the sparse literature on strategic planning in university libraries. Academic librarians considering strategic planning for their libraries will learn a great deal from this work." (Canadian Library Journal)*

Personnel Administration in an Automated Environment, edited by Philip E. Leinbach, MLS (Vol. 13, No. 1/2, 1990). *"An interesting and worthwhile volume, recommended to university library administrators and to others interested in thought-provoking discussion of the personnel implications of automation." (Canadian Library Journal)*

Library Development: A Future Imperative, edited by Dwight F. Burlingame, PhD (Vol. 12, No. 4, 1990). *"This volume provides an excellent overview of fundraising with special application to libraries. . . . A useful book that is highly recommended for all libraries." (Library Journal)*

Library Material Costs and Access to Information, edited by Sul H. Lee (Vol. 12, No. 3, 1991). *"A cohesive treatment of the issue. Although the book's contributors possess a research library perspective, the data and the ideas presented are of interest and benefit to the entire profession, especially academic librarians." (Library Resources and Technical Services)*

Training Issues and Strategies in Libraries, edited by Paul M. Gherman, MALS, and Frances O. Painter, MLS, MBA (Vol. 12, No. 2, 1990). *"There are . . . useful chapters, all by different authors, each with a preliminary summary of the content–a device that saves much time in deciding whether to read the whole chapter or merely skim through it. Many of the chapters are essentially practical without too much emphasis on theory. This book is a good investment." (Library Association Record)*

Library Education and Employer Expectations, edited by E. Dale Cluff, PhD, MLS (Vol. 11, No. 3/4, 1990). *"Useful to library-school students and faculty interested in employment problems and employer perspectives. Librarians concerned with recruitment practices will also be interested." (Information Technology and Libraries)*

Managing Public Libraries in the 21st Century, edited by Pat Woodrum, MLS (Vol. 11, No. 1/2, 1989). *"A broad-based collection of topics that explores the management problems and possibilities public libraries will be facing in the 21st century." (Robert Swisher, PhD, Director, School of Library and Information Studies, University of Oklahoma)*

Human Resources Management in Libraries, edited by Gisela M. Webb, MLS, MPA (Vol. 10, No. 4, 1989). *"Thought provoking and enjoyable reading. . . . Provides valuable insights for the effective information manager." (Special Libraries)*

Creativity, Innovation, and Entrepreneurship in Libraries, edited by Donald E. Riggs, EdD, MLS (Vol. 10, No. 2/3, 1989). *"The volume is well worth reading as a whole. . . . There is very little repetition, and it should stimulate thought." (Australian Library Review)*

The Impact of Rising Costs of Serials and Monographs on Library Services and Programs, edited by Sul H. Lee (Vol. 10, No. 1, 1989). *". . . Sul Lee hit a winner here." (Serials Review)*

Computing, Electronic Publishing, and Information Technology: Their Impact on Academic Libraries, edited by Robin N. Downes (Vol. 9, No. 4, 1989). *"For a relatively short and easily digestible discussion of these issues, this book can be recommended, not only to those in academic libraries, but also to those in similar types of library or information unit, and to academics and educators in the field." (Journal of Documentation)*

Library Management and Technical Services: The Changing Role of Technical Services in Library Organizations, edited by Jennifer Cargill, MSLS, MSed (Vol. 9, No. 1, 1988). *"As a practical and instructive guide to issues such as automation, personnel matters, education, management techniques and liaison with other services, senior library managers with a sincere interest in evaluating the role of their technical services should find this a timely publication." (Library Association Record)*

Management Issues in the Networking Environment, edited by Edward R. Johnson, PhD (Vol. 8, No. 3/4, 1989). *"Particularly useful for librarians/information specialists contemplating establishing a local network." (Australian Library Review)*

Acquisitions, Budgets, and Material Costs: Issues and Approaches, edited by Sul H. Lee (Supp. #2, 1988). *"The advice of these library practitioners is sensible and their insights illuminating for librarians in academic libraries." (American Reference Books Annual)*

Pricing and Costs of Monographs and Serials: National and International Issues, edited by Sul H. Lee (Supp. #1, 1987). *"Eminently readable. There is a good balance of chapters on serials and monographs and the perspective of suppliers, publishers, and library practitioners are presented. A book well worth reading." (Australasian College Libraries)*

Legal Issues for Library and Information Managers, edited by William Z. Nasri, JD, PhD (Vol. 7, No. 4, 1987). *"Useful to any librarian looking for protection or wondering where responsibilities end and liabilities begin. Recommended." (Academic Library Book Review)*

Archives and Library Administration: Divergent Traditions and Common Concerns, edited by Lawrence J. McCrank, PhD, MLS (Vol. 7, No. 2/3, 1986). *"A forward-looking view of archives and libraries. . . . Recommend[ed] to students, teachers, and practitioners alike of archival and library science. It is readable, thought-provoking, and provides a summary of the major areas of divergence and convergence." (Association of Canadian Map Libraries and Archives)*

Excellence in Library Management, edited by Charlotte Georgi, MLS, and Robert Bellanti, MLS, MBA (Vol. 6, No. 3, 1985). *"Most beneficial for library administrators . . . for anyone interested in either library/information science or management." (Special Libraries)*

Marketing and the Library, edited by Gary T. Ford (Vol. 4, No. 4, 1984). *Discover the latest methods for more effective information dissemination and learn to develop successful programs for specific target areas.*

Finance Planning for Libraries, edited by Murray S. Martin (Vol. 3, No. 3/4, 1983). *Stresses the need for libraries to weed out expenditures which do not contribute to their basic role–the collection and organization of information–when planning where and when to spend money.*

Planning for Library Services: A Guide to Utilizing Planning Methods for Library Management, edited by Charles R. McClure, PhD (Vol. 2, No. 3/4, 1982). *"Should be read by anyone who is involved in planning processes of libraries–certainly by every administrator of a library or system." (American Reference Books Annual)*